Decolonising the Camera

Photography in Racial Time

Decolonising the Camera

Photography in Racial Time

Mark Sealy

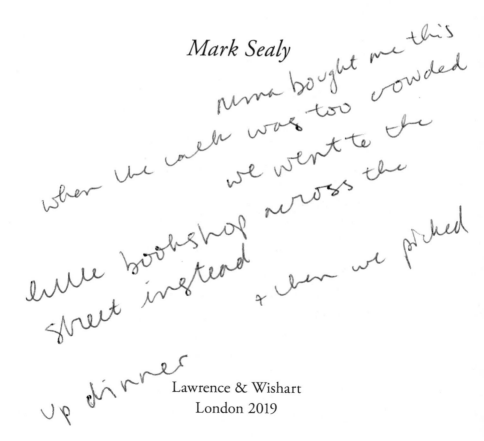

nana bought me this when the cafe was too crowded we went to the little bookshop across the street instead + then we picked up dinner

Lawrence & Wishart
London 2019

Lawrence and Wishart Limited
Central Books Building
Freshwater Road
Chadwell Heath
RM8 1RX

Typesetting: e-type
Cover design: River Design
Printing: Imprint Digital

First published 2019
© Mark Sealy 2019

Published in association with Autograph ABP **AUT◙GRAPH**

British Library Cataloguing in Publication Data.
A catalogue record for this book is available from the British Library

ISBN 978 191 2064 75 5
eISBN 978 191 2064 50 2

Contents

Introduction

This book examines how Western photographic practice has been used as a tool for creating Eurocentric and violent visual regimes. It uses the central principle of 'decolonising the camera', a process by which an analysis of photography takes place within and against the political and violent reality of Western imperialism. Through this process, it explores issues of race and cultural erasure within photographic history through the direct analysis of photographic works, informed by two underlying questions. Firstly, has photography been a liberating device, or an oppressive weapon that holds the viewer/producer and citizen/subject in a violent system of continual exposure? And secondly, what epistemic value has photography brought to our understanding of difference?

The book considers whether photographic works concerning visualisations of the 'Other' can produce different or new meanings when they are critically read through the prism of colonialism, its inherent forms of human negation, its temporalities and its violence. This is done by locating and reading the photographs discussed here within the ideologies of colonial time, space and place. Decolonising the camera functions as a critical dialogue with colonial and imperial photographic histories, and the social and visual spaces they occupy. Through the photographs discussed here, I argue that within these common types of racialised photographic spaces, we can analyse the varying levels of violence done in photography concerning the making of the Other, and from that perspective consider how these forms of violence worked in the service of Western colonial and imperial powers.

'Colonialism has been a dispossession of space, a deprivation of identity' (Barlet 2000, p.39), and it created a system of image production that maintained and disseminated its dehumanising ideologies. At the centre of this book lies the proposition that it is necessary to recognise photography as an active agent of Western colonising authority at work on the body of the Other, both in the past and in the present. It is only through this that we can begin to fully recognise the complexities and political impact of photographs in visualisations of racialised subjects.

Throughout this text I suggest that a photograph of a racialised subject must be both located in and then de-located from the racial and political time of its making and not solely articulated by its descriptive (journalistic) or aesthetic (artistic) concerns. I maintain that it is only within the political and cultural location of a photo-graph that we can discover the coloniality at work within it, and only then, through understanding this, can a process of enquiry begin into the nature of its colonial cultural coding. A key aspect of decolonising the camera is to not allow photography's colonial past and its cultural legacies in the present to lie unchallenged and un-agitated, or to be simply left as the given norm within the history of the medium. Decolonising the photographic image is an act of unburdening it from the assumed, normative, hegemonic, colonial conditions present, consciously or unconsciously, in the moment of its original making and in its readings and displays. This is therefore a process of locating the primary conditions of a racialised photo-graph's coloniality and, as such, decolonising the camera works within a form of black cultural politics to destabilise the conditions, receptions and processes of Othering a subject within the history of photography.

The notion of destabilising photography's historical past works through the lens of Stuart Hall's critical writing on race and repre-sentation, especially that concerning the British black subject's construction within photography that he wrote in the 1980s. Of particular relevance are his essays titled 'Reconstruction Work: Images of Postwar Black Settlement' from 1984, and 'New Ethnicities', from 1988. In 'New Ethnicities', Hall theorises a deci-sive turn against the Eurocentric stable and negative representations of the black subject within Western visual culture. He also articu-lates a politics in which 'unspoken and invisible' (Hall 1988, p.27) subjects in post-Second World War Britain have challenged spaces of representation, and marks the moment that black subjects begin to contest their historically fixed image. Building on the notion of the 'unspoken and invisible' black subject within Western culture, and analysing a series of complex photographic episodes drawn from various archives of Western photography, I make the case that such archives, in their myriad representative ways, are loaded with unspoken and culturally invisible subjects, and that the photographs within them work politically and aggressively as active agents locked within a colonial photographic paradigm.

Hall claimed that the 1980s were a 'critical decade' for black British photography (Bailey & Hall 1992). I assert here that the 1990s should also be read as a transformative period that heralded the arrival of the Other as photographer within mainstream Western cultural institutions. In the final chapter of this book, I consider the political and cultural conditions of both these decades as decisive periods in which the black subject entered both the domain of representation and its international art markets.

Throughout this text, I examine the visual and structural complexities at work within a given photograph's social and political formation, which I refer to as its 'racial time'. Racial time enables us to consider a photograph's function as a sign within the historical conditions concerning the 'relations of representation' that Hall discussed in 'New ethnicities'. I employ the idea of racial time to signify a different but essential colonial temporality at work within a photograph. In 'New ethnicities', Hall also presented the notion of the 'end of the essential black subject' (Hall 1988, p.28). If this is the case, then it marks an important conjuncture in history and photography where the Other is brought into focus. Hall therefore shifts the cultural landscape in the understanding of the black subject within Western visual culture and I enquire here, as an undercurrent to these chapters, how the cultural landscape in the making of race has been historically constituted and how that landscape might be read today and in the future to produce new meanings.

In my final chapter Hall's influence re-emerges through his essays 'Reconstruction Work: Images of Postwar Black Settlement' (1984) and 'Vanley Burke and the "Desire for Blackness" (1993)'. The latter, about the Birmingham-based photographer, is employed as a reminder of the rarity of visual moments concerning black intimacy and tenderness within the history of photography.

My enquiries are not limited to the context of British black cultural politics in the 1980s referred to by Hall but also extend back through the histories of the medium so that we can begin a process of understanding race at work in photography. If, as Hall suggests, the end of the essential black subject was a political reality by the 1980s, then something must have passed on or died. Further, if this is the case, then that ending affords us in the present the opportunity to do new forensic work on the historical sites and bodies of photography that concern its essentialising and racialising nature. This book aims to locate, excavate, extract and expose the slippery, ghost-like nature of the colonial in photography, so as to make the essence of the colonial legacy within photography and its dark epistemes more evident and more visible.

The images discussed here have been assembled on the basis of extensive research in key photographic archives, such as those at Anti-Slavery International, the Bodleian Library, the Black Star Archives at Ryerson University, Getty Images, Magnum Photos and the Imperial War Museum. Analysing this primary material reveals how Western regimes of scopic violence can be understood in the context of the racialised body, human rights and photographic history. I address the concept of cultural erasure against the Other, informed by a range of enquiries into history, photography, racial and cultural politics in the works of, for example, Paul Gordon Lauren, Emmanuel Levinas, Frantz Fanon, Michel Foucault, Sven Lindqvist and, as already mentioned, Stuart Hall.

Levinas invites us to look into the face of the Other as a duty of obligation and as a sign of our infinite and fundamental responsibility for the individual human Other. For Levinas, taking responsibility for the Other is the ethical site where we locate our own humanity and morality. Using Levinas's philosophy of ethical responsibility, I argue that photography made through the prism of the colonial gaze has created such a wholly dehumanising legacy of images of the colonised subject that it may be impossible to rectify.

Fanon's thoughts on decolonising the mind of the colonised subject here map onto decolonising photography, and relate to the internalising psychological damage that can occur to the human subject when constantly exposed to dehumanising representations of blackness. Fanon's view of colonial violence suggests that violence generated by the oppressor is rejected with an equal force, and with this in mind, analysing photographs of the black subject from the perspective of a decolonising critic in this book works as a process of political rejection of Eurocentric photographic practices. This opens up such photographs to different possible readings that unlock them from the fixity of the time of their making, which enables us to read, for example, Wayne Miller's photographs as a form of black performativity to white colonial privilege, rather than simply as empathetic documentary work.

For Foucault, power is a function of panopticism, in which the threat of permanent visibility causes subjects to become self-regulating and 'docile'. In the dynamics of race and violence against the black body, such power is derived from controlling the black body through the assumed cultural authority of white rights to observe and display blackness.

In Sven Linqvist's key book, *Exterminate All the Brutes* (Lindqvist & Tate 2007), he writes the history of genocide as a travelogue through colonial time. This works as a reminder of the role technology has played in Europe's domination and formation of its colonies. By presenting the tragic consequences of those technological developments for colonised subjects, he reminds us of the importance of revisiting and decoding the narratives of history that sanitise the colonial conquests.

The legacies of colonialism and racism worry the history of photography. They enable the fractures of enlightenment and humanitarian thought to haunt the present. Photography, when read within the context of European imperialism, has the capacity to function as a morbid reminder of the intense level of cultural violence that was aimed at the Other over centuries. Photographs are discussed here not just as historical documents but as images open to different interpretations of key moments in Europe's history, such as King Leopold's violent regime in the Congo, for example, or the complexity of agendas surrounding race at the end of Second World War. This form of analysis allows us to read the nuances and gauge the power of the cultural and political forces at work within the history of the genre, and to assess how these forces have impacted on photographic constructions of race, the politics of human rights, identity formations, national narratives and cultural memory.

Throughout this book, I analyse photographs and photographic practices in which issues of race, human rights and identity politics are paramount. The priority here is to analyse the extent to which the humanitarian ideals that have often animated the discourse and practice of photography have impacted on the historical conditions of race, to examine whether those ideals have supported or hindered human understandings of race within photography and to gauge how photography's dominant regimes have assisted, maintained and made possible the creation of a racialised world. The historical work that has been done in photography on constructions of race, human and civil rights has, through the ongoing institutional hegemony of European photography, failed to alter the colonial consciousness within Western thought concerning theories of and cultural attitudes towards race, even when wrapped within the context of a humanitarian concern. I explore this directly through, for example, images circulated by the Congo Reform Association, which was a powerful humanitarian organisation working at the beginning of the twentieth century on religious, political and humanitarian fronts, and also particularly through images made during and immediately after the Second World War that feature the colonised or black American subject.

I maintain that photography is dominated by the legacy of a colonial consciousness repressed in the present. If this is the case, then this ongoing imperial mindset means that the colonial visual regimes historically active within photography remain inherently intact, as the making of photography, its translations and articulations, its distribution networks and knowledge formations, continue to be critically dislocated from the perspective of the subaltern and the marginalised. Realigning photography to include a reading from subaltern or 'different' perspectives (Hall & Sealy 2001), I argue that we have to engage in a form of decolonisation work within photography concerning the Other, or consider the history of photography from within a politics of representation. In this, the primary objective is revealing the specific or latent political implications of a given photograph's production, especially its reading and its reception when the face of the racial Other is brought into focus (Levinas 1979).

The photographs by missionary photographer Alice Seeley Harris and the work of the Congo Reform Association are the subjects of Chapter 1. They are an acute reminder of the complex layers of the horrific violence that was directed at the African body in the Congo at the turn of the twentieth century. Across Europe and the United States of America, Seeley Harris's early humanitarian photographs highlighted the outrageous abuse and killings that were taking place throughout King Leopold II of Belgium's Congo Free State. They constitute some of the most politically charged images of colonial violence taken in the twentieth century. Their display in public still has the capacity to inform, educate and appal, as was evident in the exhibition titled *'When Harmony Went to Hell' – Congo Dialogues: Alice Seeley Harris and Sammy Baloji*, which I curated for Autograph ABP at the Rivington Place galleries in early 2014. Visitors to the exhibition overwhelmingly expressed limited or no knowledge of the levels of violence suffered by the Congolese people. Fewer still understood the role that Seeley Harris and her photographs played in the downfall of Leopold's regime. However, like all photographs, they carry a multiplicity of meanings according to the cultural perspective from which they are read. Seeley Harris's photographs now afford us the opportunity to enquire why they were, until fairly recently, absent from the dominant narratives of photography's history, and they enable us to address why Seeley Harris, an innovative missionary photographer, has been pushed into the background of the history of photography. These photographs, taken in Africa at the turn of century, are critical to understanding the politics of the European presence on the continent. They also performed dramatic work as documents employed in Britain promoting political and humanitarian reform in Africa. The photos' original display and reception was as theatrical lantern slides, which functioned within a specific set of scripted performative narratives working to service and expand the objectives of British Protestant missionaries based in the heart of the Belgian Catholic Congo. Locating them back within this context deepens their significance, enabling us to consider missionaries with cameras as people uniquely situated on the front line of the British empire, fuelling with their 'knowledge' the wider enterprise of British colonialism. On the surface, these ostensibly benign photographs 'humanise' the African subject by exposing King Leopold II's regime of violence. But they can also be read as rallying calls, not for the liberation and freedom of African subjects, but for the construction of a higher, morally colonising authority that was understood as uniquely British and therefore just.

Alice Seeley Harris's work and the photographs employed by the Congo Reform Association provoke questions of colonial disavowal and disingenuous imperial agendas as Catholic and Protestant missionaries fought for pole position in the race to convert the 'natives', a battle that mirrored the wider European conflicts across Africa for territorial gain and control. Through an analysis of the way these images were used by Seeley Harris and her colleagues, I make the case that essentially the Congolese were left with three choices – be converted to Christianity, become slaves or be killed – none of which guaranteed their human recognition or advanced the case of humanity for the African subject in the West. The camera in the Congo may well have highlighted the plight of the Congolese under the control of King Leopold II, but it also contributed to the increased security and certainty of the British Protestant missionary presence. Photographs displayed by the Congo Reform Association were evidently a factor in the elderly King Leopold II being pressured to sell his stake in the Congo to Belgium in 1908, just one year before his death, but the king's deluded sense of benevolence lived on through the agency of the Belgian state for at least another fifty years. The racist, dehumanising, violent ideology of Belgium's rule remained intact for decades, up to and beyond Congo's independence in 1960.

While Seeley Harris's work was produced almost half a century before the outbreak of the Second World War, it raises questions that continue to haunt the post-war moment. Sven Lindqvist's *Exterminate All the Brutes* reminds us that 'Europe's destruction of the "inferior races" of four continents prepared the ground for Hitler's destruction of six million Jews in Europe' (Lindqvist & Tate 2007, p.x). The deliberate refusal to see those regarded as Other as human subjects in their own right defines a violent literary and visual legacy that is now firmly part of the Eurocentric construction of the making of world history. Through photography, this legacy has marked those whose lives and cultures have a value and those whose do not.

The photographs taken at the Nazi death camps, discussed in Chapter 2, have had a profound effect on the consciousness of the modern world. They now count among the most iconic images of humans' inhumanity to other humans ever recorded or shown in public. Many of them first appeared in *Life* magazine on 7 May 1945 and have been discussed at length by historians of both human rights and photography (Lauren 2003; Linfield 2010). However, the specific detail and complexities of these photographs' cultural work is easily overlooked due to the grotesque nature of what they depict. Nuanced cultural work can slip by, unnoticed due to the way in which the photographs have been encoded for public presentation within larger circuits of communication (S. Hall 1973). If we accept the emergence of these photographs, published in *Life* and other Western news media in May 1945, as the origins of 'irrefutable evidence' concerning acts of mass extermination of the Jewish people by the Nazis, then it is also important to read them within a wider racial context. They act as 'irrefutable evidence' not just of Nazi horrors, but additionally of the Allied forces' disavowal concerning the plight of the Jews, the Roma, the disabled, the mentally ill and the many others who died in the death camps: photographs and testimonies were available long before Allied soldiers liberated the camps, but this visual foreknowledge gets left out of the grand narratives concerning violence against the Other.

The lack of recognition of different indigenous cultures through managed misrepresentations of their alterity in the West is a defining marker of the colonial and postcolonial eras: eras that, in various guises, continually scrutinised the 'dark races' and dismissed their capacity to rule themselves and, by extension, to fully engage with the politics of their own lives. By the end of the Second World War, Europe's and the USA's preferred political agenda was simply to maintain the old cultural racial status quo. Through its analysis of racially charged photographs produced in the West during and after the Second World War, Chapter 2 demonstrates that this agenda was also played out in the realm of photographic representation. Freedom for the colonial subject, despite that subject's major contribution to Europe's liberation, was not going to be forthcoming. Western attitudes to race in the late 1940s were resoundingly retrogressive, as was confirmed by the implementation of the Apartheid regime in South Africa in 1948 and the newly formed United Nations' inert responses to it.

Among the images discussed in Chapter 3 are those taken by the celebrated British photographer John Deakin at the fifth Pan-African Congress in Manchester in October 1945, which appeared in *Picture Post* magazine on 10 November 1945. Used in an editorial context, they allow us to take the pulse of British journalistic attitudes towards colonial subjects immediately after the Second World War, and they represent the only in-depth visual account of this significant moment within British colonial politics.

Deakin's photographs accompany an article that focuses on miscegenation rather than African liberation, recalling nineteenth-century European obsessions with racial purity (Lindqvist & Tate 2007, p.100). The *Picture Post* editorial, which was titled 'Africa Speaks in Manchester', unashamedly advocated 'white hostility' towards black subjects if the demands of the colonised carried any meaningful threat. What therefore begins to surface is the arrogant cultural assumption that the status quo concerning the empire and its subjects would be maintained violently as a European right. Within this small body of photographs, their captions and the text, we can see the early signs of a preferred national story, locating the boundaries of global freedom in late 1945 – territorially, politically and racially. Analysing the article reveals a subtle set of wider communications aimed at the British public that, when deconstructed through the prism of race, sends a distinct message that, given the end of the Second World War, there was no further need to embrace or tolerate the colonial black soldier or worker as a colleague in arms, equal in the fight against fascism. The article works as a reminder that, just six months after the end of the war in Europe, Africans could 'speak' regarding their desire for freedoms, but only according to the terms of the old empires' agendas. The article also critically inaugurates a process of cultural amnesia relating to the political promises and new images concerning colonial contributions to the war effort, which had been put into mass production and circulation. Moreover, it ignores the global significance of the transatlantic agreements that had been signed between the Allied forces that effectively promised freedom for all the world's peoples.

George Padmore, the Trinidadian pan-Africanist, is quoted in the *Picture Post* article as summing up the mood of the delegates in

Manchester: 'a Negro's skin is his passport to an oppression as violent as that of Nazi Germany's oppression of the Jews ... we don't need yellow armbands in Africa – just black skins'. As far as racial politics was concerned, across the pages of *Picture Post* in November 1945, the black colonised subject was petrified in colonial time. However, the images belie the new face of radical African liberation and highlight just how out of step the British were with the political mood and determination of their African subjects, many of whom had been hardened by their experiences of war in Europe. The presence of W. E. B. Du Bois in Manchester, probably the most influential black man on the planet in 1945, should have been a clear indicator that the political tide had turned against Europe's empires. Deakin and the editors of *Picture Post*, however, failed to recognise him in the photographs, giving his name to the face of a different delegate at the Congress.

A young German photojournalist, Robert Lebeck, was in the Congo on 29 June 1960, the eve of independence for the newly formed state of the Republic of Congo. On that day he took what has now become an iconic photograph of African independence struggles. The image shows the ceremonial sword of the Belgian King Baudouin being stolen and held aloft by an African spectator of the ceremonies. As the 'thief' turns to run away with the sword, Lebeck, fortuitously placed, takes advantage of the scene, taking a photograph that helps to establish his reputation as one of the leading photojournalists of his day. In Chapter 4, I discuss the complete sequence of photographs taken on 29 June by Lebeck, which were published in his recent monograph, *Tokyo, Moscow, Léopoldville* (2008). Examining the images that were taken before and after the sword was stolen reveals the intensity of colonial rule through the imperial signs of Belgium's symbolic order, thus directing a reading of Lebeck's work away from the traditions within photography that desire the location of a Barthesian 'punctive' moment (Barthes 1981) within a given photograph. I argue that the images are visually saturated to a claustrophobic degree with the signs of Belgium's colonialism. Reading Belgium's monuments and other colonial tropes that appear in the photographs as signs of historical violence, colonial grandeur and indulgence, offers an analysis of Lebeck's series not as a filter that works towards the making of a single decisive moment, but as images that act today as turbulent reminders of the past and visual precursors to the violence that befell the Congo just a few months after its independence. When read now, from the perspective of the known political realities of the Congo, the photographs are important not just as moments that capture African independence but as a record of the degrees of colonial oppression that were still present at the time of the formation of the new state. The sword thief may well have grabbed the symbol of power from the Belgians briefly, but the white Belgian military presence, which was managing the path to independence, rapidly restored colonial order. Lebeck's photographs from 29 June 1960 have become a unique register against which we can begin to deconstruct the damaging totalising effects of Belgium's colonial rule on the minds of both the Congolese and the Belgians.

In Chapter 5, I examine one of the first post-Second World War documentary photography projects that was funded and produced with the specific objective of changing white perceptions of the black US. As a Second World War photographer working in the South Pacific for the US navy, Wayne Miller was, by the end of the hostilities, sickened by the devastation he had witnessed. His experience of being on a racially divided ship and what he saw at Hiroshima affected his perspectives on race and humanity so much so that, on his return home to Chicago, he decided that the most pressing contribution he could make was to try and bridge the cultural and political fault-lines that divided American society racially.

Miller's ambition was to bring black Americans closer to the hearts and minds of white society, by presenting a new vision of black humanity. His project was not a self-financed endeavour; it was funded by two Guggenheim awards, which clearly indicates the Guggenheim Foundation's view of the importance and relevance of Miller's work on race. The funding enabled him to work among Chicago's black community for three years. Miller's photographs taken from 1946 to 1948 therefore represented what was then an unprecedented view of the lives of black Americans taken by a white photographer. Since their publication in 2000, these images have been celebrated as powerful examples of documentary photographs employed as a vehicle for building empathy between different people. However, given the intensity and history of racism in Chicago in the mid to late 1940s, it is pertinent to consider Miller's privileged status as a well-financed white photographer photographing black Americans, and to examine the possibilities and forms of cultural reciprocation between him and his subjects in such a racially tense environment. Cultural commentators on Miller's work have tended to ignore that the images were made within a dominant regime of representation; the fact of blackness that Miller attempted to make visible was constituted solely from a white perspective in which Miller positioned himself as the interpreter of a form of black humanity, classically aestheticised within the photographic documentary tradition. Miller does not provide any wider social context against which to gauge the levels of white oppression under which these people lived. Therefore, to read the value of the work one has to literally look outside the frame.

Enquiring into Miller's humanitarian project reveals that the photographs became virtually invisible for decades. Instead of being agents for social change in the 1940s US, they became a closed personal archive. They did not surface collectively as images in any meaningful cultural curatorial context for at least another fifty years, apart from some minor usage by the American black press to support arguments relating to black progress in the late 1940s and early 1950s. Additionally, two photographs were included as part of Edward Steichen's 1955 *The Family of Man* exhibition, one of which portrays a black man involved with a sex worker, and the other shows a depressed-looking black man dressed in his denim work clothes sitting on the edge of a double bed while a black woman lies fully clothed on the same bed with her back to the camera contemplating the condition of a fingernail.

Chapter 5 is an analysis of Miller's photographs from the time of their making against the historical background of racial politics in the midwest USA and through the period of their emergence in the public domain, highlighting the fact that they were never released into a place where they could perform the work they were funded to do. Crucially, both Miller and the Guggenheim allowed the project to effectively disappear for over half a century. Therefore, the core purpose of the photographs' making became politically redundant, or at least a failed photographic humanitarian exercise, regardless of how aesthetically successful the images are deemed to be. By not being brought into the public domain at the time of their making, the project was discharged of its original social intent and its meanings became culturally relocated into an archival story of discovery, rather than being photographs that can be read through the work they may have performed in their own time.

The emergence of black British and African photographers throughout the late 1980s and 1990s is discussed in the final chapter, which considers work that was produced in Britain by black photographers to act as counter-images to the stereotypically negative ways in which the racialised body had been positioned within mainstream cultural institutions and the media. The chapter focuses on the practices of the first wave of black British documentary photographers, then analyses a younger generation of British photographers whose production moved purposely away from the documentary tradition to create scenes where 'new ethnicities' could be imagined (S. Hall 1998). Within this context, I discuss the hybrid and transgressive nature of work by Rotimi Fani-Kayode from Nigeria, who was displaced in London on several counts. I situate his practice in contrast to the cultural business of 'discovery' and display of the Malian photographer Seydou Keita, and other African photographers who came to the attention of Western curators through the 1994 Bamako photography festival. I explore the constructions and receptions of African photography in the West and assess how African photographers and their works have been placed culturally and critically, or abstracted from their original context, to fit within Western frames of reference.

By considering the cultural and political conditions in which these photographs emerged, and through an examination of public and private agencies such as the Greater London Council and Jean Pigozzi's Geneva-based Contemporary African Art Collection, we can recognise how agency and cultural intervention change the course of photographic history. These and other powerful European and North American institutions have worked in different ways to bring black British and African photographers into the mainstream, but at what cost and for whose benefit, especially when we consider work produced from 'different' locations (Hall & Sealy 2001)? This is relevant geographically, culturally and politically, within the context of an increasingly globalised art world economy that is managed essentially by European art world elites who end up, as in the case of Seydou Keita, in legal conflicts over ownership of African artists' rights and authenticity of the work. Within these critical new domains of representation, progress is made towards a less Eurocentric photographic discourse. However, the process of control and commerce echoes the historically exploitative, competitive, colonising encounters of extraction and consumption of the image of the Other, how it is managed and how it is made real in the West.

Decolonising the camera aims to contribute to a form of theoretical uncoupling concerning the making, uses, readings and thinking of photography in Western culture. The main objective of the book is to consider how photography functions within the slippery matrix of colonial power, and to bring into sharper focus the other cultural work that photographs perform, especially if we allow them to be articulated from different perspectives, or other ways of seeing.

1

'The Congo Atrocities, A Lecture To Accompany a Series of Sixty Photographic Slides for the Optical Lantern. By W. R. (Revised by Mr E. D. Morel and Rev. J. H. Harris.) Price 6d.'

De las Casas also saw, with rare insight, the ulterior motive of many conquistadors. Though the Spanish carried the Requerimiento – a royal document that outlined Spain's divinely ordained right to sovereignty – into every battle, de las Casas believed that spreading the word of God was largely a ruse: an expedient mask. Ambition, not altruism, was the driving force; gold, not God, was their goal. He believed that the conquistadors slashed and slaughtered their way like 'ravening wild beasts' across the 'New World' not solely in homage to Christ, but to 'swell themselves with riches'. He suspected they had crossed the Atlantic not only to spread the word of the Lord, but to find the gold that washed through the rivers of Amazonia and the minerals that lay beneath their rampaging feet. 'Our work', de las Casas said, 'was to exasperate, ravage, kill, mangle and destroy'. The conquistadors destroyed lives and lands, and they told the Indians that to save their souls, they would need to become Christians.

Joanna Eede, 'For All Peoples of the World Are Men'
(Survival International 2013)

Bartolomé de las Casas (c.1484-1566), 'protector of Indians', was a sixteenth-century Spanish missionary with a passion for social justice.

Three and a half centuries after the death of de las Casas, in the early 1900s, the married missionaries John Hobbis Harris (1874-1940) and Alice Seeley Harris (1870-1970) produced what was probably the first photographic campaign in support of human rights in Africa. This was done in the form of a dramatic lantern slide show that was staged throughout Britain and the United States in the early 1900s (Figure 1). The Harrises had been stationed in the Congo Free State since 1898 and, during their time there, had witnessed the atrocities that were being carried out in the name of King Leopold II.

On returning to England in 1902 they were keen to educate and inform the world of the outrages they had seen, working with the Congo Reform Association (CRA). The CRA had been formed in 1904 by Dr Henry Grattan Guinness, Roger Casement and Edmund Dene Morel. Their aim was to highlight to the international community the levels of inhumanity towards and exploitation of the peoples of the Congo. The CRA and the Harrises collaborated to produce a dynamic lecture that was accompanied by photographic images detailing the violence being inflicted on the Congolese people.

This chapter reconfigures the original organisational structure of the lantern slide show that was produced and performed by the Harrises in the early twentieth century and, where possible, rereads the images in the order in which they first appeared in public, along with the scripted text written by the Harrises. In this way, the chapter offers a critical analysis of both the lecture and the images that made up the show. Through an extended commentary on selected slides, I discuss the complexities of the missionary messages deployed in this particular and extraordinary humanitarian campaign.

The lantern slides, notes Christina Twomey, were seen at:

> hundreds of mass meetings in Britain and the United States, the Harrises' lectures validated the photographic lantern slides they discussed through their presence as white witnesses to African suffering. In this way photographs were incorporated into much older and established methods of activism and consciousness raising.

lectures?

Twomey also states that 'the images of mutilated Congolese entered the culture as relatively novel representation of the suffering body, but they were incorporated into existing cultural practices that required the authenticating presence of whiteness' (Twomey 2012, p.50).

The Harrises' lantern slide show consists of sixty slides divided into four distinct categories. Part 1 is titled 'Philanthropy in the Making' and comprises eleven slides that provide a wide political context for the show, including the geo-specific location of the Congo Free State and an outline of the resources found there: palms, rubber and ivory. Different slides focus on the terms under which King Leopold II was given charge of the Congo by the international community: 'not for the accumulation of rubber at an infinite cost of human life and suffering, but the protection and civilization of the natives of Africa' (Slide 8). They also describe the native people in their 'uncivilised' and reputedly cannibal states. The narrative for the slides presents us with 'a closer view of the executioner', the 'native warrior', and details of 'appearances' that are 'calculated to send a thrill through most of us even at this distance'.

Part 2 is titled 'Philanthropy in Operation' and constitutes slides numbered 12 to 49. The intention of the narrative in this part of the lecture is to build a damning picture of King Leopold II. Framed as a pirate, he is accused of recruiting child soldiers and employing 'cannibal soldiers' to force people to work. As the slides progress, the narrative reveals, in detail, the disturbing horror in the Congo. A chaotic scene of blatant disregard for African life and a brutal, imperious attitude towards the death of the Congolese people is presented. Peaceful villages are flattened, children are hacked to death and eaten, and women are cut in half.

Part 3, 'Philanthropy Exposed', focuses on the revenue that King Leopold II received from the Congo, and on his lack of legitimacy as a ruler, and returns the audience to the idea that he is a pirate.

Part 4 concludes the lecture and is titled 'Philanthropy That May Be'. The narrative accompanying the final slide is effectively a plea for armed intervention from the British government:

The Great Powers have been grossly deceived and they ought to decline any longer to recognise King Leopold's flag as the emblem of a civilised administration … And if our legal and reasonable requests are refused, then let us send a man-of-war to the mouth of the Lower Congo, with orders to prohibit the entry or departure of steamers or craft of any kind until they are granted.

What is evident is that:

until photographs of mutilated Congolese were shown to the world, doubts still remained in some circles [to the effect] that reports of violence in the Congo were overblown. However, after Alice Harris circulated photos in late 1905 with dates, names and other details, Leopold found it more and more difficult to refute the charges of abuse against him. (Nault 2012, p.7)

The case against King Leopold II was critically reliant on the display of atrocity photographs from the Congo, but we can, through the analysis of the context in which these photographs were displayed, examine the complex meanings that they produced and consider the other political purposes and work that they may have served and continue to serve now. It is important, then, that we attempt to unfix these photographs from the dichotomy of good and evil colonial acts in Africa, with the Harrises representing good and Leopold representing evil. If we stop looking at them as strictly historical records, and instead read the photographs across historical time, this allows different meanings to surface and conclusions to be drawn. 'This is the power and purpose of an archive. It preserves and provides the stuff on which histories are based, even if it necessarily and always delivers a partial and particular view, based on availability, choice and chance' (Amkpa & Garb 2013, p.27).

Slide 1. Map Showing the Position of the Congo Free State

Ladies and Gentlemen,
For some time past the eyes of an increasingly large number of people in Great Britain and America have been turned upon that immense tract of country in the heart of Africa, known as the Congo Free State. Ever since the formation of the state there have

been some who have suspected the intentions and good faith of its founder; but during recent years suspicion has developed into certainty, and the revelations which are now made public surpass in horror the wildest dreams of the prophets of evil. It is high time that the conscience of this country was thoroughly aroused; and I therefore beg you to follow me closely, as I endeavour to lay before you, briefly but clearly, the startling indictment against the sovereign of this so-called Free State.

Mr E. D. Morel and Rev. J. H. Harris

The photographs taken at the turn of the twentieth century by Alice Seeley Harris and her missionary colleagues are important for understanding the dark side of European cultural and commercial encounters across central Africa (Young 1995, p.92). As archival photographs they sit in a unique, complicated place, namely at the intersection of the two deadly theatres of European encounter in Africa: commerce and religion. These aspects of colonisation are fundamental to the history of European cultural violence, 'the process where one culture subordinates another' (Spurr 1993, p.4), to the extreme where the subordinated become cultureless, and Western ideals at work in Africa dictate all forms of 'development' and articulation (C. Hall 1992, p.213).

Seeley Harris's photographs help us to address some of the complexities of this, especially when we consider the role that photography has played in the dehumanisation of African and other non-European subjects. Her photographic works are usually discussed in the context of human rights and atrocity photography, with Christina Twomey's essay titled 'The Incorruptible Kodak: Photography, Human Rights and the Congo Campaign' being a recent example (Twomey 2014). However, little analysis has been done on the work that they perform across the wider discourse of racial theory, particularly at the time of their display, or how they may have functioned as a narration on race for their diverse audiences. Not much attention has been paid to the actual language of the lectures that accompanied the photographs when they were displayed as lantern slides at the beginning of the twentieth century. Seeley Harris's photographs are not only early documents of atrocity but are also pioneering portrayals of the black body as a site of excessive violence in Africa (Figure 2). They contain the ideas, images and fantasies of an ostensibly benevolent form of colonisation.

The Harris archive is currently in a fragile state and largely in a condition of disarray. However, there is one facsimile of a document that represents a record of the lecture that the Harrises and E. D. Morel delivered to their audiences. Its full title is 'The Congo Atrocities, A Lecture To Accompany a Series of Sixty Photographic Slides for the Optical Lantern. By W. R. (Revised by Mr E. D. Morel and the Rev. J. H. Harris.) Price 6d.' This document provides a critical starting point from which to contemplate the photographic archive of Alice Seeley Harris. To date there has been no analytical work done that locates the images directly within the context of the lecture, yet to ignore this vital element when reading the images dislocates them from the conditions of their delivery. Because they ran alongside the lecture, as images they were as much heard as seen.

The lecture enables us to enquire into the undercurrents of meanings that accompanied the presentation of the photographs. Within the Harris archive, there is currently no index correlating the images and text. The archive, then, 'ceases to be a univocal, flat, and incontestable indexical trace of what was, and becomes instead a completely textured artefact (concealing many different depths) inviting the viewer to assume many possible different stand-points – both spatial and temporal – in respect to it' (Pinney & Peterson 2003, p.5). Now, Seeley Harris's photographs are not only objects of political agitation but are also moments that expose the myriad forms of colonial violence. It is also clear from the structure of the lecture that other visual aids, such as maps and extracts of texts from political treatises, were used, as well as the lantern slides, in order to build an intricate web of meaning.

Seeley Harris's photographs were either presented by the Harrises themselves or through an international network of Protestant missionaries and members of the humanitarian CRA to thousands of people across Britain and the US. They played an influential role in what Western audiences saw, heard and experienced with regard to interpretations and representations of colonial atrocity in Africa. Her photographs were critical and political images that attracted, mobilised and affected large crowds of people when they were presented in public spaces (Thompson 2012, p.194), and they were agents for change within the European imagination over a period of nearly a decade.

'Considering the long-term significance of the Congo Free State controversy for human rights history, leading human rights historians have devoted little attention to the subject' (Nault 2012, p.1). Seeley Harris's photographs were clearly critical to the success of the CRA in bringing an end to Leopold's hold on the Congo. Published literature indicates that they had an influence on many prominent figures across Britain and the US. While the photographs encouraged humanitarians to voice considerable opposition to Leopold's regime of violence (Nault 2012, p.7), it is only recently that Seeley Harris's work has begun to surface in debates concerning the study of atrocity photography and its histories (Twomey 2014).

Seeley Harris's images hold a unique place within the history of photography. That she was one of the first women photographers to pick up a camera in the cause of humanity represents a critical turn in the history of photography, and forces us to rethink how it has been written in relation to gender, religion, race and empire. Her photographs also show important early images of African victims of violent direct colonial rule. The work they perform across the history and visualisation of violence in Africa is fundamental to the visual, physical and political pressures to which the African body has been subjected in colonial and postcolonial encounters. Seeley Harris's images demonstrate European photography at work in Africa and trace the genealogy of photographic practices and representations that frame the African subject in crisis.

For European photographers, Africa is historically a carnivorous affair. The image that stands out from the Harris archive is that of a young man, Nsala, sitting in front of the remains of his daughter who had been eaten by violent tribes in the service of King Leopold II (Figure 3). It is clear from this, and the vast archives of photographs held in Western collections, such as the photographs taken by the Catholic missionaries Paul Schebesta (1887-1967) and Martin Gusinde (1886-1969) that are owned by the Weltkulturen Museum in Frankfurt, that missionaries and colonial photographers found it difficult to resist the temptation and far-reaching pleasures of capturing African or racialised flesh on film for consumption by audiences at home (Deliss & Mutumba 2014, p.11). The legacy of this visual desire for African flesh is still very much alive and is clearly evidenced today through the outputs of Western media and charitable institutions that use broken black bodies to raise funds for their causes.

Seeley Harris's photographs encouraged people to take action: to directly or indirectly challenge King Leopold II. In this sense, they mark an important visual moment in the photographic framing of Africans. Many of the photographs sit comfortably within the tradition of ethnographic and missionary photography (Maxwell 2000; Edwards 2001); there are, for example, images of prayer meetings held by the missionaries, of Congolese people working for the missionaries or sitting childlike around them.

However, 'many modern writers on missionaries in the Congo fail even to mention Alice Harris' work' (Thompson 2012, p.184). This may well be because, as works that emerged out of a missionary agenda, they offended the missionary sense of purpose, that is, they represented an archive of missionary failure and could therefore be read as problematic within the visualisation of missionary history. Their portrayal of such raw violence implicates the missionary presence in the scenes of devastation.

Missionary proximity to the violence combined with isolation from home, along with interdependence on aggressive rubber traders and agents for basic survival, would suggest a degree of missionary compliance with and tolerance of the levels of violence being acted upon the Congolese. While W. J. T. Mitchell argues that 'the psychological forces that lead people to be offended by an image are invisible and unpredictable' (Mitchell 2006, p.126), it remains valid to ask: at what point in the theatre of violence in the Congo were the British missionaries offended? And what actually constituted the nature of that offence in order for them to begin to act against the atrocities?

Offending images do not all offend in the same way. Some offend the beholder, others the object represented. Some offend because they degrade something valuable or desecrate something sacred, others because they glorify something hateful and despised. Some of them violate moral taboos and standards of decency, while some are politically offensive, insults to national honour or unwelcome reminders of an ignoble past. Some offend because of the manner of representation, so that a caricature or stereotype offends not because of *who* but *how* it represents. (Mitchell 2006, p.131)

Seeley Harris's photographs clearly evoke the image of an 'ignoble' British slave-owning past from which the Protestant church profited. As images presented in a religious setting, they also prompt the questions of how long and why British Protestants stayed silent in full knowledge of the atrocities taking place in Leopold's Congo (Hochschild 2000, p.114).

As Kevin Grant has argued:

The missions' problems intensified at the turn of the century on two fronts. Firstly, the rubber industry in Congo grew rapidly after the mid-1890s and the increasing labour demands of the state and concessionaire companies interfered with the missionaries' access to African communities.

Grant also notes that:

more importantly, the State refused to grant new stations to British Protestant missions, at the same time as it encouraged the growth of Belgian and French Catholic missions, which took a more circumspect view toward its brutal practices. It is noteworthy that even under these circumstances the Protestant missions did not establish a closely united front of opposition to the state's policies, nor did the majority of members in any given mission participate actively in public protest against the regime. (Grant 2001, p.32)

Protest against the atrocities in the Congo by the British can therefore be read through the lens of self-serving interest, because: 'It was only after years of failed attempts to expand inland that the executive of the Congo Balolo Mission condemned the

Congo State in the British press in April 1903, with the Baptist Missionary Society following suit in October 1905' (Grant 2001, p.32).

African bodies subjected to brutal violence, torture and death were tolerable to British missionaries as long as the missionaries' aims in the Congo were being carried out. Only once it was obvious that British Protestant missionaries' progress was being stifled in the Congo did they begin a campaign against Leopold's atrocities.

As noted above, Seeley Harris's photographs are increasingly being referenced in debates concerning atrocity, memory and photography. They surface as part of a growing interest in the study of atrocity by academics from various disciplines when examining the work that photographs perform in understanding and memorialising past violent events (Sliwinski 2006). However, even within contemporary readings, her photographs more often than not continue to perform 'reassuring symbolic work' concerning atrocity for predominantly white humanitarian-type audiences (Berger 2011, p.6). This work amounts to endorsing a legacy of images of Africa in Europe that maintain the presence of violence and helplessness as acceptable.

The photographs produced by Seeley Harris cannot be viewed solely as isolated moments of humanitarian Christian benevolence in contrast to Belgian atrocities. Politically and culturally they sit in a more ambivalent location. The work the photographs do now is unstable, as overall, they exist within a dynamic form of British colonisation. Simply repositioning these photographs within the context of *The Violence of the Image* (Kennedy & Patrick 2014) denies the fact that the Harrises and their presence in the Congo were themselves a component of a violent penetrating phase of aggression that propagated white supremacy (Headrick 1981, p.12). The images were used at home to raise not only awareness but also money, to further assist the missionary work in the Congo. They therefore have to be read as one of the earliest examples in photography of the black broken body being put to work as part of an economy of display, to service and extend a preferred vision of British colonialism.

This visual work has a foundational core in abolitionist images trading in emblems of black suffering and passivity. Such images are typified by the well-known picture of 'Gordon', which was produced as a *carte-de-visite* in the US in 1863. Here, the back of 'Gordon' is presented to the camera showing the mass of his keloid scars, which became symbolic of the violence of slavery in the US. The photographs portraying Congolese people with missing limbs came to represent a form of renegade or crazed colonial brutality in Africa. They encourage the viewer to think of these moments in isolation, away from the broader questions of colonisation and cultural oblivion. Seeley Harris's photographs are not deployed as images against Europe's wider colonial enterprises in Africa. They focus on the more singular and intimate forms of violence that were being conducted by the agents of King Leopold II.

The Harrises as humanitarian activists were clearly at ease with the manner in which the British conducted their own colonial business. British colonialism was a much more mechanised affair. Its violence was practised through 'the art of killing from a distance' (Lindqvist & Tate 2007, p.46). In 1898, the same year in which the Harrises arrived in the Congo, 'The Battle of Omdurman' took place, where 'technical superiority provides a natural right to annihilate the enemy even when he is defenceless' (Lindqvist & Tate 2007, p.65). At Omdurman, Winston Churchill, who participated in the campaign, noted that the act of killing became 'tedious ... after five hours of fighting, twenty Britons, twenty of the Egyptian allies and 11,000 Dervishes lay dead' (Headrick 1981, p.118). The final appeal to the audience at the Harrises' lecture was for the navy to send a man-of-war to the Congo to act as a blockade and force King Leopold II to comply with the Congo Reform Association's demands.

Seeley Harris's 'Congo Atrocities' photographs expose the social tensions surrounding Europe's conflicting 'civilising' practices at work in Africa at the turn of the twentieth century. They opened up a critical space in which their audiences were able to voice their outrage. They moved the viewer to a potentially different state of reception of images produced in Africa, away from the securities of benevolence and enlightenment and into an uncomfortable situation of violent abstraction in which blame for the atrocities is easily located. The photographs could be read as traumatic markers situated on a public platform to generate an immediate act of interrogation into the previously unseen violent conditions in the Congo. When we read the Harrises' lantern slide show now, we can establish that there is a distinctive, ideological, two-faced aspect to it: one face scorns the violence of King Leopold II; the other wilfully accepts the violence of British imperialism as natural and right. Neither face recognises the human condition of the African as fully equal.

Therefore, Seeley Harris's photographs are important because they changed the field of perception concerning European encounters in Africa. They present an unacceptable outcome of European presences in Africa to the coloniser. The photographs offend audiences because they act as representations of the savage face of Europe at work. They also excite viewers because they claim a morally higher ground over the Belgians and reinforce British colonial presences as a more pure and divine form of subjugation.

The photographs destroyed the prevailing popular myth that all was well with the programme of modernisation of Africa by Europe. We cannot, however, simply view them as basic evidence of actual violence. They are more than the sum of the victims' stories. They also allow us to see the outcomes of King Leopold II's totalitarian regime. The body, as Foucault noted, is 'directly involved in a political field; power relations have an immediate hold upon it; they invest it, mark it, train it, torture it, force it to carry out tasks, to perform ceremonies, to emit signs' (Foucault 1991, p.25). Monarchies and totalitarian systems, according to Foucault, 'function through the overt exercise and display of punishment for the violation of laws, such as public execution' (Sturken 2001, p.96), while the modernising, post-Enlightenment states of nineteenth-century Europe eschewed such spectacular displays of violence and instead found non-coercive ways to discipline the body.

The emphasis on the display of overt violence in Seeley Harris's photographs suggests, though, that the modernisation process can easily revert to premodern forms of the exercise of power, signalling the failure of both missionary Christianity and, more importantly, of the Enlightenment as an over-arching concept. They provoked the audience, who, as I discuss later, would have had some knowledge of the violence that had been taking place in the Congo for at least a decade. The photographs rendered the religious conversion of the African subject useless before the very eyes of those with the greatest investment in the idea of 'saving' African souls. What Mark Twain in his celebrated 1905 satire of Leopold's rule *King Leopold's Soliloquy* referred to as 'the incorruptible Kodak' symbolically revealed the absence of God, the failure of the Europeans as a civilising force, and the disastrous complacency of the white missionary (Twain 1970, p.73).

The opposing ideological forces of commerce and religion are exposed in these photographs, which reveal so much of what has been historically ignored. Through these images we can see the impact of both these forces on the African subject, in different but equally violent conditions of oppression. For King Leopold II, colonisation was primarily concerned with the continued domination of the African body by the tradition of slavery. His method was to break the African body by any means possible in order to profit. His unique power lay in the fact that he did not actually own the enslaved subject. His regime was based on traditional forms of domination, deception and violence, rendering the African ultimately disposable (Bales 1999). In contrast, the British missionary preferred to use a more subtle form of domination to coerce the African subject, focusing on their moral and religious condition, saving their souls or moulding an ontological new African into an imagined Eurocentric being. Seeley Harris's photographs depict the individuals caught in this no-win space of objectification and cultural oblivion. Some of those photographed are named, thus bringing them closer to the idea of a distinctive identity for the audience. However, the naming process only marginally reduces the distance between the subject and the audience, unaccompanied as it is by any reference to those photographed as fully developed human subjects in their own right. Thus the deployment of a single name in effect becomes a patronising term of colonial endearment.

The 'Congo Atrocities' lecture assumed that its audience had little or no knowledge of the Congo. The Congolese were presented as having no history and their vast country enters the audience's imagination as if the beginning of time in central Africa came about by the discovery, presence and absolute mediation of the missionaries. The Congo in this context has no indigenous perspective, no cultural articulation or expression; it becomes, in fact, the story of one man: Henry Morton Stanley (1841-1904). Stanley's discovery gave meaning to the region in terms of assets, time and place. For the missionaries and their audience, even though Seeley Harris's photographs relayed this as a devastating encounter, what the 'Congo Atrocities' lecture marked was the moment of birthing of modernity for the Congo, a most violent introduction to the industrial world. The photographs therefore become representatives of 'the point at which the West began to universalise itself'; they are 'connected with the attempt to construct the world as a single place, with the world market, with globalisation, and with that moment when Western Europe tried to convert the rest of the world into a province of its own forms of life' (S. Hall et al. 2001, p.18). The key colonising objective was to remake Africa as a form of temporally backward European state, ripe for subjugation and economic exploitation, with a black workforce that was lower in human value than Europe's peasants, and which would naturally, with the assistance of force and superstition, serve white supremacy.

Slide 2. H. M. Stanley

> Mr. H. M. Stanley was the first to trace the Congo River from the Great Lakes to its well-known mouth in the Atlantic, and he it was who described with natural enthusiasm the possibilities of this great division of Equatorial Africa. He foresaw quite clearly that under the influence of civilisation the country could be made to yield immeasurable stores of animal, vegetable and mineral wealth, to the mutual advantage of the white and coloured races ... We shall see how the advent of the European, which Stanley naturally encouraged, has 'ameliorated the condition' of the 'moderately industrious' native.

The sarcasm in the text accompanying Slide 2 allows blame to be apportioned to those who were from the outset employed in the service of King Leopold II. Stanley is identified as Leopold's agent in the field, and he here becomes a disingenuous man and a betrayer of good Christian values. Therefore, and by implication, the 'Congo Atrocities' were, at their very core, a British problem. This is because it was the great British characteristics of tenacity, invention and endeavour that gifted Leopold his colony.

Slides 3, 4 and 5. The Wealth of Country

These three slides share the same main title, followed by the word 'Palms', 'Rubber' or 'Ivory', and each one carries a detailed narrative of these natural resources available in the Congo. Regarding palms, Slide 3 relays that:

> in some districts there are entire forests of it and as one tree yields annually from 500 to 1000 nuts it will be seen at once that great wealth was being wasted … The natives knew nothing of their value in Stanley's day, but they have learned a good deal since.

Here, Stanley is credited as being responsible for the shift in local understanding of the value of palm oil in Europe, albeit a value that increased the risk of exploitation of the natives.

Slide 4 discusses the abundance of rubber:

> But more important by far is the gum of the India-rubber plant; and the great vines which produce the sap which we call rubber grow here in luxuriant profusion. I do not profess that the picture represents the rubber vines, but in forests such this they are found in large numbers.

This slide works as a scene-setter to help the audience imagine the density of opportunity that the Congo forests offered. The narrative continues:

> As great creepers they hang in festoons from tree to tree, and said Stanley, 'if every warrior living on the immediate banks of the Congo and its navigable affluents were to pick about a third of a pound of rubber each day throughout the year and convey it to the trader for sale, five million pounds worth of vegetable produce could be obtained without exhaustion to the wild forest production'.

Stanley is once again cited as the main protagonist in the fantasy of the commercial opportunities the Congo offers for trade.

Slide 5 focuses on ivory, and acts as a damning marker of Stanley's enterprise. The lecture reads:

> One other source of wealth cannot be overlooked ... the picture shows a couple of young elephants shot at Lomako ... Stanley calculated that there were some 200,000 elephants in the Congo basin, each carrying an average 50lbs weight of ivory on his head, which would represent, when collected and sold in Europe, some five million pounds.

The photograph accompanying the slide, of two dead baby elephants, sits uncomfortably with the narrative, as the ivory yielded from this kill would have been zero, the elephants being too young. The dead baby elephants are shown in the foreground, laid out side by side on a well-kept path as if they have been trained in a circus to lie down simultaneously. Even in death, they remain cute creatures of curiosity, and the fact of their killing becomes a facile representational moment of European power in Africa. The baby elephants could not have been shot for any other reason than sport, but as sporting trophies they make a pathetic display. The photograph reveals a powerful and wasteful culture of destruction rather than industrious cultivation and benevolence. This is the first image of death presented in the 'Congo Atrocities' lecture and marks the transition from the topographic to the evidential use of photographs to show 'real' violence. The wastefulness becomes emblematic of the violent culture of destruction in the Congo. It reads as an unnecessary form of colonial excess. The killing of these two young elephants sets the scene for the ensuing critique of violence against the people and the environment. The heroic figure of Stanley is ridiculed through this photograph; he is transformed into an ironic, tragic, Grim Reaper-like figure that brings death and destruction to the Congo. He is ultimately positioned as naïve regarding the rich natural resources of the Congo, and the narrative brings into focus King Leopold II's intentions and greed. The lecture highlights this in claiming that:

Stanley, however, was keen-sighted enough to place Ivory 'fifth in rank among the natural products of the basin'. He foresaw its extinction in the most distant future. What he did not foresee was the methods by which this would be brought about. He did not reckon on the vigour of the royal trader.

Seeley Harris's photographs and the accompanying lecture work within ideological parameters that are concerned primarily with exposing wrongs relating to forced slavery on the African body. The archive builds on the foundational critical misgivings expressed by other missionaries who were attempting to raise public awareness of the existence of forced labour in the Congo. One early opposer of King Leopold II was a French Catholic missionary to Africa, Cardinal Charles Lavigerie (1825-92), who, during a sermon at St Sulpice in Paris in 1888, 'shocked his audience by describing the horrors of the Congo slave trade: villages surrounded and burnt; men captured and yoked together; women and children penned like cattle in the slave markets' (David 2011). Another dissenting missionary voice was that of George Washington Williams (1849-91). Williams was an African American journalist, pastor, historian, lawyer and Civil War veteran, and in 1890, he visited King Leopold II in Belgium, and went to the Congo, with the intention of seeing the benevolent Leopold's regime at work. Horrified by the violence he witnessed, from the Congo he wrote a comprehensive open letter to the king, in which he invited the international community to take action against Leopold and to hold him to account for his criminal acts. In his long and detailed letter, he delivers a profound humanitarian message:

I now appeal to the Powers which committed this infant State to your Majesty's charge, and to the great States which gave it international being; and whose majestic law you have scorned and trampled upon, to call and create an International Commission to investigate the charges herein preferred in the name of Humanity, Commerce, Constitutional Government and Christian Civilisation. (Williams, in Kilson & Hill 1969, pp.98-9)

Williams's appeal was circulated widely: 'Copies [were] sent to the British Secretary of State for Foreign Affairs, the US Secretary of State, and newspapers and magazines throughout Britain and the United States, commencing the international debate over the Congo Free State' (Nault 2012, p.2). His letter seems to have been well received but without the added weight of photographs, it did not attract great public attention, and was easily negated as merely the subjective point of view of a disgruntled or ill-informed black missionary. Photographs would have helped Williams to demonstrate an objective distance from his campaign by creating a 'real' picture of the atrocities with which audiences could engage. However, the lack of visual evidence cannot be the only reason why his appeal did not strike an even deeper chord with the political powers in Britain and the US. Williams's appeal took place within a wider field of contemporary transatlantic racial politics; he was a black American in Africa, offering a damning critique of the royal-blooded European Leopold. Especially given these circumstances of his racialised political and cultural weakness, Williams's criticism of the king was an extraordinary political act. He refused to be an accomplice in this theatre of non-recognition (Levinas 1987, p.109). At the time of his writing, the US was locked into the segregationist Jim Crow laws, and a humanitarian appeal of this magnitude from a relatively disenfranchised black voice could not carry the political weight to effect the changes Williams demanded. Unfortunately, Williams died in 1891 in England on his way back to the US. His contribution to exposing Leopold may well have been more significant had he lived longer (Thompson 2012, p.171). What is certain is that his race would have hindered greatly his protestations against Leopold's blatant disregard for life, culture and international agreements.

The complex position of black missionaries and the realities of their race are clearly defined through the experience of William Henry Sheppard (1865-1927). Sheppard was fully aware of his designated role as a subordinate to white missionary authority in Africa. He was in no doubt about the disadvantages of being black and how this would impact on his being recognised as a valid concerned voice commenting on the atrocities. In 1899, Sheppard had reported and photographed a massacre in the Pianga region but when pressed as to why he was not more vocal about making public his report he stated that, 'Being a coloured man, I would not be understood criticizing a white government before white people' (Austin 2005). Unlike Williams, Sheppard was fully aware that, as an American of African descent, his humanity was politically, ideologically and culturally vulnerable, and he recognised his subaltern position in the missionary world.

The question of the state of African American humanity and American racism at the time Sheppard was photographing atrocities in the Congo is evidenced most clearly in the photographic and theoretical work produced by W. E. B. Du Bois at the turn of the twentieth century. In 1900, as part of the Paris Exposition Universelle, he displayed his 'Georgia Negro' portraits for the first time, as an interventionist cultural act to oppose the archives that registered the 'Negro' as inferior. Du Bois was deliberately working 'against the scientific archives that constructed a visual racial typology at the turn of the century' (Smith 2004, p.23). 'The introductory chart that framed Du Bois's social study of "The Georgia Negro" for visitors at the Paris Exposition of 1900 carried his lasting declaration: "The problem of the twentieth century is the problem of the colour line"' (Smith 2004, p.22). For those subjected to King Leopold II's rule around 1900, the problem was not just that of the colour line; it was the age-old chattel slavery, the unstoppable force of European colonialism in all its guises.

Slavery as a period of shame across Europe had been put to rest and advocates of the abolition movement well celebrated and honoured. Seeley Harris's photography produced emotive rememory work, by reawakening the spectre of European slavery. The images critiqued the Western world's sense of progress and, as archival records of Western endeavour, now allow us to peek into the dark side of Enlightenment thought.

There has been much discussion about photographs and their capacity to trouble the subconscious, as well as the unfixed nature of their meaning and reception. 'A photograph might be a fixed image but its meaning is much less stable' (Campany 2007, p.20), and its reception cannot be guaranteed (S. Hall 1973). Photographs do not carry universal meanings. 'Rather, an image "speaks" to specific sets of viewers who happen to be tuned into some aspect of the image, such as style, content, the world it constructs, or the issues it raises' (Sturken

2001, p.45). It is important to recognise time, place and emotive voice in the location and reception of photographs, especially when looking at the Other and the cultural positionality of the different people in the imagination of those doing the looking. Colonial curiosity had dangerous outcomes, and is not to be underestimated as a mild-mannered, passive act of engagement. The 'Congo Atrocities' lecture and photographs constructed a politics of visualisation of the Other that was specifically deployed to engage the force of white moral outrage and religious conviction surrounding the knowledge of the atrocities taking place in the Congo. This locked these pictures and their subjects into a tight form of visual exchange. The question of a less stable visual meaning is suffocated by the narrative descriptions that focus on King Leopold II's deceptive political manoeuvrings and violence. The lecture keeps the portrayal of colonial violence coupled with King Leopold II and, by extension, frees the missionaries of guilt. The photographs within the context of the lecture do two distinctive types of cultural work. They overtly demonise King Leopold II and they covertly erase British missionary knowledge and inertia regarding the atrocities in the Congo.

Slide 6. Leopold II from Stanley's Standpoint

In this slide, the narrative positions King Leopold II as a monarchic magician who cast a spell over the world, stating that:

> He captivated everybody by his philanthropic schemes for regen-erating and saving the African races ... Stanley fell under the spell of the philanthropic monarch. So did the British Chambers of Commerce. So did the Protestant Missionary Societies. So did everybody – almost everybody, for there were just a few notable exceptions.

The lecture does not mention who these exceptions were. Williams's and Sheppard's contributions to the knowledge of the atrocities are conveniently absent, marking a historical erasure of their attempts to raise awareness of the situation in the Congo. Sheppard's analysis of the futile nature of his expression of concern against the violence of Leopold is here validated. In 1890, Williams in particular acted in the moment of discovery of slavery; responding immediately and directly to what he had seen in the Congo, and reaching a broad public platform in doing so. Therefore, the British missionaries could not, with any secure justification, claim the same sense of humanitarian urgency and responsibility that was clearly evident in the work of Williams.

The early part of the lecture's narration and display of photographs would have disturbed Britain's religious circles' sense of organisational political confidence, a confidence that was part of the legacy of the abolitionist movement. The Congo Free State afforded the merchant classes a free trade zone, and there would have been much anticipation of this economic potential. The Harrises' lecture can thus also be read in the context of British religious and commercial opportunities in the Congo that were being denied; that is, the other emotive and real issue at hand was not the welfare of the Congolese people but the welfare of the British nation state. Britain saw itself as being cheated by King Leopold II's illegal commercial exploits in the Congo, which clearly broke with the terms and conditions under which he had been granted custodianship of the Congo by Europe's more powerful countries. The unstated subtext of the lecture's demand for military intervention by the British, then, was that a blockade mounted for humanitarian motives would have decidedly beneficial side effects for British commercial interests.

Slide 7. Extracts from the Articles of the Berlin Conference

This slide reminded the audience of the 1884 conference in Berlin, which the narration claims 'resulted in the recognition of the new state and the eulogising of its author; and all the powers congratulated themselves and each other on their humanity and self-abnegation'. Nowhere in the rest of the lecture is there any mention of the other outcomes of the conference, in which the foundations for Europe's colonisation of Africa were put in place. The narration continues with a focus on the conference's Article VI:

> All powers ... bind themselves to watch over the preservation of the native tribes, and to care for the improvement of the condition of their moral and material well-being, and help in suppressing

slavery, and especially the slave trade. They shall, without distinction of creed or nation, protect and favour all religious, scientific, or charitable institutions and undertakings created and organised for the above ends, or which aim at instructing the natives and bringing home to them the blessing of civilisation.

The critical point here was to illustrate how completely King Leopold II had broken his agreement with Europe. The lecture and Seeley Harris's photographs therefore appear intended to disrupt the benevolent self-image of their intended Western audience, which believed fundamentally that, as Europeans, their governments, religious institutions, charities and science had a natural right over the African body and African resources, but which nevertheless was shocked to be confronted with the continuation of violent slavery as part of that dispensation.

The photographs, then, do much more than just put the mutilated and distressed African body on display. They represent the colonised black body as victim, as well as perversely and critically reflecting the colonisers back onto themselves as they display the outcomes and effects of corrupt colonisation on the African body. The coloniser as spectator is present in each frame taken and each photograph is framed for the spectators at home. The colonisers in all their forms – religious or commercial – are signified most powerfully by what is violently cut away from the black body. This in turn creates a record against which the coloniser gauges himself as a competent, civilising authority. The black mutilated body on display in Seeley Harris's archive is in fact emblematic of the failed authority that the coloniser has over the black body, for the black body has to be whole in order for the colonising ideal of civilisation to be fulfilled. The colonised must reflect fully his state of conversion to the colonising condition. This is why it was important for King Leopold II to try and create a counter-positive image of the black subject to those that were presented by the Harrises.

As a broken subject, the image of an African slave serves no real purpose in the post-abolition world; it is an image that must be denied and repressed within the psyche of the European enlightenment programme. The transformation from native savage to enlightened black subject must be done with the body complete.

Any mark of violence against the black body becomes inadvertently a mark of violence against the righteous Europeans, a representation of the failures in their mission. The humanity of the African subject is therefore not all that is at stake when looking at the photographs that accompany the 'Congo Atrocities' lecture, but also, critically, Europe's idea of itself. The Harrises' campaign was not about the liberation and freedom of the Congolese; it was essentially concerned with eradicating the physical brutality towards a 'recognised' lesser African being. The image of the contented African subject under European rule works as a sign of European superiority, like taming a wild beast, and this as an act of power is much more productive than the act of killing.

> What is left of the colonized at the end of this stubborn effort to dehumanize him? He is surely no longer an alter ego of the colonizer. He is hardly a human being. He tends rapidly toward becoming an object. As an end, in the colonizer's supreme ambition, he should exist only as a function of the needs of the colonizer, i.e., be transformed into a pure colonized. (Memmi 2003, p.130)

A broken colonised body therefore suggests colonial failure in an enlightened colonising mind, a mind that denies the presence of violence as being the essence of colonial rule. This is the condition within which the Harrises were trapped.

Through a now well-established photographic colonial gaze and its empirical systems of knowledge exchange (Maxwell 2000, p.9), and despite false European claims to recognise the condition of the African that are clearly evident in the detail of article VI of the Berlin conference, we can gauge from Seeley Harris's photographs the tragic scene and the devastating outcome of this historical and internationally ratified European encounter with Africa. Rather than bringing the African subject closer to Europeans, photography often titillated and facilitated the European fascination with difference. 'This led to a particular genre of African colonial photography which aimed to contrast European progress with African backwardness' (Thompson 2012, p.34). Much of the work contained within Seeley Harris's photographic archive reinforces a sense of African backwardness. What surfaces is an acultural being on the edge of life, complicit in its own destruction.

The 'Congo Atrocities' images are part of a chain of violent connections that bind the colonising missionary, King Leopold II and the African body together. The lecture and its photographs are capable of producing 'an over-determining definition of "context" [that can] obscure readings against the grain and obliterate the space for counter-narratives' (Edwards 2001, p.108). Neither of the European forces present in the Congo offered a space for African wellbeing to develop. The missionaries actively worked to erase that which they considered unholy, and Leopold worked to erase that which he thought unproductive. As external forces with core conflicting values, methods and ideologies, which clearly had a different understanding of the nature of benevolence and how it should be applied in Africa, neither the missionaries (Christianity) nor Leopold (capitalism) could accommodate a sense of value in the alterity of the Africans' humanity. Cultural recognition in European encounters with Africa, as is evident in these two positions, exists only in a hierarchical construct of racial difference.

The African Other when seen from the European standpoint is not met with parity. The African subject is faced with forces of persistent conversion, exploitation and brutality. Seeley Harris's photographs are a critical part of the story of photography in Africa, in that they alter our perception of the way colonisers acted on the African body. When Leopold considered the African, he embodied the violence of the colonising gaze, but saw no human presence. In the work of Emmanuel Levinas, taking responsibility is an infinite act of humanity towards the Other, when we look into the face of the Other (Levinas 2006). Leopold culturally and ethically could not recognise the face of the Other, revealing his absolute inability to take responsibility for the humanity of the Congolese. In this significant racial blind spot, both Leopold and the Other were doomed, locked in a violent struggle that would, over time, as Frantz Fanon states, finally end through acts of extreme anti-colonial violence (Fanon 1963). Leopold was metaphorically doomed to carry on killing, even after his death, via the Belgian state, and the Other was doomed to cultural and physical oblivion as part of a process of liberation. As Levinas states:

The other man commands by his face, which is not confined in the form of its appearance; naked, stripped of its form, denuded of its very presence, which would again mask it like its own portrait; wrinkled skin, trace of itself, presence that at every moment is a retreat into hollow of death with an eventuality of no return. The otherness of the fellow man is this hollow of no-place where, face, he already takes leave (*s'absente*), without promise of return and resurrection. (Levinas 2006, p.7)

Seeley Harris's photographs disturbed the coloniser because they revealed his capacity for oblivion: 'colonisation is not merely satisfied with holding a people in its grip and emptying the native's brain of all form and content. By a kind of perverted logic it turns to the past of the oppressed people, and distorts, disfigures, and destroys it' (Fanon 1963, p.170).

Slide 8. The Ideal Congo – A Civilised Country

This slide bolsters its critique of King Leopold II by stating that:

The late Under Secretary for Foreign Affairs, speaking in the British House of Commons on June 9th, 1904, expressed the international view quite clearly: When the United States first, and European governments subsequently, recognised the existence in the Congo Basin of a government possessed of a national status, that recognition was accorded not to the Congo State, but to an Association professing an international character, and proclaiming before the world as the object of its being, not the accumulation of rubber at an infinite cost of human life and suffering, but the protection and civilisation of the natives of Africa.

The narrative builds a strong sense of international political commitment to 'protection and civilisation' of the Congo natives and provides a powerful appeal to those in the audience who may have been of a more secular persuasion. What was at stake was of global political significance; a treaty defaulted upon, and 'Signatory Powers' needed to be mobilised against Leopold. The civilising mission in the Congo could not be fulfilled without a close alignment between the state and the church, and here the lecture requests a greater degree of state intervention to clear the path for British missionary work to continue, work that was being blocked by Leopold.

At this stage in the politics of the presentation of the 'Congo Atrocities' lecture, the missionaries evidently felt compromised. From their perspective, they had not been allowed to succeed because of the other external colonising forces at work around them. What they failed to recognise, even at the height of this humanitarian moment, was that all these colonising presences were in part responsible for the conditions that had developed since the Congo Free State was formed. The intensity of Leopold's violence had been known for years, and had been tolerated as a necessary evil. While Protestant missions up the Congo River were made possible, British missionary silence regarding the atrocities became a convenient historical revision of the humanitarian concerns voiced in the lecture. This compliance incites an important counter-reading of Seeley Harris's photographs, which became a double-edged marker of accusation against both King Leopold II and the cohort of British missionaries present in the Congo from 1885 to 1904.

The photographs, then, prompt a level of enquiry that is common to much analysis concerning colonisation and extreme levels of violence. Albert Memmi describes the condition of seeing the colonising self from a position of privilege:

> for how long could he fail to see the misery of the colonized and the relation of that misery to his own comfort? He realises that this easy profit is so great only because it is wrested from others. In short, he finds two things in one: he discovers the existence of the colonizer as he discovers his own privilege. (Memmi 2003, p.51)

Although Seeley Harris produced critical work, it was informed from an absolute position of privilege. The Harrises did not seem to recognise themselves as colonisers, and Alice's position as a colonising force complicates the idea of her photographs as an instance of what Sharon Sliwinski has called the 'childhood of human rights', that is, early examples of the use of photography for humanitarian causes (Sliwinski 2006).

Images of violence, either as a form of cultural ridicule, titillation or caricature against the African or other indigenous peoples, have a long and well-documented history, as do those produced to generate sympathy for the victims of colonisation and slavery (Wood 2000). In 1904, atrocity in photographs, especially those that focused on violence by Europeans against Africans, was a new development. As far as public encounters with photography were concerned, Seeley Harris's photographs were foundational for a new way of seeing twentieth-century Africa, and they marked a new chapter in the visual consumption of Africa in the Western metropolis. When the native was photographically rendered, they were mediated into a subject of curiosity, a lower human form, out of harmony with European capitalist ideals or, alternatively, posed on the edge of humanity: a raw savage reproduced for voyeuristic pleasure, staged as ripe for religious indoctrination, primed for hard industrial labour or ready to be tamed for domestic work. These representations cumulatively construct an authentic but lesser human form, producing these figures as primarily on earth for European benefit. In 1904, the savage native was very much alive in the Western imagination: 'savages – whatever their supposed racial origins – were said to be characterised by "ferocity" and "treachery", their bodies were self-mutilated, and they lacked language and ate people' (Pinney & Peterson 2003, p.59).

Within the realm of the Western public imagination, the Harrises' slide show thus sat within a wider set of dominant colonial narratives that were at work in Europe and the US in this period, narratives which helped to shape perceptions of the Other. This phenomenon is tragically seen through the treatment of Ota Benga in 1904. Benga, a Congolese Pygmy, was put on display as part of the St Louis World's Fair. Within two years he could be seen at the Bronx Zoo, New York City, sharing a monkey house with an orang-utan. The event was an international sensation making headlines in Europe and across the US (Newkirk 2015). Effectively, as can be seen in the treatment of Benga, commercial gain dictated the context in which the colonised subject was exhibited. *just egg?*

The context of colonial encounters within the West was dominated by fantasy, display, the rhetoric of discovery and new forms of pseudo-knowledge production surrounding race. Encounters between the colonised subject and the colonisers at home was primarily through the spectacle of world fairs such as that held at St Louis, which contained human zoos from the colonies, and through the circulation of anatomical or anthropological photographs that focused on 'primitive' races billed to audiences as being near extinction. These images were sold in the form of affordable and collectable cards. 'Photographs produced for the mass tourist market were wedded even more firmly to the stereotype' of the exotic or savage Other because they were commercially viable commodities (Maxwell 2000, p.10). Through commercial outlets, they rapidly became the dominant set of visual tropes that created, objectified and distanced the colonised subject from European time. The colonised black body on display at this time became a living relic of humanity. Therefore, with the Harrises presenting mutilated black bodies within a political and cultural climate of extreme fascination with the African body, part of the work the lantern slide lecture may have performed, when shown to its white public, was providing another layer of voyeuristic pleasure generated by the spectacle of fragmented black bodies on the edge of life. *this is heavy*

Slide 9. Entrance to a Cannibal Village

Bringing forth the image of the savage cannibal, the main narrative of this slide highlights that:

> the Congo was not a region of ideal happiness and peace for the Negro before the advent of the white man. It was, in fact, a region of isolated tribes and communities, almost the whole of which, except in the south, were confirmed cannibals. In the northern half of the Congo Free State incessant wars and slave raids took place, not with a view to supplying labour, but with the intention of obtaining wives, and above all, victims for the cannibal feast. But then, where is ideal happiness to be found in this world?

The accompanying image 'shows the cage-like entrance to a Cannibal town – an entrance which could easily be made to act as a trap on occasion'. The 'Congo Atrocities' lecture animated the image of a base civilisation, with men having multiple wives and eating other people. The slide does not actually show an image of a cannibal; this is left to the imagination of the audience. The cannibal presence instead appears here through the context of a dwelling's entrance, which also serves, according to the lecture, as a possible human trap, a powerful emotive context.

Subsequently, the lecture takes a distinctive turn away from the Congo cannibal, back to a place that brings the native closer to the European. The final part of the narrative for this slide contradicts the information previously shared with the audience when it announces that, 'The missionaries, however, state that many of the native tribes, even in the north, have never been cannibal'. Clearly, sympathy would not be forthcoming, if a strong impression of the native as cannibal was left with the audience, as it would leave the humanity of the Congo native open to counter-interpretation and would risk arguments that their extinction was desirable because they were non-human and beyond redemption. The construct of the cannibal created the ultimate and most charged justification for colonial presences in Africa and, when required, a cannibal threat would justify the use of violence.

A variant image of the savage cannibal in Africa that was often reproduced by missionary photographers in the Congo:

> served one of two purposes: either to show aspects of missionary work, including the transformative power of that work on the African converts, or to show various studies of Africans who had not come under the influence of the mission – the purpose here being predominantly one of contrast with the converts. (Thompson 2012, p.13)

Seeley Harris's photographs portray violence but they also carry an embedded message of the African subject as being a cultureless, helpless child who would, with proper guidance and missionary application, become a good hardworking African Christian, and who would thereby mirror the colonising missionary ideals and character 'to the point where Africans are walking abstractions, inanimate things or invisible creatures' (West 1987, p.23). The objective was

when does protection become erasure?

the production of a Christian, industrious, happy African, who was nurtured out of cultural darkness and into the light of modernity. Or, put another way, the objective was to coerce the idle African into becoming a profitable, productive being through "religious" enlightenment.

> The mythical portrait of the colonized therefore includes an unbelievable laziness and that of the colonizer, a virtuous taste for action. At the same time the colonizer suggests that employing the colonized is not very profitable, thereby authorizing his unreasonable wages. (Memmi 2003, p.123)

Whatever the issue, the outcome is the same: force of some kind must be applied to the African. The success of such colonising work would leave only one remaining cultural marker of difference in place, one that cannot be erased, that is, the irresolvable epidermal scheme of things, 'the fact of blackness' (Fanon 1986, p.109).

Everything else regarding African cultural life in missionary and capitalistic terms was scheduled for oblivion.

> Modernity, or at least that component of it represented by economic expansion of the capitalist process of production, produces cultural amnesia not by accident but intrinsically and necessarily. Forgetting is built into the capitalist process of production itself, incorporated in the bodily experience of its life-spaces. (Connerton 2009, p.125)

The process of capitalistic production clearly aided King Leopold II's amnesia regarding his proposed and designated position in the Congo.

The thousands of people attending the 'Congo Atrocities' lectures would have expected to see images of violence. The title of the lecture prepared by the CRA contained those key words 'Congo' and 'Atrocities', clearly with the intent of whetting the appetites of those interested in violence or spectacles from Africa. By 1900, lantern slide shows were well established throughout Europe. The earliest reference to something resembling a projection lantern dates from around 1420 ('An Introduction to Lantern History: The Magic

Lantern Society' n.d.). From the very beginning, lantern slide shows were used to entertain audiences in darkened spaces and, over time, images projected onto screens came to depict biblical scenes, X-rated striptease and popular horror in shows known as 'phantasmagoria'. 'The exhibition/performance of magic lantern shows was considered entertainment not much different than the motion picture today' (Peres 2007, p.803). The darkened room allowed for a large degree of 'voyeuristic phantasy' to be generated in the audiences that attended the Harrises' lantern slide show (Mulvey 1975). This positions the slides uneasily within an erotic economy. The slide show traded in part on the anticipation of seeing naked black bodies, fuelling further European sexual fantasies surrounding Africa and other indigenous peoples, which, at the time, were being brought to public attention through 'the quasi-scientific ethnographic, presentation [that] excused what would have been unacceptably pornographic under other circumstances' (Maxwell 2000, p.158).

Seeley Harris's atrocity images thus sustain many counter-narratives when read within the wider context of photographic representations from Africa at the turn of the twentieth century. These early encounters with blackness, even those that claimed to champion African rights, are framed through an ideological framing that was busy constructing and propagating ideas of race and racism. This ideology emerged primarily through sciences based on an obsession with empirical evidence, of which photography played a major part, and a desire to dissect the natural world for greater internal knowledge of it and its peoples, of which the African subject was central. The development of Europe and its advancement could be considered only when pitched against the Other, the Other being the subject against which Europe measured and viewed itself.

The African body within the Harrises' lantern slide show is also put to work against the industrial and technological developments in Africa, developments which denied the urgency of the missionaries' religious purpose. The images of atrocities highlighted Belgium as a power that not only committed violence against people and the environment but that also negated the missionaries as agents of God. Through their work the Harrises prioritised religious conversion over industrial extraction and greed. Within this context, the broken African body put on display in the West through the theatre of lantern slides became a haunting sign of the perceived absence of God, as manifested through technology. As Cornel West reminds us, this historical period of white supremacy was constructed out of:

> a scientific racist logic [that] rests upon a modern philosophical discourse guided by Greek ocular metaphors, undergirded by Cartesian notions of the primacy of the subject and the pre-eminence of representation, and buttressed by Baconian ideas of observation, evidence, and confirmation that promote and encourage [the epistemologies associated with colonialism classically through] the activities of observing, comparing, measuring and ordering physical characteristics of human bodies. (West 1987, p.23)

West also states that:

> Given the renewed appreciation and appropriation of classical antiquity, these activities were regulated by classical aesthetic and cultural norms. Within this logic, the notions of black ugliness, cultural deficiency, and intellectual inferiority are legitimated by the value-laden yet prestigious authority of science. (West 1987, p.23)

This form of modernity when put to work against the African subject in the Congo relieved the colonisers of any moral responsibility for violence against the indigenous African because it represented this as merely a result of the natural order that Western science and progress required.

The Harrises' lantern slide show was the first significant international photographic campaign directly in support of Protestant missionary development in Africa. The photographs bring to the fore the issue of Africans caught under intense regimes of violent colonisation. The critical question here, however, is whether African human rights, or the European coloniser, gained more from these campaigns led by white British missionaries. In terms of the European penetration of the African continent, history would suggest the latter. Nonetheless, Seeley Harris's photographs can be read as a moment in Western culture that was, in the visual sense, historically groundbreaking: they were an attempt, though problematic, to build a condition of empathy for the African subject from within a difficult Western visual paradigm. That visual paradigm was swamped in a culture of racist imagery, which had commodified African bodies in debasing ways for centuries (Mirzoeff & McClintock 1998).

The photographs marked a shift in the West's understanding of itself as a presence in Africa that could no longer be constructed as mutually beneficial. By working through the power structure of the CRA, the Harrises became key players in Western audiences' realisation of the violent events that were taking place in the Congo. Through the production of Seeley Harris's photographs, we can gauge the power inherent in photography to affect social attitudes at the turn of the twentieth century. This campaigning use of photographs is a clear example of what could be achieved politically when graphic images of violence were presented directly to audiences who were willing to engage with the violence and to take responsibility for what they were shown. The horror of the photographs was profoundly influential, not just on the general public, but also on wealthy captains of industry. In 1905, William Cadbury of the cocoa company Cadbury Brothers Ltd donated £1000 to the CRA, the equivalent of around £100,000 today. This massive act of support from Cadbury, along with the Harrises' direct participation in lecturing, changed the course of the CRA. Money was of course needed to fund the campaign, but so were influential individuals, and Cadbury had influence over the Society of Friends (Quakers), 'whose long-standing antislavery committee embraced the issue and, in turn, mobilized local Quaker structures' (Stamatov 2013, p.6). The CRA thus gained access to thousands of people through this. However, Cadbury was also a controversial figure. The charge of hypocrisy was levelled at him in a newspaper editorial in 1908, because of the business's ongoing links to slave labour despite Cadbury's supposedly ethical stance. This led to a famous court case in which Cadbury Brothers won a libel suit, but the jury only awarded them derisory damages of one farthing (Satre 2005, p.127). This left doubt over the credibility of Cadbury as an ethical business given that it still had connections with slavery.

The CRA sought 'to secure for the natives inhabiting the Congo State territories the just and humane treatment which was guaranteed to them under the Berlin and Brussels acts' (Grant 2001, p.39). With Seeley Harris's photographs in circulation across Europe and the US in such a progressive way, the atrocities they portrayed were the central component in this CRA message. Exposing Western audiences to King Leopold II's brutalities had a substantial visual impact, but the extent of such audiences' understanding of the scale and scope of violence being carried out across the Congo Free State is less clear. The CRA's campaign was maintained for eight years, mainly through direct public engagement with Seeley Harris's photographs and other associated publications.

Seeley Harris's photographs served primarily as new documents of critical visual evidence to support claims of atrocities happening in the Congo. Their radical nature as photographs was that they introduced to the British and North American audiences a visual dynamic that disturbed the normal flow of images produced in Africa. They created a seismic shift in the Western viewer's perceptions of Africa, moving past the staged fantasy of the cannibal, shifting away from the exotic or pornographic postcards and towards a new domain of visual pleasure, one that engages in the spectacle of horror and violence enacted on the black body as a form of consumption. Seeley Harris's images introduced a degree of pathos within the photographic rendering of the African subject; they aimed to generate viewers' sympathy above their curiosity. However, they emerged in the context of other historical renderings of colonial atrocities, such as in an earlier phase of European colonialism. Writing of the humanitarian activities of Bartolomé de las Casas, Stephen Eisenman notes:

> The engraved illustrations by the Flemish artist Theodore de Bry for the *Brevissima relacion de la destruycion de las yndias* commissioned by the Spanish humanitarian priest Bartolomé de las Casas, such as his print of 'Punishments met out by the Spanish upon unruly slaves', were indictments of the *encomienda* systems of New World plantations and were instrumental in establishing the 'black legend' of brutal and superstitious Spain. But there is no reason to believe that his extravagant images of tortures and atrocities engendered sympathy for Indian victims so much as stimulated hatred of Catholic Spain. (Eisenman 2007, p.69)

In light of Eisenman's statement, we have to question how much sympathy for the African victims the 'Congo Atrocities' lecture produced, as a parallel and equally dominant reading works as a direct assault on the greed of King Leopold II and his support of the Catholic missions. More importantly, the photographs revived centuries of religious conflict in Europe being played out in Africa and on the African.

Slide 10. Execution of Slaves

This slide provides a graphic description of:

> the execution of slaves on the occasion of the death of a chief, and Mrs Harris's photograph strikingly depicts the scene. The doomed men were made to sit or kneel, their arms and legs being securely bound. A young tree was bent like a bow and a rope was lashed to the top. The rope was then passed round the man's head, drawing up his form and straining his neck, and almost lifting the body from the ground. Then the executioner advanced with his short broad-bladed falchion, and after measuring his distance, severed the head clean from the body. The spring of the released tree sent it bounding several yards away. But whilst this is revolting enough, we must not forget that this is no worse than what took place in Europe in the Middle Ages; and the condition of those people is, naturally, one of primitive barbarism.

This detailed account pushed the audience back in time. It established a fictional temporal equivalence between the Congo and the Middle Ages in order to help the audience locate themselves across the place in discussion. It also served to remove King Leopold II's regime, and its actions, from the age of 'civilisation' and put it in the past. The critical accusation here is that Leopold held the Congo back in a place from which the missionaries wanted to progress, which located progress in the Congo within the work of the British missionaries and not in King Leopold II's preferred paths of development within the region.

Discussing lynching photographs from the US, Shirley Samuels states:

when, more specifically, the act of seeing is presented as an act of witnessing violence, and, most specifically, witnessing the conversion of bodies into objects, viewers become parties to a reverse anthropomorphising. Here those who were previously human have lost their humanity, and the very staging of viewers within the frame reinforces the violence of a dehumanising that does more than make impossible the category of the human. (Samuels 2006, p.126)

Seeley Harris's photographs worked to establish and make real the dehumanisation process that was taking place at the hands of the European colonisers. The central moment is not just the shock of the body present but also the incriminating nature of the power absent. The photographs bring forth that which is invisible or denied. Here within the Harrises' slide show, the power of incriminating presence can also be aimed at the missionary.

Slide 11. An Executioner and a Warrior

The lecture at this stage provides a short but detailed description of an executioner 'and their appearance is calculated to send a thrill through most of us, even at this distance' (Slide 11). We are presented with a fantastic image of a native man and the thrill for the audience is having the opportunity to come face-to-face with a 'savage'. The distance between the viewer and the subject in the frame represents a space in which there is no form of recognition. The face of the 'savage' symbolises all that Western audiences found threatening in the indigenous, tribal culture of the Congo. The image deployed in this context drives a wedge between liberty (the ending of slavery) and equality (a recognition of shared humanity) (Gilroy 2007, p.23). The photograph also creates for the European a superior image of the self. It becomes part of a process of 'remaking the world according to the timeless order of the Ideas' (Levinas 2006, p.19), which translates into Eurocentric fantasies of philosophical and humanitarian progress through ideas of enlightenment that have an imagined or real genealogy within classical Greek scholarship. The photograph therefore acts as a tool to sweep away Europe's violent past because, in this moment in time, when confronted with the image of the savage, nothing else is rendered more barbaric in the mind of the coloniser. Here both the image and the text induce a form of amnesia about Europe's dark past. The narrative about the uncivilised executioner and the warrior concludes Part 1 of the lecture.

In Part 2, titled 'Philanthropy in Operation', the level of violence intensifies for the audience.

Slide 12. Village Scene and Chief's Compound

The lecture builds on the case against King Leopold II, further arguing that he is duplicitous and untrustworthy: 'By the stroke of the pen nearly a million square miles of country and all its produce became the personal property of one man'.

Slide 13. Types of Congolese Warrior

This slide introduces the hidden force with which Leopold was able to take control of the Congo: 'A large number of troops [were] recruited from the most savage tribes in the Upper Congo, and were equipped with modern rifles of precision. Imagine this native warrior instructed in the use of the Albini Rifle!' It is made clear that this modern weapon in the hands of primitive soldiers would naturally have disastrous consequences, and thus the act of giving natives rifles served to underline further the madness of Leopold. The narrative continues, 'A little later, when it became known what a good time the soldiers had, recruiting presented no more difficulties. Many of these savage men preferred, and not unnaturally, to be the hunters rather than the hunted.'

Slide 14. Types of Irregular Cannibal Soldiers

At this point, the lecture presents us with a greater sense of the conditions in which the 'cannibal soldiers' emerged. 'These cannibal soldiers (types of whom you see upon the screen) were required to force the natives to work for the philanthropic King'. The text describes the 'fiendish' methods used by King Leopold II to dominate the natives by force. Photographs of the 'cannibal soldiers' are not prominent throughout what remains of the archive and the one that may have illustrated this narrative has become among the more widely used of Seeley Harris's works. It shows four standing men, three of whom have rifles and wear well-worn European clothing, including hats. Two of the men wear the same type of clothes: wide baggy trousers and sleeveless crew-neck pullovers. The soldier on the far right wears a pullover bearing a five-point star, which was the central motif of the Congo Free State flag (Figure 4).

The two men on the far left and far right are in what could be described as the uniform of the Anglo-Belgian Indian Rubber Company (ABIR), which transforms them, so that they no longer belong to the world of the native, but have made the journey into colonial service. They now represent a different kind of colonised subject: one that acts out violence on behalf of the coloniser. Through their makeshift uniforms, which are a symbol of the disorderly violence present in the Congo, and their framing as 'cannibal soldiers', they have become neither native nor soldier but a hybrid of the two. In this state, they lose all sense of identity as they can no longer be viewed as the 'pure natives' that they were before their conscription into service for Leopold; at the same time, they cannot be fully recognised as 'real' (i.e. European) military men. The violent acts they performed in these uniforms became abstracted, as they belonged to a construction of the 'savage native' in relation to Leopold. As perpetrators of Leopold's will, they visually fulfil the image of both the savage native and the colonised subject. The image then reads as an analysis of power and an illustration of the 'mechanisms of repression' at work in the Congo (Foucault & Gordon 1980, p.90).

From the moment of their presentation as objects of scrutiny, the men in the photograph and the violence they represent are no longer native in nature, but European by design.

> The colonial world is a world cut in two. The dividing line, the frontiers are shown by barracks and police stations. In the colonies it is the policeman and the soldier who are the official instituted go-betweens, the spokesman of the settler and his rule of oppression. (Fanon 1963, p.29)

The other soldier central to the image wears a more tailored jacket and trousers; he also wears shoes, suggesting that he is of higher status than his fellow barefooted soldiers. The soldiers on the left of the frame are leaning in a relaxed and confident manner on their long rifles, which here become the ultimate symbol of their transformation into agents of violence 'that speak the language of pure force' (Fanon 1963, p.29). The third soldier, on the right of the photograph, stands with his rifle held close to his side in a more formal pose. All three soldiers stare directly back at Seeley Harris's camera in calm but inquisitive contemplation of the photographic moment.

The central figure in the photograph is the man held captive. He is near naked apart from a piece of cloth just visible around his waist. Around his neck hangs a bunch of ropes, which, although not physically restraining him, work as a sign of his bondage. His hands are clasped together and held under his chin in a prayer-like or begging gesture. Looking at the detail of his body we can see that he has considerable scarification or self-mutilation across his torso and shoulders. His expression is one of distress, generating sympathy in the viewer as he stands powerless between his captors. This image is temporally and symbolically charged as it recalls a more famous image and slogan that were made popular by the British abolitionist movements from the late eighteenth century onwards: 'Am I Not A Man and Brother', in which a slave is seen kneeling begging for his freedom. Seeley Harris's photograph of the native captive offers the audience a disturbing face-to-face confrontation with the great historical abolitionist and humanitarian crises that were at the heart of evangelical concerns.

The ABIR soldiers in the photograph become symbolic characters in King Leopold II's benevolent civilisation mission, in which the indigenous people were encouraged to become active players in their own exploitation and destruction.

> Colonialism pulls every string shamelessly, and is only too content to set at loggerheads those Africans who only yesterday were leagued against the settlers … Sometimes American Protestantism transplants its anti-Catholic prejudices into African soil, and keeps up tribal rivalries through religion. (Fanon 1963, p.129)

Slide 15. A Savage ABIR Sentry

Here, E. D. Morel is introduced into the story of the atrocities for the first time, highlighting his work in proving that 85 per cent of the rubber 'has been forced out of the Congo native in the last seven years at the point of the bayonet'. The focus, though, is still on the 'savage': 'When they come to a town no man's property or wife is safe, and when they are at war they are like devils'. The orchestration and demonisation of the savage is thoroughly rendered for the audience.

Slide 16. Mr E. D. Morel

A photograph of Morel is presented, in which he is seen sitting at his desk, a figure of studious contemplation in his grey waistcoat, black tie and white shirt. Morel sports a broad thick moustache that mirrors the centre parting of his well-kept hair. His form is that of the archetypal clerk. On his desk are piles of papers that indicate the amount of research Morel has done. His backdrop is a large-scale 'Philips New Map of Africa'. His head is located in the middle of the map, symbolising his authority over the continent. His eyes look into the distance, fixed in reflective contemplation. He holds a pipe, a sign of his sophistication and maturity of thought, which links him directly to an older, more established form of British colonial history: the tobacco plantations of the American South. His sleeves are rolled up, signifying a hardworking nature and commitment to his task, with a mass of papers spilling from the in-tray on his desk, suggesting the intensity of the work he has to manage. He is presented as a modest, honest and well-dressed man of steely determination, who symbolises the ideal of European righteous reason.

Slides 17-60

Seeley Harris's images from the Congo act to complete an African visual trinity: the exotic, the ethnographic and the horrific. In future renderings of Africa, these three perspectives became the guiding principles of a doctrine that formed the foundations for a European way of seeing Africa at home: a doctrine of European visual superiority in which the church of photography reigned supreme.

With the support of the Congo Reform Association, Seeley Harris's photography, and her and her husband's work as missionaries, the plight of millions of Africans was brought literally into focus. Through the presentation of a few intimate moments of violence, the Harrises were able to generate an image of atrocity far beyond the visual evidence they actually presented within the lantern slide show. As a result of the international outrage these photographs sparked, the Congolese were eventually delivered from the direct rule of King Leopold II's regime of indiscriminate killing and mutilation. As far as Leopold was concerned, his colonial management, civilising methodologies and economic strategies were enlightened and necessary (a view that was endorsed by his grandson, King Baudouin I, over half a century later on the Congo's day of liberation from Belgium) to maximise the profit from Congo's core assets, namely rubber and ivory. Leopold did not have to purchase his slave labour; for Leopold and his agents, rubber and ivory were clearly seen as more valuable than the expendable and seemingly limitless supply of worthless people who were forced to collect them. Quotas of rubber and ivory were well measured, recorded and valued. Those killed during the atrocities were rarely named, seen or remembered.

Looking at the corpus of photographs that Seeley Harris produced, the complexity of her position as a missionary, photographer and campaigner is evident. Yet her work as a pioneering woman photographer, who contributed to the use of photography to effect political change in Europe and the US, has slipped away from the grand narrative of social reform photography history. Her time in the Congo pre-dates Lewis Hine's (1874-1940) 1908 labour project in the US but they share the desire to put a human face on the exploitative nature of capitalism and those most vulnerable to its excesses. Rarely is Seeley Harris acknowledged as one of the world's earliest photographic activists who recognised the capacity of the photograph to work as a visual aid in effecting change, especially within British and American attitudes towards conditions and violence in Africa.

Through an evangelical sense of purpose and identification with her subjects, primarily through photography and testimony, she helped to change the view of European colonisation of Africa. Therefore, while Seeley Harris's photographs are foundational within the context of imaging atrocity, they also form part of a unique index of colonial violence and sexual fantasy that emerged beyond the graphic nature of the scenes depicted. In effect, her photographs broke the supposedly sympathetic aura of colonial welfare and care for the native. The critical work that they performed was not to address or redress the question of African inferiority or human rights. They laid no claim to championing the equality of Africans. Instead, they framed a perspective that highlighted the unfairness of the treatment of Africans not as equals but as recognisable inferior beings. The question of African rights is an absent part of the moral dilemma in the photographs, as the objectives for Seeley Harris and her missionary colleagues were the pacification and control of the African body and, more importantly, its soul. The Harrises operated under missionary codes of conduct:

This means at least that the missionary does not enter into dialogue with pagans and 'savages' but must impose the law of God that he incarnates. All of the non-Christian cultures have to undergo a process of reduction to, or – in missionary language – of regeneration in, the norms that the missionary represents. This undertaking is perfectly logical: a person whose idea and mission came from and are sustained by God is rightly entitled to the use of all possible means, even violence, to achieve his objectives. (Mudimbe 1988, p.47)

In the context of human-rights discourse, the question remains as to whether there was any examination of the colonial self in the generation of the images, or if indeed there was any sense of power being altered, or a critique of the photographer's presence and position. Seeley Harris's work did not create a shift in the ontological relations between the European and the African. The essential construct of an inferior African being remained intact. The historical past of the encounter between the African and the European outweighed its future possibilities as a visual form. The missionary sense of ultimate responsibility for the African would have to be relinquished for African humanity to be fully recognised.

This recognition was therefore essentially blocked by evangelical thought and the sense of divine purpose. Although Seeley Harris created a visual space in which to engage with the morally bankrupt regime of King Leopold II, her photographic work has an inherited ideological and flawed basis that fixed her present to a past through an identifiable cultural trait, so that in the moment of her photographic instance Seeley Harris's core duty was not to demand acceptance of African humanity. Seeley Harris's responsibility comes from a belief in her divine purpose and righteous commitments, and is anterior to all the logical deliberation summoned by reasoned decision. African human rights were not the primary issue driving the production of these images. That sense of responsibility is imposed on them by later readings (Sliwinski 2006; Thompson 2012).

Seeley Harris's photographs did not emerge because the international public lacked awareness of atrocities in Africa (Nault 2012, p.2). However, it was Roger Casement (1864-1916), the British consular official who had just completed a 'damning investigation of atrocities' in the Congo (Grant 2001, p.33), who established the conditions necessary for Seeley Harris's photographic representations of atrocity. This could be read as an opportune moment of missionary visual sophistication.

Casement's report carried several photographs that had been taken by missionaries working in the area. These included the Reverend W. D. Armstrong and the Faroese missionary Daniel J. Danielsen, the skipper on the American Missionary Union steamer *Henry Reed*, which Casement used for his expedition in the Congo. Danielsen may well have been the first person to bring back and publicly display staged atrocity photographs from the Congo (Jacobsen 2014, p.16). In recent research regarding the authorship of the photographs reproduced in Casement's report, the Faroese scholar Óli Jacobsen cites Danielsen as being the actual photographer of some of the key images. On his return to the UK from the Congo and prior to Casement's arrival back in the UK, Danielsen, outraged by his experiences, began lecturing in Edinburgh on the atrocities, possibly with the aid of lantern slides (Jacobsen 2014).

Key to some of the publications and displays was that they contained oral testimonies gathered by missionaries directly from the victims of King Leopold II's regime. As an act in and of itself, this represented a rare but small moment when the Congo subjects were given a voice and name.

Scholars across the fields of photography and human rights have only recently begun to recognise the strategic and historical significance of the Harrises' work, together with other key photographic images authored by missionaries that emerged out of this critical period in colonial history. Sharon Sliwinski's essay, 'The Childhood of Human Rights: The Kodak on the Congo' (Sliwinski 2006), marks a significant enquiry into the cultural relevance of Seeley Harris's photographs taken in the Congo at the turn of the twentieth century with regard to how they assist current understanding of violence, colonial memory and ideological formulations concerning the construction of atrocity theories. She highlights that:

> What is invariably underplayed in the histories of this movement is the impact of photography. The CRA was not only the largest humanitarian movement of the era, it was also the first humanitarian movement to use atrocity photographs as a central campaign tool. (Sliwinski 2006, p.334)

Sliwinski here comments on the significant 'underplay' in photographic history of Seeley Harris's photographs and how they contributed to humanitarian and human rights visual culture. However, these works, although they are now gaining in recognition as agents of change by some commentators on photography and colonial history, have become critical images that slip into a variety of different fields of enquiry. They have more recently become partially accommodated into the history of photography, but only through what could be described as a looser or marginalised photographic history outside of the main narrative of the medium, and have come to light mostly through the study of human rights and atrocity. They are not marked as a significant photographic contribution in their own right, but merely as examples of photography for a specific cause.

Christina Twomey covered some similar ground to Sliwinski in her essay 'Severed Hands: Authenticating Atrocity in the Congo,

1904-13', published in *Picturing Atrocity: Photography in Crisis* (Twomey 2012, pp.39-50), in which she states that 'Photographs were an essential element of the Congo reform campaign, which was one of the most successful instances of a humanitarian revival at the turn of the century'. Twomey, however, lays greater emphasis on testimony:

> The creation of the Congo photographs, then, can be viewed as an initial act of collaboration between missionaries and Africans, in which missionaries reserved for themselves the right to speak on behalf of their subjects. The photographs were given meaning by the words that surrounded their creation, publication and performance and almost always those words were spoken or recorded by non-Africans. (Twomey 2012, p.48)

The question of the African not having a voice is clearly identified by Twomey, and I would suggest that this position has not predominantly changed in the practice of photography across the African continent since its first arrival. It was not until the late 1980s that we began to witness in Europe and the US the emergence of an indigenous African-orientated critical photography voice that carried a different emphasis when reading into the history of photography in Africa. African scholars during the late 1980s began to claim that photographic history was primarily a European discourse. 'The camera', as Olu Oguibe reminds us, 'was a decidedly ideologically positioned tool on the side of incursion' (Oguibe 2002, p.566). These incursions arrived from many perspectives, including both the military and the missionary points of view. The end result, however, is often the same: a visual power relationship that is inherently ideologically weighted towards the cultural superiority of the Western gaze and its image interpretation.

Seeley Harris's photography did not just reduce the African subject to a generic representational African body; she did to some extent 'privilege the body as evidence of atrocity' (Grant 2001, p.34), but what is significant is the move towards a space of greater identification with the subject in the frame through close engagement with the intended audiences. This is primarily achieved by the fact that many of the photographs included in the lantern show offer a direct visual exchange between the subject of the photograph and the viewer. Often the victims glare straight back at the camera. When this return of the colonial gaze is underpinned by a narrative of violence against the subject, which is delivered from an outraged missionary perspective, the capacity to identify with the subject as victim becomes increased as the distance required for complete objectification of the African subject is shortened through a more engaged theatre of encounter and knowledge transfer of the situation presented.

When we consider the photographic construction of Africa as a place in the European imagination, it becomes clear how absent the human subject is from the frame throughout the history of photography. The author of the work, rather than the purpose of the image, is the critical point from which we read the image of Africa. Africa as a visual place has predominantly been authored from outside or from positions of white authority.

The photographs taken by Seeley Harris and her missionary colleagues in the Congo could represent historical visual milestones for a way of seeing Africans in distress. What surfaces from the images as we look back at them with the benefit of hindsight is that a multiplicity of meanings emerges, the most obvious being the scopic pleasures in looking at the African as both the exotic Other and the photographic origin of the image of the helpless victim.

These historical photographs of violence in the Congo provide the perfect photographic moment for benevolent Christian ideology to work within a continued visualisation and infantilisation of the African subject. Seeley Harris's photographic work emerges not out of a human rights discourse but primarily out of a discourse grounded in a traditional British Christian abolitionist movement that was well versed in the use of images to influence public opinion. These were communication strategies that would have been very familiar to Seeley Harris and her husband. Therefore, when we consider John Harris's response to seeing the photograph of Nsala with the remains of his daughter (mentioned in the section on Slide 1, above), it is clear that his main concern was with the photograph's potential impact on audiences: 'The photograph is most telling, and as a slide will rouse any audience to an outburst of rage, the expression on the father's face, the horror of the bystanders, the mute appeal of the hand and foot will speak to the most skeptical' (Grant 2001, p.27). His analysis of the photograph, coupled with his wife's staging of this moment, illustrates a high degree of understanding in relation to the theatrical impact that the image would have at home. It would join a long line of outrageous images of violence on the black body.

We now know that at the time of their display in public theatres as lantern slides, the photographs from the Congo produced by Alice Seeley Harris and her fellow missionaries had a far-reaching influence, as is best illustrated by Joseph Conrad's *Heart of Darkness* and in Mark Twain's now celebrated 1905 critical text on King Leopold II's Congo, titled *King Leopold's Soliloquy.* Twain writes in Leopold's imaginary voice, lamenting the use of photography to attack his colony:

> The kodak has been a sole calamity to us. The most powerful enemy indeed. In the early years we had no trouble in getting the press to 'expose' the tales of mutilations as slanders, lies, inventions of busy-body American missionaries and exasperated foreigners ... Yes, all things went harmoniously and pleasantly in those good days ... Then all of a sudden came the crash! That is to say, the incorruptible kodak – and all harmony went to hell! The only witness I couldn't bribe. (Twain 1970, p.73)

Seeley Harris's photographs functioned as vital visual evidence across Europe and the US concerning the disasters taking place in the Congo under King Leopold II, but for the Belgian imperial rulers the photographs worked against them only temporarily as an uncomfortable source of political embarrassment. Over time they came to register as a historical blip across their overall 'civilising' mission in the country. Belgium's rule continued in the Congo for over fifty more years and, even after the Republic of Congo gained its independence, Katanga Province was too irresistible a source of natural resources for Belgium to discontinue its exploitation. The Belgians could not and would not let go of the desire to extract from the Congo its mineral assets or to allow democracy to flourish post-independence.

Three Speeches on Independence Day, 30 June 1960, for the Democratic Republic of the Congo

When Leopold II undertook his great work which today reaches its crowning moment, he did not come to you as a conqueror but as a civilizer. Since it was founded the Congo has opened its borders to international commerce, and Belgium has never exercised a monopoly in its sole interest.

(King Baudouin I)

Belgium had the wisdom not to oppose the tide of history and, understanding the greatness of the ideal of freedom imbuing the hearts of all the Congolese people, transferred our country, directly and without transition, from foreign domination to independence and full national sovereignty, an action quite without precedent in the history of peaceful colonization.

(President of the Republic, Mr Joseph Kasavubu)

Although this independence of the Congo is being proclaimed today by agreement with Belgium, an amicable country, with which we are on equal terms, no Congolese will ever forget that independence was won in struggle, a persevering and inspired struggle carried on from day to day, a struggle in which we were undaunted by privation or suffering and stinted neither strength nor blood. It was filled with tears, fire and blood. We are deeply proud of our struggle, because it was just and noble and indispensable in putting an end to the humiliating bondage forced upon us. That was our lot for the eighty years of colonial rule and our wounds are too fresh and much too painful to be forgotten. We have experienced forced labour in exchange for pay that did not allow us to satisfy our hunger, to clothe ourselves, to have decent lodgings or to bring up our children as dearly loved ones.

(Patrice Lumumba)

These statements are extracts from formal speeches delivered on Independence Day for the Republic of the Congo. The first two, although delivered from different sides of the colonial experience, work to deny the decades of colonial violence and the atrocities that were carried out across the Congo by Belgium's imperial rulers, and both speakers act to construct a benign colonial memory. King Baudouin I (1930-93), like his grandfather, King Leopold II, before him, offers a civilising gift, while Kasavubu (1910-69) is a willing recipient. These speeches demonstrate that the colonial power relationships were secure and entrenched both within the mind of the liberator and the liberated at the time of Congo's independence, clearly illustrating the damaging psychology of colonisation on the colonisers' and the colonised mind. They are an example of history being abstracted from the experience of the individual and the mass of people concerned, and represent fine examples of modernity's capacity to forget: 'Modern space is, as it were, space wiped clean' (Connerton 2009, p.40).

The presence of two powerful forces – religion and commerce – from Europe in Africa wreaked havoc in the Congo and they were at their most potent under King Leopold II's rule. The result of this great European act in the Congo still resonates today. It is an intense geopolitical zone of conflict and is now fixed in the European psyche as being emblematic of all that is culturally deficient in Africa. The very idea of the Congo represents a sign that is both negative and hostile across notions of development throughout the continent, especially when discussed within the context of Africa as a European invention (Mudimbe 1988). Therefore, Alice Seeley Harris's photographs reveal a record of the disasters of European self-interest and they are foundational in the evidencing of the violence of those conflicting colonial missions.

2

Race, Denial and Imaging Atrocity

PART 1. HORROR IN TIME AND *LIFE*

If at the beginning of the war and during the war twelve or fifteen thousand of these Hebrew corrupters of the people had been held under poison gas, as happened to hundreds of thousands of our very best German workers in the field, the sacrifice of millions at the front would not have been in vain.

> Adolf Hitler, 'The Right of Emergency Defence', *Mein Kampf*
> (Hitler 1925)

ATROCITIES: CAPTURE OF THE GERMAN CONCENTRATION CAMPS PILES UP EVIDENCE OF BARBARISM THAT REACHES THE LOW POINT OF HUMAN DEGRADATION

...

Dead men will have indeed died in vain if live men refuse to look at them.

> Headline and feature text, *Life*, 7 May 1945
> (*Life* 1945, p.33)

The much-anticipated United Nations Conference on International Organisation that opened in San Francisco on 25 April 1945 was, according to *Life* magazine, full of 'a typically American setting of elaborate arrangements, public excitement and swarming cameramen' (*Life*, vol. 18, no. 19, 7 May 1945, p.39). During this, an extraordinary event in relation to the reception of photographic images took place. *Life* magazine published on 7 May 1945 a six-page feature of photographs showing the horror the Allied forces faced when they captured the German concentration camps.

Human rights historian Paul Gordon Lauren, in his celebrated book *The Evolution of International Human Rights: Visions Seen* (which was nominated for a Pulitzer Prize), claims that these photographs made an important contribution: they created a real sense of urgency during the conference and acted as catalysts for change among the delegates, encouraging them to support the development of international human-rights legislation as a global political necessity for the future security of the world's people after the Second World War (Lauren 2003, p.186).

For Lauren and the many other scholars (Zelizer 1998; Lowe 2012) who have since referenced this powerful series of photographs, the 7 May 1945 issue of *Life* and the 'Atrocities' photographs from the German concentration camps published within it, command a very special place in discourses and ethical debates that attempt to theorise images of violence and of war. In particular, they have defined how we picture atrocity, and the extent to which Western audiences have become anaesthetised to such images. They also force considerations of the role that aesthetics play in the making of photographs of violence for the media, the gallery and the many other sites of cultural production and display that photographs now occupy.

One of the key points of ignition for this debate was the now seminal work by Susan Sontag, *On Photography*, in which she stated: 'The ethical content of photographs is fragile. With the possible exception of photographs of those horrors, like the Nazi camps, that have gained the status of ethical reference points, most photographs do not keep their emotional charge' (Sontag 1973, p.16). Sontag here suggests that most photographs are temporarily and culturally charged with ethical power at the time of their production and initial consumption, but then later become transformed into petrified moments of atrocity whose ethical power is degraded. The exception to this rule, for Sontag, are photographs from Nazi concentration camps. Perhaps such images resonate across time whenever mass acts of violence shown to us, but the context of their original display and meanings produced will always be open to deconstruction. It is clear that there is a degree of memory management at work when we consider what constitutes the central motif of discussions on the theme of atrocity.

Our memory bank of atrocities thus works backward in time – using the past to stand for the present. Ultimately it reaches the first major killing fields to have been extensively and elaborately depicted in photos in the daily press – the concentration camps of the Second World War – and it is those killing fields that are replayed in discussions of contemporary atrocity. (Zelizer 1998, p.210).

In discussing the photographs from the concentration camps within the context of the San Francisco Conference of 1945, Lauren seems to see them as revelatory. He informs us that during the conference and 'in the midst of all this discussion and debate, a powerful and emotional element suddenly appeared', and that 'it was captured with particular poignancy in a single issue of *Life* magazine'. Lauren then describes vividly how the reader encountered the photographs, stating that this issue of *Life*:

begun normally with letters to the editors, ads, humorous cartoons, stories on the events of the previous week, that the readers quite naturally anticipated full coverage of the start of the San Francisco Conference. Then, without any warning they turned a page and saw something they had never seen before in their lives. In an article entitled with the single word 'Atrocities', readers looked in horror at the photographs of piles of emaci-ated corpses and prisoners with bodies deformed by malnutrition found by Allied forces as they liberated Nazi extermination camps. (Lauren 2003, p.186)

Much work has also been done by other scholars, who have commented that when the images were first shown in 'newspapers, magazines and public exhibitions ... they inspired a feeling of intense and profound shock almost universally amongst the people they reached' (Lowe 2012, p.190). Although Lauren's analysis of the text that accompanied the photographs in *Life* is more than half a century on from the original publication, he asserts that 'the accompanying text still speaks for itself' (Lauren 2003, p.186). It is worth noting that for Lauren, time has not altered the editorial interpretative possibilities of *Life*'s deeply encoded humanitarian lexicon: the communicative process and the system of signs that the magazine employs to contextualise the photographs for its 1945 audience remain fixed and temporally transferable to the present intact. In choosing to frame these images as if seeing them solely within the context of their historical past, Lauren negates the idea that the meanings generated in the 'Atrocities' feature may have shifted over time. His perspective suggests that, even when originally seen in the context of their first display in *Life*, and given the complexity of the scenes of violence presented, the visual language used cannot be read as a simple and unmediated reflection of the crisis at hand.

More than most, images that act as witness to atrocities need to be read as constructions and distortions simultaneously, as they are presented as events produced for our benefit and on our behalf. Such constructions and distortions work on us as part of a set of cultural values that we may, or may not, be aware of at the time and place of the encounter with the photograph (Procter 2004, p.59). For Lauren, the political and cultural infrastructure that lies above the production of these photographs – the photo apparatus – is not a historical concern (Cramerotti 2009, p.97). The danger in not addressing that infrastructure of highly charged emotive images of atrocities, is that they become fixed as objects that simply transmit the history of their making as a dead piece of knowledge that we periodically unearth.

The German atrocities as a visual revelation in 1945, a revelation which is bound up with Allied ignorance or doubt about the horror in the camps, is a dominant idea that emerges from historical readings such as those of Lauren: 'The most important trope in memory is forgetting. It exists against a background of what has been forgotten' (S. Hall 2008). If this is the case, then it is important that we continue to peel back the layers of time and look through the details of those repressed moments. Considering *Life*'s 'Atrocities' feature requires an interpretation of the backstory of what has been ignored, reinvented or culturally forgotten. When regarding the feature from the advantageous place of our present, what seeps out of the photographs is not just the barbaric Nazi acts of genocide but also the violence of Allied abandonment of the most vulnerable people caught up in the horror of German fascism.

Lauren lays emphasis on a universal response to the images,

which found them 'absolutely shocking' (Lauren 2003, p.186). He shares this with a range of academic texts that examine the reception of these photographs by the Western public when they were exposed to them for the first time (Lowe 2012, p.193; Willsdon & Costello 2008, p.222). The theme of horror that Lauren and others support serves to encode the 'Atrocities' feature with a moral authority that is commonly associated with the golden age of photojournalism – the 1930s to roughly the end of the 1950s – an era when cameras became very portable and magazines began to invest heavily in reportage photography. Therefore, Lauren's historical perspective on *Life*'s publishing of the photographs encourages a reading that recreates the original condition, in which the magazine was venerated, affirming it as a bastion of reportage photography for groundbreaking and truthful journalistic work.

Across photographic history, however, it is possible to formulate an alternative reading of the way in which *Life* and the Western news media managed the use of the atrocity photographs. In the case of *Life*, it is a reading that works against the grain of the magazine's revered place in photographic history (Martens 2000, p.245): it used the feature in this specific context to conceal criticism of its historical editorial past. *Life* had chosen not to pursue many other opportunities to present to the American public earlier atrocity photographs from the German camps, which were well known to picture editors of the period, and this feature sought to erase that. When we see events like these through photographs, their 'universal' effect as shocking images of violence may still be intact, but as an act of looking into humanity's violent past one can 'see things you never thought you would see when you stop looking at the image as a strictly historical record' (S. Hall 2008).

It is clear that *Life* magazine and the Allied media had ample opportunity to publish photographs that evidenced German atrocities, which had in fact been in circulation since 1933. As American academic Susie Linfield states, 'Western Governments, embassies, newspapers, and antifascist organisations were flooded with atrocity images' (Linfield 2010, p.71). What is more relevant now is to examine *Life*'s editors' inertia in not taking the opportunity to publicise the horrors in the camps much earlier. This shifts the emphasis in interpreting the use of atrocity photographs in time and in location, thus enabling a different set of readings across the ideologies and ethical positions of *Life* magazine and its editors. The much-discussed shock and horror relating to the photographs might then be read as a critique of Allied forces' alien-entry policies, and of those in positions of media power who refused to publicise the images sooner. This throws into doubt the assumed humanitarianism of *Life* and the Allied high command, both military and political, hinting that it might have largely been a false sentiment and that, prior to 1945, the magazine simply did not prioritise the German death camps enough to warrant publishing anything from them, choosing instead to ignore the mass of photographic evidence that was available.

Given this, it seems logical to ask if *Life* was politically or culturally restrained from publishing previously known atrocity photographs from the death camps, or, if other motives were at work, what might they have been. In other words, how do these photographs of atrocities help us to understand *Life*'s refusal to display previously known atrocity photographs? If 'the photograph formally evacuates the signs of its own productive hence ideological location, its purpose' (Willsdon & Costello 2008, p.221), then it is necessary to relocate culturally a photograph's connotative meaning in the present. When we choose over time to put the photograph back to work, its original dominant meaning could become redundant, allowing a secondary reading to surface more clearly. The photograph then becomes enabled to do different cultural work.

The lack of recognition of Western denial in the editorial of *Life*'s 'Atrocities' feature forms an essential part of the impact this article has on the reader. The feature, and its capacity to profoundly shock, enables *Life* to create a safe moral barrier between it and the sceptical American public, which the magazine accuses of being at the core of denying German brutality: 'Last week Americans could no longer doubt stories of Nazi cruelty' (*Life* 1945, p.39). *Life* empowers its own editorial voice to be read as a credible and legitimate source in restoring truth and faith back into the reality of the 'Atrocities' photographs and therefore presents its editorial as a valid body of evidence against the German camps.

The framing of the 'Atrocities' photographs by *Life* can be read as an editorial moral finger being wagged at a denying and cynical American public. By giving the public the opportunity to empathise with the victims through engaging with the photographs, the magazine provides its readership with a place to focus any feelings of remorse that being doubtful of the atrocities' existence might have generated. However, *Life*'s editorial pages leave open the question of who we are actually looking at and how they got to the camps.

Life's failure to act earlier to publicise the stark reality of those caught in the camps is congruent with the moment when many German people turned a blind eye as their neighbours were being rounded up. The moral stance of the text that accompanies the photographs allows the editors of *Life* to detach themselves from the sceptical American public. It is the American public, according to *Life*, who doubt the violence of the camps, not the powerful and influential editors and owners of the magazine. In 1945, *Life* sold over a million copies weekly and during the war greatly influenced American public opinion; this was a position of substantial editorial power. This issue of *Life* is culturally important, because it allows us to see the nature of hegemonic media forces at work as 'what was a site of resistance to publishing photographs of atrocities from the camps at one moment becomes a site of incorporation at another' (Procter 2004, p.26). However, Lauren and indeed this issue of *Life* magazine do not address why doubts regarding German atrocities were so prevalent among both the American and British publics throughout most of the Second World War. It remains unclear why a culture of doubt was manufactured and what political or historical end might this have served. After the 'Kristallnacht' in 1938:

> Foreign consulates in Germany found themselves flooded with urgent and tragic pleas for visas from those seeking to escape Hitler's persecution. But Switzerland and most of the Latin American countries closed their doors by actually making their existing laws on entry for refugees more restrictive. None of the major powers, including Britain, France, the United States, and the Soviet Union, would permit any large-scale Jewish immigration into their borders ... In some cases diplomats proposed that these victims of the Nazis be settled among blacks somewhere in Tanzania, Northern Rhodesia, Uganda, or Madagascar. (Lauren 1988, p.133)

It is clear that in some diplomatic circles Jewish culture was regarded as being closer to that of Africa than Europe, echoing the deadly theories of eugenics that ranked Jewish and black people together as inferior races to the Aryan. Eugen Fischer, who served as the director of the Kaiser Wilhelm Institute for Anthropology, Human Heredity, and Eugenics from 1927 to 1942, minced no words when he stated in a 1939 lecture: 'I do not characterize the Jew as inferior, as Negroes certainly are, and I do not underestimate the greatest enemy with whom we have to fight. But I reject Jewry with every means in my power, and with reserve, in order to preserve the hereditary endowment of my people' (Bachrach & Kuntz 2004, p.10).

By 1945, the people that the fascists had an explicit interest in killing were well known among the Allied forces and media. Historians have amassed evidence showing that the Allies clearly knew, and in great detail, about the industrial nature of Nazi killing (Shephard 2006, p.25). Strong historical links between German and American eugenicist movements meant that it was widely acknowledged that the Nazi programmes of racial hygiene had at their core violent anti-Semitic policies. Stefan Kühl notes that it was only after September 1935, with the passing of the Nuremberg Laws, that relationships between German 'racial hygienists' and American eugenicists began to be less enthusiastic (Kühl 1994, p.97).

Contrary to *Life* magazine's insistence that the camps were denied, in various Western locations from 1935 onwards, wave after wave of people advocated that action should be taken against German policies of Jewish extermination. As early as 1936, Victor Gollancz, George Orwell's publisher, produced *The Yellow Spot: The Extermination of the Jews in Germany*, an anonymous text detailing Nazi policies against the Jews. Herbert Dunelm, the Bishop of Durham, a well-respected public figure who was outspoken in his condemnation of Nazi anti-Semitism, wrote an introduction to the book. In it, he urges European states to take action against the 'resuscitation of medieval barbarism', and he makes very clear that 'A new principle of persecution has had to be discovered. Not religion but race has provided the requisite plea. No longer the error of the mind, but the poison of the blood is to stamp the Jew as unsafe for German citizenship' (Dunelm 1936, p.8). The book's title refers to the legacy of Jewish persecution by European churches and states that historically required Jews to identify themselves by marking their clothes with a yellow spot. In 1942, *The German New Order in Poland* was published by Hutchinson & Co. in London for the Polish Ministry of Information, and in December 1942 the Houses of Parliament observed a minute's silence after the Leader of the House of Commons, Anthony Eden, informed the house of mass Jewish executions in Germany. In 1943, *The Black Book of Polish Jewry: An Account of the Martyrdom of Polish Jews Under the Nazi Occupation*, by Jacob Apenszlak, was published in Russia and the US, aimed specifically at an English-speaking audience. In October 1944, the *Illustrated London News* published eleven photographs from Majdanek, the camp on the eastern front liberated by the Russians: 'More than the earlier photographs, these images hinted at the scope and industrial nature of the Nazi atrocities' (Zelizer 1998, p.52).

We now know that:

> throughout the war, though, Western governments and the Western press tended to see these images of atrocity and the reports that accompanied them as examples of untrustworthy, exaggerated Soviet or Jewish propaganda; only a minuscule portion of the available images was ever published. (Linfield 2010, p.72)

With so much evidence and military intelligence surrounding the horrors taking place in the camps, it was clearly manipulative, disingenuous and misleading of *Life*'s editors in its publication of these photographs to hide behind the shield of not having 'irrefutable evidence' of German atrocities. When Lauren states that the text used by *Life* 'speaks for itself', this can be read in the present as representing a different articulation: one that asks a critical question relating to the depths of denial, inertia and racism that ran through the Allied political powers and their media concerning the horrors of the concentration camps.

When addressing the historical, cultural and humanitarian impact of the 'Atrocities' photographs reproduced by *Life* and other news media in 1945, a wider frame, or uncropped knowledge, reminds us of the overarching attitudes regarding the construction of Jewish and other 'alien' identities that were dominant throughout American and British social and political cultures during the Second World War. Matthew F. Jacobson, in his essay published in *Theories of Race and Racism* in 2009, titled 'Looking Jewish Seeing Jews', reveals that:

> In America an *Atlantic Monthly* piece entitled 'The Jewish Problem in America' (1941) could still assert that the Jew had become 'European only in residence; by nature he did not become an Occidental; he could not have possibly done so'. Comparing Jews to another problematic 'Oriental' group, Armenians, this writer went on to wonder 'whether (differences) can be faded out by association, miscegenation, or other means of composition'. When Nazi policy began to make news in the 1930s and the early 1940s, too, headlines in journals like the *Baltimore Sun* and the *Detroit Free Press* revealed the extent to which Americans and Germans shared a common lexicon of racial Jewishness. (Jacobson 2009, p.313)

The Nazis were clearly not alone in their fundamental ideological commitment to the cruelty of racism during this tense period.

PART 2. THE RUSSIANS

The impact of the 'Atrocities' article in *Life* was further enhanced by the editorial feature immediately preceding it, which created what looked like a warm and optimistic picture of camaraderie during the war. Two features run from page 27 to page 31. The first is titled 'War in Europe Draws to its End'. The main photograph used across half a page is captioned 'Russian Major General Rusakov and American Major General Reinhardt drink a toast in vodka as their divisions meet on the banks of the Elbe River' and shows the two generals with rather stern-faced expressions in a moment that does not quite convey celebration or friendship, as if they are reluctant guests at the party (*Life* 1945, p.27). The Russian Rusakov is holding a drink, his eyes slightly averted from the camera. He looks bored. The American Reinhardt carries a similar expression, although he appears to be in a more reflective mood; his look is to our left out of the frame. Four Russian soldiers are standing directly behind the two generals. The Russian soldier nearest to Reinhardt seems to be singing or shouting in celebration of the occasion. The opening lines of *Life*'s editorial text frame the global significance of the moment for the reader:

> The end of war was close in Europe. Rumors spread across the continents, over the oceans. The people of Verona in Italy celebrated the coming of peace. So did the people of Paris. In the U.S., Senator Tom Connally, vice chairman of the U.S. delegation to the San Francisco Conference, told a reporter that Germany's surrender was expected momentarily. Two hours later the resulting roar of national excitement was silenced by President Truman's announcement that there was no foundation for the report. (*Life* 1945, p.27)

The text then goes on to describe a scene that clearly references the dark moments of the 'Atrocities' feature that follows shortly. It states that:

> through the desolation of the cities still smouldering with a smell of death and across the countryside green with spring, streamed wandering hordes of humanity – looting, drinking, fighting, begging. Most were slave laborers, now suddenly free. Others were Germans escaping the Russian armies or crawling from the cellars and caves in which they had been living. (*Life* 1945, p.27)

The scene portrayed in the text associates the freeing of those held in camps with a vision of hell and damnation, as if the act of release in and of itself has created a mass of zombie-like creatures devoid of any moral substance as they loot and drink across the decaying city. The Russians are cast as an indiscriminate deadly force sweeping across Germany. They here do not liberate; they terminate. Meanwhile, the slave labourers in this editorial shaping move from victim to parasite in a few short lines, homogenised as an amoral living dead. In this context there is clearly little, if any, sympathy for the slaves or the victims of the camps. They simply become part of the wider story of Germany's defeat, and are, as far as the writer is concerned, a problematic presence. The fact that many of the slave labourers would have been Jewish or Slavic, though this is never explicitly stated, may have a bearing on their description; casting them as vermin leans on old racist stereotypes. The text goes on to further emphasise the hell-like scenario as Berlin crumbles: 'In Berlin dust and the smoke of guns and the cries of the dying echoed through the sewers and subways'. Throughout *Life*'s reporting, there is a systematic failure to differentiate between Jewish victims of Nazism, Slavic forced labourers and German 'victims' of the advancing Russians.

The next two pages present a series of seven photographs featuring Reinhardt and Rusakov along with American and Russian soldiers in various forms of exchange and celebration. The photographs themselves are a fairly generic record of the meetings that took place between the two armies. Both sets of soldiers share drinks and shake hands in different formal and informal settings, all clearly staged for the camera. However, *Life*'s captioning of the photographs focuses on the ideological differences between the political regimes that the soldiers represent. One of the more formal photographs of an American soldier shaking hands with a Russian soldier is framed against the backdrop of a poster that mirrors the actual exchange taking place (*Life* 1945, p.29). The real replicates the imagined painted event. The painted mural shows the soldiers standing in front of their respective national flags and standing on a fallen Nazi swastika. The poster is inscribed in English, 'East Meets West'. *Life*'s full caption reads:

> One of the first four Americans to make contact with the Soviets, Pfc Frank Huff of Washington, Va., shakes hands with a Russian before a poster signalizing the event. Less formal Russian greet-ings included guitar playing, bear hugs, handshakes that left Yank hands aching.

The aching grip of Russia becomes a bruising cultural encounter – something for the Americans to be mindful of as an early indicator of the ideological gulf that exists between these two emergent superpowers.

Another caption that builds on the ideological tension across the meetings of the Russian and American forces is one in which three soldiers are seen standing in what looks like relaxed conversation. A US lieutenant is in the centre of the image. On his left is a female Russian soldier and on his right is a male soldier. The caption reads:

> Russian Wac, U.S. Lieutenant and Red Soldier try to converse despite their lingual difficulties. One Russian with a smattering of English called everyone "my dear". But when a GI tried to buy a Russian officer's cap insignia, he got instead a thundering tirade against capitalism.

This small encounter between the soldiers becomes for the editors of *Life* a 'thundering' ideological exchange between Russian communism and American capitalism. Each seemingly friendly encounter between the two armies shown in the photographs is laced through with exaggerated cultural and political differences via the captions used, underpinned by a fear of aggressive communism. The Russians salute with heel clicks, turn up late for meetings with the generals, drink captured alcohol and ogle American women journalists. Their enthusiasm for the Americans is rendered crass and crude, and it forms part of a national narrative concerning fear of subversive communists who may be active in American government, Hollywood and news media. The post-war years in the US went on to rapidly become a hysterical period in which Senator Joseph McCarthy crusaded, through the House Un-American Activities Committee, to rid American society of communists.

Pages 30 and 31 carry no advertising and constitute a continuation of the previous feature. The text on page 30 is titled 'The End of the War in Europe'. It carries with it a prominent subtitle that reads, 'Coming at a Gas-Engine Clip, it Out-Marches our Ability to Think About Peace'. A single full-bleed photograph accompanies this article on the facing page, with the caption: 'At the Elbe River a U.S. and Russian Lieutenant meet to link the American and Soviet armies' (*Life* 1945, p.31). The image shows two soldiers embracing each other in mirror-like fashion. Both smile warmly and look directly into each other's eyes; each places an arm around the other's shoulders and they clasp hands to complete the embrace. The photograph represents a tender exchange between the two men, and the similarities in the men's features is striking: in other circumstances they could have passed for brothers. Only their uniforms indicate their differences. The image is *Life*'s 'Picture of the Week' for this edition.

The editorial, which is the final text before we turn the page to see the 'Atrocities' photographs, focuses on the concern that the US is not planning for peace quickly enough:

> The diseases of social unrest that come in the wake of starvation do not respect geographical boundaries, and it is to our advantage to halt them before they develop and leap the ocean. We must plan our rehabilitation measures quickly if only to save Europe ... There have been indications that a U.S. chief 'hand outer' is about to be dispatched to Europe to look after the equity of rehabilitation distribution. One hopes that an able man will be chosen, someone who is neither a milk-to-Hottentots dreamer on the one hand or a person with a ward politician's view of the world on the other. (*Life* 1945, p.30)

The reference here to 'milk-to-Hottentots' conjures up an image of inappropriate misguided political acts, and plays to the myth that what 'Hottentots' really want is to eat white missionary meat, not to drink milk. The editorial's allusion to African cannibalism within the context of Europe on its knees serves to revive age-old myths of black savages eating Christian missionaries and their need for European civilising presences. In 1945, the term 'milk-to-Hottentots' seems to have been used as a common point of reference for journalists discussing flawed political initiatives directly or indirectly endorsing racial stereotypes, a language that may have been noticed by the non-European delegates at the San Francisco Conference.

PART 3. THE ATROCITIES PHOTOGRAPHS

British and American newspapers and picture magazines exchanged photographic material and 'This created a shared visual narrative record for both countries, somewhat neutralizing the differences between the nearby war in Britain and the more distant one experienced in the United States. The record produced was massive yet uniform' (Zelizer 1998, p.88).

Life was a large-format publication, approximately 36 cm by 26 cm, and with some of the highest-quality printing available at the time. So, even by today's standards, the 'Atrocities' feature can be recognised as an immense photographic moment and a dynamic visual statement. This being the case, *Life*'s article is clearly one of the key moments regarding public awareness of the death camps, in the context of the historic significance of the horrific events that took place in the German concentration camps with the recognition that 'the Holocaust has become for humanitarians the crime against which all else is measured – the un-comparable, to which all else is compared' (Weizman 2012, p. 39).

Page 32 is the opening left-hand page of *Life*'s 'Atrocities' spread. It is the only place within the 'Atrocities' article where a photograph fills the complete page. This image is one of George Rodger's more well-known photographs from Belsen and as such deserves particular attention.

The photograph is captioned 'A Small Boy Strolls Down a Road Lined with Dead Bodies Near Camp at Belsen'. When the same photograph was reproduced subsequently elsewhere the caption stated that the boy was German. However, according to research by the German Historical Museum, the boy was in fact a Belgian Jew named Sieg Mandaag (Bernard-Donals 2004, p.382). In *Humanity and Inhumanity*, Rodger's retrospective photography book published by Phaidon in 1994, the caption reads, '1945 Belsen. A Dutch Jewish Boy Walks Through the Camp'. Rodger was meticulous in his research notes and diary-keeping when it came to captioning his work. However, in the photograph's original use in *Life*, the boy's cultural identity was uncertain; the meaning generated by the photograph shifts significantly depending on whether he is cited as being German, Jewish, Belgian or Dutch. If identified as German, he becomes part of a wider German problem of ambivalence towards Nazi atrocities. His stroll can be read as a nonchalant and familiar encounter with the scene of horror, making him a representative of the German nation and therefore associated with the perpetrators of these violent acts. The abnormality of the scene becomes a metaphor for the fascist state. However, if the boy is identified as Jewish, then the difficult question to ask is: what are the conditions of his survival – or how has he survived when he is surrounded by death?

Retrospectively, the photograph's appearance in *Life* is further complicated by the fact that we now know from both Rodger's book and the *Life* archives that the image has been cropped down its right-hand side. Apart from a couple of young women, who are also walking down the forest road in the distant background, there are few signs of human survival when we look at the photograph as reproduced by *Life*. The cropping reduces both the foreground and background of the photograph's content on the right-hand side of the frame. When the photograph was reproduced in full in Rodger's book, the right-hand side opens up the scene; it is much more than the story of the boy, revealing in clear detail the explicit body parts and faces of many victims (Rodger 1994, p.137). In particular, a dead woman stares out at the viewer with unseeing eyes, from underneath the fully-exposed body of another woman, whose face is covered by her clothes. In the uncropped version of the photograph, the dead woman's expression eclipses the punctive power contained in the small boy's inquisitive look. This version also reveals a well-populated scene. In the background on the right-hand side, survivors are clearly evident throughout a woodland area of the camp, many of whom appear to be squatting, huddled together in small groups. Given the angle of the sun and the length of the boy's shadow, we can assume that it is around midday. It is possible, then, that the people are preparing some kind of meal. What is evident, though, is that the presence of the boy, and the two women following him further down the road, seems less significant, less at odds with the scene, as we can interpret these individuals as being some of the many survivors hanging on in the chaos of the camp.

Life's decision to crop the photograph suggests that there was a real desire to visually exploit the presence of the boy, so as to emphasise the level of inhumanity operating in and around the camps. However, the cropping denies us access to the wider scene of the chaos surrounding survival and death across the camps and shuts down some of the uncomfortable aspects of simultaneously seeing people dead, on the edge of life or in moments of survival.

Rodger was so sickened by the experience of trying to make

aesthetically pleasing photographs for news media from the horrors that he had encountered at the camps that he never returned to photographing in war zones again. He is much quoted as saying:

> It wasn't even a matter of what I was photographing, as what had happened to me in the process. When I discovered that I could look at the horror of Belsen, 4000 dead and starving lying around, and think only of a nice photographic composition, I knew something had happened to me and I had to stop. I felt I was like the people running the camp, it didn't mean a thing.
> (Rodger, quoted in Shephard 2006, p.102)

What Rodger states here is of profound importance when we think about the role of photography and the making of images of violence for popular consumption. He tellingly reveals that his act of photographing the results of the camps with his aesthetic eye equated to a fascist act of violence. Rodger recognised the power of his situation above the vulnerable dead or living, who were caught in the most extreme circumstances. This relationship for Rodger was so profoundly disturbing that he aligned his fully exploitative gaze with that of Nazi prison guards, a form of extreme objectification at work.

On page 33 there are four photographs of equal size. The two at the top are from Belsen and were also taken by Rodger. They portray the sick, the dying and the dead lying around the enclosures at the camp. The lower two are from Buchenwald and are by Margaret Bourke-White. Like that of Rodger, Bourke-White's work from the camps has become iconic. Her two photographs are taken from inside the barracks and portray emaciated, starving and deformed men on the edge of existence. In one of the photographs some of the men smile and wave back at Bourke-White's camera in acknowledgement of her photographic act. It is an example of a human moment when, even in the harshest conditions, one of the default positions for people in the presence of a camera is to smile or wave. They clearly see her looking at them and now, from the archive, they wave back at us. Her use of flash adds an increased sense of exposure to an already harsh scene. Bourke-White reflected on her time making photographs at the death camps:

I saw and I photographed the piles of naked, lifeless bodies, the human skeletons in furnaces, the living skeletons who would die the next day because they had had to wait too long for deliverance, the pieces of tattooed skin for lampshades. Using the camera was almost a relief. It interposed a slight barrier between myself and the horror in front me. (Bourke-White, quoted in Feinstein 2005, p.4)

Not all who saw the prisoners could hide behind their cameras. When many of the 'soldiers looked into the camp ... one after another, they threw up. Seeing this, the inmates became embarrassed and turned away' (Shephard 2006, p.23). Ben Shephard's text argues that the prisoners, once liberated, saw themselves through the eyes of the liberators as being human again but in debased form. Seeing the reactions of the liberating soldiers and watching the response to their condition relocates the victims' sense of self outside the violent gaze of the Nazi regime, which clearly derives pleasure from their destruction. According to Shephard, the gaze of the liberator returns the victim back into a difficult place of self-consciousness and embarrassment concerning their condition, when they register that they have been seen as human once again.

At Gardelegen camp, William Vandivert took the photographs that appear on pages 34 and 35. Page 34 contains four photographs, each roughly a quarter-page size. They show in detail the remains of people who were locked in a warehouse when the camp guards set it on fire; some of the corpses are still smouldering. The image filling page 35 illustrates the enormity of the overall atrocity from inside the warehouse at Gardelegen. The almost full-page photograph on page 36 was taken by Johnny Florba at Nordhausen. It shows thousands of prisoners laid out, waiting for burial in neat rows across a bombed-out street. American soldiers can be seen surveying the scene.

The final photograph, on page 37, provides a detail of German guards being forced to bury the dead. The first part of its caption reads 'Two German Guards, knee-deep in decaying flesh and bones, haul bodies into place in the Belsen mass grave' (*Life* 1945, p.37). The photograph is once again by Rodger. This image takes the reader full circle back to Belsen, but this time with the perpetrators enclosed in the making of their own horror. The lack of horizon in this photograph creates the impression of an unending mass of dead people. You cannot see past the corpses that fill the image from top to bottom. The guards appear to rummage like scavengers as they pick through the bodies. The caption informs the reader that one of the guards is a 'strong-armed German SS girl wearing leather jack boots'. The dead bodies in which the guards are knee-deep, and the way they are framed as they handle the corpses, render the dead as symbolic lost souls collectively caught, even in death, in Nazi hell. They have become a mass of nameless players in a horrendous theatre of death that visually recalls Francisco Goya's etchings *The Disasters of War*, produced between 1810 and 1820 to illustrate the destructive violence of conflict in Europe during this period. The horror in Rodger's photograph, however, is intensified because these images are not etchings but photographs and as such they share all the realism associated with the medium.

In 1945, because these photographs were displayed in this particular magazine, they would have been regarded by the American public as being images that 'transmit immutable truths ... it is clear that photographic meaning depends largely on context ... Meaning is always directed by layout, captions, text and site and mode of presentation' (Sekula 2002, p.445). This issue of *Life* illustrates well Allan Sekula's argument that, over time, linkages in meaning may be weakened and unhinged from their original dominance. Now, these photographs cast a dark shadow across Allied attitudes towards Jews during the war.

PART 4. OMISSIONS (BACK TO LANGUAGE)

Life's editorial tone is rich with righteous condemnation and moral authority, and evokes a nationalist tone. The text is peppered with the symbolic meaning of judgement. Words such as 'evidence', 'charges', 'witness' and 'doubt' reproduce the logic of a courtroom trial in process. Part of the work that *Life*'s text performs for its readers, then, is in calling forth these evidential photographs as primary collective chief witnesses from the scene of atrocity. According to this text, before this issue of *Life*, photographs of German atrocity, especially those from Soviet or Jewish sources, did not carry the authoritative power to make the charge or to substantiate the existence of the camps. An analysis of the text exposes *Life*'s attempt to deflect its twelve-year legacy of refusing to address Nazi brutality back onto the American people, reconstructing the public as the primary source of doubt that drove the 'sceptical' perspective that the magazine highlights.

In discussing the importance of these photographs as active agents in the development of human-rights politics, Paul Gordon Lauren edited *Life*'s text for his readers, laying emphasis on the notion of the shocking discovery. His version reads:

> Last week the jubilance of impending victory was sobered by the grim facts of the atrocities which Allied troops were uncovering all over Germany. For 12 years since the Nazis seized power, Americans have heard charges of German brutality. Made sceptical by World War I 'atrocity propaganda', many people refused to put much faith in stories about inhuman Nazi treatment of prisoners. (Lauren 2003, p.186, paraphrasing *Life* 1945)

Lauren continues his quotation from *Life*: 'Last week Americans *could no longer doubt* stories *of Nazi cruelty. For the first time there was irrefutable evidence*, as the advancing Allied armies captured camps filled with political prisoners and slave laborers, living and dead' (Lauren 2003, p.186). The first point to note is that the italics are not in the original *Life* text. More significantly, Lauren's own reproduction of *Life*'s critical factual omissions, of which more below, creates a gap in understanding the magazine's editorial stance, especially when the text and photographs are considered through the prism of the evolution of the history of human rights.

A retrospective reading of *Life*'s full 'Atrocities' text reveals a most disturbing absence that is crucial to both the debates on the representation of atrocities within the concentration camps and the development of human rights in spring 1945: the lack of any reference to the ethnicity of the prisoners. This omission is also evident in the twelve photographic captions. The critical aspect of the Jewishness of many victims of the camps is withheld and totally denied throughout the 'Atrocities' feature. *Life* states that the 'camps are filled with political prisoners and slave laborers'; given the high moral standing that *Life* adopted throughout this powerful editorial moment, this omission or refusal to discuss the Jewish presence can only be understood as a deliberate withholding of information. The photographs therefore evidence a refusal to address the specifics of German policies of extermination aimed at Jews at this critical time in developing public awareness of the specific details of these events. A question then that surfaces here is, did *Life*, like its British media counterparts, have concerns when it came to highlighting the violent treatment of Jews by the Germans? When discussing the British media in her essay, 'Horror in Our Time', Hannah Caven states that:

> One of the biggest difficulties for newspapers appears to have been how to refer to the Jewish populations within the camps. In some ways it almost seems as if there was an attitude that everyone knew that the Jews were the main victims and that no more needed to be said on the subject. (Caven 2001, p.234)

Read from the perspective of racial politics, this could also have been motivated by a fear that highlighting the fact that the majority of the victims were Jews might reignite old anti-Semitic attitudes and alienate readers; veiling the presence of Jews in the camps could have been perceived to render the photographs more emotive for generic Western public consumption. In short, and given Allied state and public attitudes to Jews, as 'the worst period of American anti-Semitism was sandwiched between the ends of World War I and World War II' (Dinnersten 1993, p.212), might the audience be less inclined to identify with the people in focus if they considered them alien and apart from themselves?

PART 5. RACE AND INFORMATION

Paul Lowe informs us that in Britain it was well known that 'the majority of the inmates at Belsen were Jewish', but:

> by the time the reports reached the general public this fact had largely been censored from the material. This was mostly the result of attitudes of the British Ministry of Information and the Foreign Office who rarely mentioned Jews in their reports on the camps preceding the liberations. (Lowe 2012, p.193)

The text in *Life* appears to mirror this policy of censorship adopted by British state information services. By withholding references to ethnicity from the 'Atrocities' feature, *Life* may well have thought it could maximise the potential to extract an emotive and sensationalised response from its readership. If this was such a deliberate act of erasure aimed at creating wider public empathy for the victims of the camps from among *Life*'s readers, then this was gained at the expense of denying the victims their Jewish identity:

> Images carry out the incessant work of a formulation of archaic passions. Warburg proposed an iconology (a method of reading the work performed in images) of the interval, the symbolic space between thought and the deepest of emotional impulses that is produced and remembered by the formulation of affect in the image. (Pollock 2012, p.66)

In May 1945, could the symbolic order of the work produced in the 'Atrocities' photographs have had such a wide emotional impact if the ethnicity of the Jews was part of the narrative of the feature? This cultural erasure becomes a denial of the historical reality to which the images belonged.

Lauren draws our attention to the parts of the text in the 'Atrocities' feature that highlight the eyewitness accounts of those who entered the camps. He states that, 'Eyewitnesses were quoted as saying, "Anything you hear ... will be an understatement. The full truth would get ... so low you couldn't print it." "The memory of what we saw and heard will haunt us."' Lauren continues:

> The editors then concluded by informing the readers that, 'With the armies in Germany were four *Life* photographers whose pictures are printed on these pages. The things they show are horrible. They are printed for the reason [that] ... Dead men will have indeed died in vain if live men refuse to look at them' (Lauren 2003, p.186).

He concludes his analysis of the photographs by stating that:

> The images on the pages that followed were absolutely shocking, especially when seen by the public at large for the very first time,

and revealed the power of photographs to arouse the conscience and thereby serve as a catalyst for action ... the juxtaposition of the knowledge of the Holocaust entering the public consciousness at the same time as the creation of the United Nations ... added still another powerful force to a volatile mixture of politics and diplomacy at the San Francisco Conference. (Lauren 2003, p.186)

The key emotive, catalytic action that these photographs generated was, according to Lauren, in helping to create a sense of political urgency among the delegates at the San Francisco Conference, encouraging them to subscribe to the formation of a new global world order that would prevent the disasters of war that had been laid out before them on the pages of *Life* magazine. However, if the photographs had revealed the identity of the clear majority of people who had suffered in the death camps, then they would have performed different political work. They would have supported with greater emotive charge those at the conference who wanted to ensure that anti-racism was enshrined in any new universal declarations on human rights. The image work that Lauren claims this feature in *Life* carried out contains a fault, as the Holocaust as an idea was not fully formed in international political consciousness as the Second World War drew to its end.

PART 6. WIDER SCENE OF EVENTS AND THE ABSENCE OF RAGE

As discussed, *Life* had a massive circulation and an influential editorial news position in the US and beyond, and its presentation of the photographs took place within wider reporting on the conference and other contemporaneous political events. As Lauren states, readers of *Life* 'quite naturally anticipated full coverage of the start of the San Francisco conference' (Lauren 2003, p.186). This was the main political event of the period and represented the possibility of a new dawn in world affairs.

At the conference there was a variety of different and complex political agendas being worked through in the grand settings of the San Francisco Opera House, but one of the more poignant questions was how the world's smaller nations, colonial subjects and other peoples that had been historically oppressed would fare in a new post-Second World War global politic. What would freedom and liberation look like for the colonised subjects of the world after the defeat of the Axis powers, and would the Allied powers live up to the promises made, for example, at the signing of the 1941 Atlantic Charter? Fabien Klose captures the expectations raised by the Charter for the leaders of colonised peoples:

> The Atlantic Charter of 1941, signed by Roosevelt and Churchill, reaffirmed faith in the dignity of each human being and propagated a host of democratic principles. Some in the West saw the Charter as empty promises, but not those of us in Africa. Inspired by the Atlantic Charter and the fight of the Allies against tyranny and oppression, the ANC created its own charter, called African Claims, which called for full citizenship for all Africans, the right to buy land, and repeal [of] all discriminatory legislation. We hoped that the government and ordinary South Africans would see that the principles they were fighting for in Europe were the same ones we were advocating at home. (Klose 2013, p.22)

Expectation that the Allied powers would deliver was therefore high, and political aspirations were real and substantial. Political autonomy throughout the colonies was demanded as the war in Europe was entering its final phases. In describing the events that took place at the Fifth Pan-African Congress in Manchester 1945, George Padmore noted that 'The Second World War had led to an almost universal feeling among Africans and people of African descent that colonial liberation was the order of the day, and that this struggle would be achieved by force if necessary' (Padmore 1947).

Racism and imperialistic attitudes among the Allies were clearly in evidence at this time. America's black soldiers served in a segregated Jim Crow army, and American racism during the war was not reserved for its own citizens. American high command specifically ordered that French African colonial soldiers be excluded from taking part in the victory parade through Paris to celebrate French liberation in August 1944. The order came from General Walter Bedell Smith, who was President Eisenhower's Chief of Staff. The face of victory over fascism in France, as far as the US was concerned, had to be white (Deroo n.d). The assumption here is that black faces liberating white Paris would have had a negative impact on race relations back at home in the US.

Eisenhower visited the camp at Ohrdruf just a few days after its liberation on 4 April 1945. He played an important role in publicising the events unfolding in the camps and stated:

> I had never felt able to describe my emotional reactions when I first came *face to face* with indisputable evidence of Nazi brutality and ruthless disregard of every shred of decency ... I have never at any other time experienced an equal sense of shock ... As soon as I returned to Patton's headquarters that evening I sent communications to both Washington and London, urging the two governments to send instantly to Germany a random group of newspaper editors and representative groups from the national legislatures. I felt that the evidence should be immediately placed before the American and British publics in a fashion that would leave no room for cynical doubt. (Charny 1999, p.296)

In the immediate aftermath of the discovery of the camps, both the American and the British editorials would indeed be fashioned to clearly suit the Allied political perspective on how to manage their public perception. However, not all senior Allied army staff that visited the camps felt or displayed the same compassionate need to act as Eisenhower did, despite Eisenhower's failure to come to terms with America's racist policies towards colonial soldiers and black American service personnel.

Leslie Hardman, a Jewish British soldier, 'recalled that a visiting officer to the camp made the tasteless comment "Bloody Jews it's good for them". Hardman was understandably incensed, disbelieving that in the sight of such tragedy people could still be so callous towards the Jews' (Caven 2001, p.212). It is clear from Hardman's experience that not all those in positions of authority in the Allied forces carried with them a sense of outrage regarding the dehumanising conditions faced by Holocaust victims. The absence of rage is historically evident through the lack of military and political action by the Allied forces and is made manifest by Hardman's experience in the camp:

It is no doubt possible to create the conditions under which men are dehumanised – such as concentration camps, torture, famine – but this does not mean that they become animal-like: and under such conditions, not rage and violence, but their conspicuous absence is the clearest sign of dehumanisation. (Arendt 1970, p.63)

The 7 May 1945 issue of *Life* stands out in this highly influential magazine's famous legacy, primarily because of the 'Atrocities' feature. However, also important is the full visual aspect of this issue, for example the cover story and its specific reference to the 'the German People', and the images immediately preceding and following the 'Atrocities' article that focus on the other visual and textual aspects of the conclusion of the Second World War. One of these was, as discussed, the hugely symbolic moment when the Russian and American armies met in Germany. Similarly, consideration should be given to the way the 'Atrocities' photographs may have influenced the reading of the feature about the San Francisco Conference.

PART 7. THE COVER STORY

The environmental photographic portrait, taken by William Vandivert, of three German men, which appears on the cover of this issue of *Life*, has an air of menace (*Life* 1945). The men all stare challengingly back in the direction of the photographer. Given their age, they are likely to have done some military service and they therefore appear to be demobbed army personnel. The youngest of the three looks straight ahead but very slightly off camera; assured, inquisitive and confrontational in his gaze. He has an injured left hand, which has been freshly bandaged; it is not soiled in any way. Standing slightly behind his right shoulder is a man of roughly the same age; behind his left shoulder, further back in the frame, is an older man, who is gaunt, in a black hat and overcoat. The text to the left of the photograph reads 'The German People'. The three men could be interpreted as presenting an image of a wounded, defiant, but still dangerous, nation.

This sense of defiance and lack of remorse is carried through the article about the cover, which appears some twenty-three pages after the feature titled 'San Francisco Security Conference Starts'. Between the feature on the conference and the cover story we are presented with a feature titled 'Baseball', followed by one called 'How America Lived – Six Old Houses Give a Realistic Record of the Past'. There is then a photo feature: 'Freudian Ballet "Undertow" is a Choreographic Study of Frustration and Violence'. On page 69 the cover story unfolds. The title is repeated, 'The German People', but this time we have a sub-heading too: 'A Few Anti-Nazis Face the Appalling Job of Redeeming a Country that Feels No Guilt or Shame' (*Life*, vol.18, no.19, 7 May 1945, p.69).

A photograph accompanies this text, occupying more than half the page, taken by the now legendary Robert Capa. It shows an elderly German couple dressed in dark overcoats, scarves and hats squatting in a foxhole in the middle of a field. It is mildly comical, as the couple appear to pop out of a muddy grave. The surreal nature of the image is further enhanced, because Capa's close framing gives no indication as to why they are there and where the foxhole is located. The caption reads: 'German and his frightened wife squat in a foxhole. Unlike the young, older Germans were friendly and anxious to please the Americans' (*Life* 1945, p.69). The caption does not cohere with the image, and the image tells us nothing about the older German people in relation to the Americans. What the image does do, though, is echo back to an earlier sequence of photographs from the 'Letters to the Editors' section on page 6. These were sent to *Life* by an American soldier returning from Europe. He reports finding the three photographs in Germany:

Sirs: To supplement your pictures of what the Germans did to their prisoners of war I submit three pictures I found in Germany. They evidently give a photographic record of a typical German execution, one in which the condemned man dug his own grave before being cut down by rifle bullets. Not a very pretty practice, is it? Sgt. Earl E. Rauscher. (*Life* 1945, p.6)

The 16 April issue had carried photographs of American prisoners of war in a state of starvation and Sgt Rauscher sent in the photographs he had found in response to seeing the emaciated

American men. The letters to the editors also carried another interesting response. The reader commented that she could not bear to look at the starved American soldiers. She criticised *Life* for publishing the images, stating:

> But I cannot conceive of the psychology behind the publishing of such pictures as these of starved American prisoners of war ... There is enough realism and foresight in the average American to convince him that these murderous enemies must for ever be silenced. We can do without the pictorial examples until our men have returned. Our hearts have quite enough burdens to carry ... Jane M. Smith. (*Life* 1945, p.6)

Jane Smith's point illustrates how difficult it may be to look at a subject caught up in violence when the person in the frame is readily recognisable as one of our own. Two of the American soldiers photographed were emaciated and close to death. Both the images were produced as empathetic documents of humanity in distress. They render the American servicemen with dignity and are loaded with pathos. The subject of American soldiers held in prison camps was clearly handled by *Life* with national sentiment in mind, even at this mild level of exposure to their debasing condition. The difference between these images in the 16 April 1945 issue of *Life* and those in the 7 May 1945 issue is that the men are clearly identified as being American, and the detail of their capture is part of the caption, as is the length of their captivity. The men isolated in the frame become the sole focus of our gaze rather than part of a mass of violence, with the result that they are presented more from the perspective of an intimate visit than as being part of an overall scene of disaster. In these frames we are encouraged to be with them as men rather than as mere observers of their condition.

Nevertheless, as Jane Smith illustrates, reader reaction could be quite strong:

> The language of these magazines revealed a true concern for social problems but from a reformist point of view: 'there is a real rhetoric of change and improvement there, of people capable of resilience and courage; but there isn't anywhere a language of

dissent, opposition or revolt'. *Life* magazine proved most influential during this period; it had a major, long lasting impact on the very conception of the photographic document in the West. (Ribalta 2008, p.22, quoting Hall 2001, pp.71-2).

'The German People' article runs from page 69 to page 76 and claims, through the writer's experience, that there is no sense of guilt, shame or responsibility for the war among the German people themselves. The article concludes with a photograph by Margaret Bourke-White of an older man dressed in a trolley-car inspector's uniform, leaning assertively on his bicycle, taken from a low position at an upward angle, thus elevating his status in the frame. In the context of Germany's defeat, the inspector becomes a parody of German military might, which now renders him a tragic but sinister comic figure as if Hitler himself is reduced to riding a pushbike. If the reader is in any doubt, the caption affirms his clownish status: 'A Hitler moustache still decorates Paul Pelzer, Cologne trolley-car inspector. A typical small Nazi, he had confidence in Germany's victory until bombing stopped his cars' (*Life* 1945, p.76).

PART 8. THE SAN FRANCISCO CONFERENCE

There were hundreds of thousands of African Americans and those caught in Europe's colonies who had contributed to the war effort, and these men and women were not going to revert to being treated as second-class citizens living under the old segregationist or Jim Crow laws, nor would they continue to succumb to colonial regulations that condemned them to servitude. Given that black soldiers and civil-rights activists had key roles both throughout the Second World War and in the subsequent anti-colonial, pro-civil rights and Cold War-based ideological confrontations that emerged throughout the twentieth century, then one of the key outcomes of these conflicts was that the racialised and disenfranchised subject's sense of self – and of being a valued human being – was profoundly altered by the direct experience of war, the concentration camp and the struggle for political recognition. This is intricately linked to the argument that conflict has the capacity to cause both national and personal trauma. Walter White, the executive secretary of the National Association for the Advancement of Colored People in 1945, was 'convinced that the Allies simply could not grasp that if they tried to trot out the same old discredited peace plan, especially a peace based on the perpetuation of white overlordship ... another war is inevitable'. To save the Allies from committing 'the folly of another Versailles Treaty', the NAACP, 'on behalf of the Negroes not only of America, but Africa, the West Indies and other parts of the world', was going to have to make its 'voice heard' (Anderson 2003, p.17).

A self-contradictory political and ideological front opened during the Second World War, in that Europe wanted to maintain or re-imagine the old imperial structures but at the same time had to espouse libertarian and humanitarian propaganda to mobilise the colonies to support the war effort. The United States faced a similar predicament and, throughout the war, it maintained a policy of racial segregation in the army and at home. The Allied forces' essential propagandist message was that they were fighting for universal freedoms and that extreme fascist aggression, which targeted all those who did not meet the Aryan model of human worth, was a collective, moral and shared human concern for all the world's peoples. So, for example, the Atlantic Charter of 1941, adopted by Britain and the US, served as the guiding principle of this moral and political position that the Allied forces held throughout the war. The third point of the charter was particularly relevant to the colonised and disenfranchised peoples around the world. Its signatories 'respect[ed] the right of all peoples to choose the form of government under which they will live' (Atlantic Charter 1941); however, the Allied forces appeared not to have taken account of the actual political reality of delivering self-determination for all the world's people after the war.

The Atlantic Charter was critically important in that it marked the beginning of the end of European colonisation, at least psychologically for many people, and represented a milestone by proposing self-determination for the colonised nations. It also played an important part ideologically as a key point of contention for the non-European and African American delegates at the San Francisco Conference. 'For African Americans ... the Atlantic Charter was revolutionary. It was something, as NAACP Board member Channing Tobias declared, that black people would be willing to "live, work, fight and if need be, die for'" (Anderson 2003, p.17). However, what was becoming most evident to the black delegates was that the major powers would fight:

> tooth and nail over the definitions and priorities of human rights, they unanimously agreed that these rights could not be used to pierce the shield of national sovereignty ... The most powerful states, through the human rights discourse, made their priorities the universal concern of others. (Douzinas 2000, p.119)

The construct of universality as an idea among dominant Allied forces maintained its fundamental Eurocentric essentialist origins.

After the Second World War, 'subjugated voices from across the black world accrued into a new kind of colonised peoples' political reconstruction work' (Bailey & Hall 1992, p.106), a work produced from within an increasingly unified subaltern and shared body politic that demanded autonomy. The colonial subjects' participation in the war against the fascist threat therefore evolved into a continuous, complex web of interconnected struggles for freedom that would resonate around the world for decades to come. These utterances of real freedoms were turned into political articulations during the San Francisco Conference. However, faith in change began to slowly dwindle during the course of the event, which led W. E. B. Du Bois to comment later that 'San Francisco was a beginning, not an accomplishment' (Du Bois, quoted in Anderson 2003, p.55).

> For the historically oppressed person of colour, having rights and scrupulously following legal procedures offers much more than the actual contents of these rights; it offers the respect of others and the self-respect that legal recognition ensures but which has been systematically withheld. Being admitted to right-holding is a symbolic admission to the dignity of humanity and a very real introduction to the legal recognition of (formal) equality. (Douzinas 2000, p.295)

So while the fresh cool wind of Cold War politics was beginning to be felt around the collars of delegates attending the conference, American black activists such as W. E. B. Du Bois, Walter White and others were pushing forward the questions of race, decolonisation and equality beyond the politics of civil rights and into the theatre of human rights.

'As feared by some, and hoped for by others, the question of race came up immediately at the San Francisco Conference. The mood and interests of the delegates differed sharply from those of the Americans, British and Soviets at the Dumbarton Oaks Conference in 1944' (Lauren 2003, p.109). As voiced by Du Bois:

> Today as we try in anticipation to rebuild the world, the propositions of Dumbarton Oaks center their efforts upon stopping war by force and at the same time leaving untouched, save by vague implication, the causes of war, especially those causes which lurk in rivalry for power and prestige [and] race dominance. (Du Bois 1945, p.103)

As long as these exist, he declared, 'there can be neither peace on earth nor good will toward men'. Now was the time, argued Du Bois, to shift from the old 'for white people only' policies and to recognise that 'the day has dawned when above a wounded and tired earth unselfish sacrifice, without sin and hell, may join through technique, shorn of ruthless greed, and make a new religion, one with new knowledge, to shout from the old hills of heaven: "Go down Moses!"' (Du Bois 1945, p.103). Du Bois and other active observers and participants conveyed an intensity that far surpassed Secretary of State Edward R. Stettinius's first general expression of the need to work towards 'greater freedom and greater opportunity for all peoples of every race, creed and colour' (Lauren 1988, p.163).

Page 38 of *Life* follows George Rodger's photograph of the German guards pulling bodies around in the Belsen mass grave. This page features a wide photograph taken from high up in the opera house looking down at the stage and the theatre packed with conference delegates. The caption reads, 'Conference Opens in San Francisco Opera House'. It is a fantastic grand setting in which the future security of the world is being dramatically addressed. The old opera house is rendered a fitting location for the reality of this political drama.

Page 39 is divided into three sections. The first has a photograph in which the USSR's Foreign Commissar Vyacheslav Molotov is speaking to the conference. The text states that, 'Molotov showed himself to be a master of both stubbornness and surprise'. The caption reads, 'USSR Foreign Commissar V.M. Molotov tells the conference that his country believes in a security organisation and will help set it up now' (*Life* 1945, p.39).

It is a typical conference setting with note-takers and the chairman of the conference, Edward R. Stettinius, with his distinctive head of white hair, watching over the proceedings. A colleague is seen whispering in Stettinius's ear. The text for the feature occupies the centre section of the page, with the final third of the page showing a photograph filled top to bottom with the seated delegates applauding. The caption informs us that the three delegates closest to the camera are from Brazil: 'Delegates at the first session applaud the address of welcome by Governor Warren of California. In the front of the photograph are seated three of the delegates from Brazil' (*Life* 1945, p.39). The unnamed delegates, though solemn in expression, appear mildly appreciative of the speech. The photograph is revealing not so much because of its focus on the three Brazilians but because it highlights just how few black faces made up this section of the conference, despite the fact that over 750 million people were under some form of colonial control at this time.

Page 40 has two photographs positioned on the left-hand side, one above the other. The right-hand side of the page is dedicated to a text titled 'The Russians'. The top photograph shows Anthony Eden, the British Foreign Secretary, speaking at the podium caught in a statesman-like gesture, his right hand held high, while he addresses the delegates. We have been informed on the previous page that he gave 'the most eloquent speech' in which he 'reminded the big powers of their responsibilities to the world' and that the 'conference should conclude its work within four weeks' (*Life* 1945, p.40). The photograph below this is of T. V. Soong, the Chinese Foreign Minister. He is also photographed standing at the podium. The caption for both photographs reads:

Addressing the conference, Anthony Eden, British Foreign Minister, declares that 'we must succeed' in solving disputes by agreement. Below T.V. Soong, Chinese Foreign Minister, says that 'China, perhaps more than any other nation, understands the necessity of success of this conference'. (*Life* 1945, p.40)

In direct contrast to the relatively positive messages used in captioning the photographs of Eden and Soong, *Life* includes a text that focuses on the difficulties and cultural gaps that exist between 'the Russians' and the Americans. The title of the editorial carries a sub-heading: 'A *Life* editor finds they got off on the wrong foot because they did not understand the Americans' (*Life* 1945, p.40). The article is written by Fillmore Calhoun, a *Life* foreign corre-spondent. The opening paragraph states,

> For reasons of which they seem entirely unaware, the Russian delegates at San Francisco started out by losing friends and jeopardizing its influence at toboggan speed. Either the State Department, their own people who have lived in the U.S. or a competent public relations man should have filled them in on a few facts. What they probably needed was a little booklet similar to those which introduced the GIs to various European coun-tries, titled *The Americans: a Strange People.* (*Life* 1945, p.40)

Calhoun's article constructs an image of the Russians as a suspi-cious, hostile, secretive people, locked out of foreign techniques of diplomacy and courtesy. The article continues:

> The trouble began when word got round that the Russians had brought a shipload of vodka and caviar for their own pleasure. The 'proof' was that anyone could go to the top of Telegraph Hill and see the ship at anchor. Actually the ship was there primarily for communications and to provide living quarters for some of Russia's delegates, but the everlasting secretiveness of the Russians made it all seem mysterious. Idle tongues clacked away. (*Life* 1945, p.40)

Russian photographers seemed to have upset American photog-raphers by breaking out of the designated 'pool' of photographers:

> Screams of rage rose, 'Is San Francisco running this conference
> or is Moscow?' Just before Molotov's plane arrive[d] the whole
> mob was allowed to move out to take their pictures where they
> wanted to, each and every individual feeling he had struck a firm
> resounding blow for liberty. (*Life* 1945, p.40)

A chaotic photographic press moment at the airport is rendered
as a fight for liberty against the Russians. The article goes on to
further ridicule the Russians when it states that, 'Part of the Russian
difficulty lies in the fact that they have been so busy ironing out
a revolution and winning a war that they have paid no attention
to the mores of other nations. The conference marks the Soviets'
first real emergence into the outside world' (*Life* 1945, p.40). The
Russians at the conference are ultimately infantilised through *Life*'s
article, which creates a sense of a Russian nation lacking the cultural
confidence to cope with the modern developed 'outside world', as
represented by San Francisco.

The article also pokes fun at the Russians' appearance: 'Their
clothes are poorly cut, their shoes badly worn ... men whose courage
has won them the Hero of the Soviet Union medal look half-scared
to death' (*Life* 1945, p.40). The statement mocks the integrity of
their status as having contributed to the war effort, questioning
whether these shabby characters can be genuine 'heroes' if they are
so easily 'frightened' at a world peace conference. In closing the
article it is evident that *Life*'s editors would have preferred to have
had a Russian delegation that was prepared to sing and dance to the
tune of American politics, and they clearly had an expectation that
foreign diplomats and soldiers should have the capacity to entertain
Americans: 'If the Russian soldiers had brought out balalaikas the
crowds would have cheered, traipsed around with them as they do
when Scots bagpipers parade on New Year's Eve' (*Life* 1945, p.40).
Equating the Russian delegation at a world peace conference with
Scottish bagpipers on New Year's Eve reveals a form of deep-seated
cultural arrogance and insensitivity from the editors of *Life*, who,
by trying to elevate the Russians' obvious trivial differences into
significantly political events, ultimately inform us of *Life*'s own
hysterical fears.

Breaking up the coverage of the San Francisco Conference, on pages 41 and 42 there are full-page advertisements for Campbell's Soup and Snider's Tomato Catsup respectively. These interject with a flavour of American domestic values across the scene. There are caricatures of women positioned on different days of a calendar wearing aprons, and one of the women stands out, as she is dressed for a formal occasion.

Page 43 continues with further coverage dedicated to the Russians. There is an almost full-page photograph of the Soviet Foreign Commissar Molotov. Its headline reads 'Molotov Holds First Press Conference' (*Life* 1945, p.43). The photograph shows him talking to the press in an open and inviting manner, his gesticulating hands wide apart and with what appears to be a glint of excitement in his eyes, and he is presented as a 'graying, dark-suited Russian of medium height with a mustache and pince-nez' (*Life* 1945, p.43). We are informed that 'he is usually completely surrounded by bodyguards ... Reporters knew him only by reputation – a stern-visaged early Bolshevik, twice exiled to Siberia, once editor of *Pravda*, once 1930-1941 Premier of the U.S.S.R. They understood him to be a capable but colorless administrator' (*Life* 1945, p.43). The editors of *Life*, though, did discover that Molotov 'had a sense of humor' and they offer some additional respite to the coldness of their description by conveying to the readers that the Russian delegation is not beyond negotiation: 'Russia was willing to amend the Dumbarton Oaks plan'. However, the article lays strong emphasis on Molotov's dogmatic character when he is quoted as saying that 'it was "only just" for Russia to have three seats in the Assembly' (*Life* 1945, p.43). Molotov, as far as Du Bois and his colleagues were concerned, was hardly a 'colorless administrator': for the black delegates at the conference, Molotov and the Russians were a source of inspiration and hope because, as 'Du Bois noted, at San Francisco, it was painfully obvious that "not a whisper against colonialism could be heard except from Molotov"' (Du Bois & Aptheker 1997, p.14).

The articles in *Life* give strikingly little detail about the critical political issues at stake during the conference. Much of the coverage is dedicated to reinforcing ingrained xenophobic attitudes towards different cultural and political perspectives. The British are described as 'natty Etonized' characters although Anthony Eden is photographed as statesman-like at the podium (*Life* 1945, p.40). The Saudis later on in the article provide an exotic presence by wearing long brown robes (*Life* 1945, p.46).

The final four photographs from the San Francisco Conference appear on pages 44 and 46. The first, on page 44, shows Clement Attlee, British Deputy Prime Minister, holding a press conference. It seems to be a rather informal affair as there is no podium for the speaker and it is taking place outside the main delegates' hall. One of his colleagues sits on the small raised stage from which Attlee is speaking, while another leans back, confidently smoking a pipe. We are informed by the text that Attlee is in favour of Russia having three votes on the Assembly and also 'that said means must be provided for removing conditions in which wars breed. This would require improvement of the economic conditions and social well being of all peoples' (*Life* 1945, p.44). Attlee's comment mirrors Principle 5 of the Atlantic Charter, which states a 'desire to bring about the fullest collaboration between all nations in the economic field with the object of securing, for all, improved labor standards, economic advancement and social security' (Atlantic Charter 1941); a position from which the imperial powers and the US were progressively retreating during the conference.

The photograph immediately below that of Attlee shows Prime Minister Jan Christiaan Smuts of South Africa. He is looking down in a reflective pose from the heights of a balcony at the Fairmount Hotel over the San Francisco Bay area. 'Now 74, he was in Lloyd George's cabinet during the last war, and helped shape the League of Nations. This time, he thinks, the world is "ready" for a peace organisation. "We have learned our lesson now", he told reporters in San Francisco' (*Life* 1945, p.44). Smuts had been a good friend of Churchill since the First World War and, 'His presence in San Francisco can be seen as the start of a precipitous political decline, a process highlighted by his (and his political peers') failure to comprehend fully the democratizing environment of postwar internationalism' (Dubow 2008, p.46). The inclusion of Smuts in *Life*'s feature brands him as a significant political elder statesman in attendance at the conference who, like many of his political peers, Churchill included, is out of time and out of step with the speed of change occurring across the world. In reading the photograph of him today, Smuts becomes symbolic of the many white statesmen present at the conference whose 'ideas had been formed in the First World War context of the League of Nations', the vast majority of whom were clearly 'adrift in the post-1945 world order, as the language of anti-colonialism and democracy challenged' white world authority (Dubow 2008, p.47). Within a year Smuts would be facing a different set of concerns at the United Nations. 'At the very first session of the General Assembly, in 1946, South Africa was charged by India with discriminating against citizens of Indian descent' (Dubow 2008, p.47). It is evident from Smuts's comments that the sovereign state of South Africa had learnt some lessons from its participation in the Second World War. However, it would take South African statespeople nearly fifty years to acknowledge the social injustice and cruel inhumanity of white supremacist policies that promoted segregationist racism and the economic and cultural disenfranchisement of black Africans, under its regime of Apartheid. Apartheid was implemented in 1948, the same year in which the United Nations came fully into being.

The last two photographs and the end of the coverage from the San Francisco Conference are on page 46. The photographs take up the right-hand side of the page and are presented with extended captions. The first portrays a chef sitting on a stairwell lined with filled plates. He strikes a jovial figure in his chef's whites and his button mushroom hat as he poses on the steps smiling at the food. It is a seemingly banal photographic moment. The caption reads:

> George Mardikian, owner of San Francisco's Omar Khayyam restaurant, is semi-official Conference chef. On Wednesday he will serve Armenian dishes at the Opera House itself. Above, he poses with some of his favorites: shish kebab, cracked wheat and rice pilaf, yaprak sarma, harpout keufte, kouzou kzartma, derevapatat, paklava. (*Life* 1945, p.46)

The offering of an Armenian dish at the conference would have literally served to remind the delegates of the historically benevolent nature of American foreign policy and charitable acts towards minorities caught up in state-sponsored violence against them. Between 1915 and 1930 the American-based charity that became known as the Near East Relief Fund raised millions of dollars to provide critical aid for the Christian Armenians being systematically slaughtered by Turkish nationalist forces.

The final photograph and last editorial comment are positioned immediately under the photograph of Mardikian. The caption reads:

> Sayyid Jamil Daoud, advisor from Saudi Arabia, is cornered by autograph fans. At first the Arabians, along with the Russians, refused to give autographs, but before long they caught on to the American custom. The Fairmont Hotel, where they are staying, was alarmed when told that their brown robes had to be pressed every night. (*Life* 1945, p.46)

The photograph shows Daoud smiling back at the photographer enjoying his newly found celebrity status, surrounded by mostly women autograph hunters, some of whom also return a smile to the photographer. It is obviously a light-hearted moment for most of the people present. *Life*'s mention of the Saudi robes, however, encodes the delegate as an exotic rather than a political presence at the conference. For *Life*, the issue is not what the Saudi delegate stands for ideologically and politically but what he potentially represents in the mind of *Life*'s editorial and its readership. The reference to his brown robes unlocks larger circuits of oriental fantasy in the West. The political reality of the Saudi situation was that they were instrumental in the formation of the Arab League, just a few weeks previously. The Arab League went on to play a significant part in post-Second World War world affairs and at the time of its foundation was most concerned with ending European colonial influence in the region: 'the issues that dominated the league's agenda were freeing those Arab countries still under colonial rule, and preventing the Jewish community in Palestine from creating a Jewish state' (BBC 2011).

CONCLUSION

In a telegram sent to American magazine magnate Henry Luce in 1936, the poet and essayist Archibald MacLeish wrote, 'The great revolutions of journalism are not revolutions in public opinion but revolutions in the way in which public opinion is formed' (Briggs & Burke 2010, p.194). MacLeish gauged the role that *Life* was to play in American society profoundly and accurately, as, by 1945, the magazine was in a powerful position to shape public opinion through its wide national and international circulation. Opinion-forming is clearly evident in the way *Life* used these 'ethically' stable and emotionally charged photographs from the Nazi concentration camps (Sontag 1973, p.16). However, their ethical stability and emotional charge when first presented to the Western public was far from fixed.

Life's use of these 'Atrocities' photographs represents a cultural and media milestone in the representation of atrocities. According to Paul Gordon Lauren, the *Life* editorial played a significant role in knowledge of the Holocaust entering the public realm, and he further claims that it was a 'catalyst for action' (Lauren 2003, p.186). What action did it cause and what purpose did this action serve? On closer scrutiny of the 'Atrocities' feature we can observe subtle but significant cultural management in the way the photographs are presented: race is omitted from the feature and is markedly absent or decoded out of their meaning, yet this was the essential element concerning the construction of the death camps.

'[T]he relationship between photography and reality is not perfect evidence but it is nonetheless a substantial link to what-has-been, like a footprint or a death mask' (Taylor 1999, p.296). Given this, reading *Life*'s 'Atrocities' photographs through the time of their publication, as Lauren invites us to do, would historically reposition them and alter the precise nature of the work they performed on the audiences that read this issue in early May 1945. In the ways that the photographs are used by *Life*, they cannot deliver the vital knowledge relating to the Holocaust with which Lauren retrospectively empowers them (Lauren 2003, p.186). They fall foul of a form of atrocity supervision over *Life*'s readership, because, within the editorial and historical time and context of their original display, reading these photographs as records of violence against Jews was not possible unless the reader had access to or prior knowledge of the extreme levels of ethnic cleansing that had taken place.

The editors of *Life* can therefore be charged with a large degree of misrepresentation and race management through the use of the photographs from the death camps, because they did not provide their readers with the critical information concerning the majority of the victims. The 'Atrocities' photographs, which flow seamlessly into those taken at the San Francisco Conference, can now be read as working more to aid American national and foreign policy during the conference than as working to highlight the core violent and racial realities of the death camps. If *Life* had seen fit originally to position these images within the context of the racist violence to which they now belong, then it is possible that those campaigning for the rights of the black Americans and subject peoples at the conference would have had a powerful visual tool to assist their cause. They aimed to enshrine anti-racist clauses fully within the formulation of any new universal declaration, but anti-racism and colonial freedoms were omitted from the outcomes of the San Francisco Conference. This created despair among key black political activists such as Max Yergan and Walter White. The latter commented that 'the San Francisco Charter provided "scant hope for liberation" for the 750 million people in non-self-governing areas' (Anderson 2003, p.56). *Life* had the opportunity to explain that race was integrally part of the concentration camps, but they did not. And thus, even with the increasing amount of visual evidence that was emerging from the camps, the dominant powers driving the formation of the United Nations failed to recognise the catastrophic disasters of race-orientated violence.

3

Violence of the Image

PART 1. RACIAL TIME

Equal recognition is not just the appropriate mode for a healthy democratic society. Its refusal can inflict damage on those who are denied it ... The projection of an inferior or demeaning image on another can actually distort and oppress, to the extent that the image is internalized.

Charles Taylor, 'The Politics of Recognition'
(Taylor 1994, p.36)

We forget the things that shape us and all those things that made us.

Stuart Hall, 'The Missing Chapter – Cultural Identity and the
Photographic Archive' (S. Hall 2008)

Archival photographs are a message from the past. They open and adjust our understanding of the way we were. Photographic archives, such as those held at the Royal Anthropological Institute in London and the Weltkulturen Museum in Frankfurt, when read from outside the dominant narratives of their making, offer different points of departure from which to translate the past. As we can only read the past, as it were, in our present, and as the present is never still, then it makes sense to read the past as always being in transition, constantly redefining us in the present as we learn more about the historical conditions of our existence back then.

As Stuart Hall suggested in 2008, trawling through the archive often means 'we have to take one step back and go through the imaginary to enter the domain of culture' (S. Hall 2008). Archives are highly cultured spaces, making them rich and attractive places within which artists and curators of photography may make critical interventions, as was seen in the exhibition held in 2008 at the International Centre for Photography in New York, titled *Archive Fever: Uses of the Document in Contemporary Art*. The press release states:

> One of the most compelling issues explored by artists in recent years centers on the nature and meaning of the archive, that is, how we create, store, and circulate pictures and information. This widespread investigation examines the archive as both a conceptual and physical space in which memories are preserved and history decided. (International Centre for Photography in New York 2008)

The exhibition, which included works by Walid Raad, Thomas Ruff, Anri Sala, Fazal Sheikh, Lorna Simpson, Eyal Sivan, Vivan Sundaram, Nomeda and Gediminas Urbonas, Andy Warhol and many other internationally respected names, owed its title and curatorial framing to Jacques Derrida's book *Archive Fever* (Derrida & Prenowitz 1996).

The place of race in the archive is a highly contested area of investigation, one which W. E. B. Du Bois was at the forefront of articulating, through his work on the visual and race. In discussing the work of Du Bois, Shawn Michelle Smith states that, 'In Du Bois's early writings, the colour line represents not only the systematic inequity of racialized labour but also a visual field in which racial identities are inscribed and experienced through the lens of a "white supremacist gaze"' (Smith 2004, p.24). Archival photographs put to work in the present can now help us recall, rearticulate, manage and make visible the systems of visualisation that have brought the racialised body into focus and question how that focus has contributed to Western ideas on human progress and understanding.

Archival photographs constitute a place in which we can continuously engage with important cultural memory work, which helps us reread the actual making of the past and therefore reconfigure different historical narratives concerning the stories that make up history, race, rights and recognition: four vital stations in our understanding of humanity that remind us of the power relationships between the 'observer and the observed' (Ribalta 2008, p.38).

Old photographs from colonised and oppressed regions of the world can influence our current sense of place. They have the potential to become key markers in understanding how colonisers have, in different temporalities and political conditions, chosen to engage, make visible, control or erase the colonised subjects' claims for recognition, reminding us that in many instances the political space of progress is nearly always framed as a modern space and that 'modern space is, as it were, space wiped clean' (Connerton 2009, p.121). Modern space often denies the racial spectres that live in museums and among the photographic archives. It is a space where time seems to start afresh and memories are suppressed. It is critical to consider that when archival photographs focusing on the black subject are set free to be read in the present they have the capacity to resist the pace and process of photography's and modernity's desire to forget. In using Derrida's seminal *Archive Fever* as a point of departure from which to discuss the distancing nature of archives, Ariella Azoulay highlights that 'in the archive constructed as ex-territorial and as a receptacle for the past, that which has been cruel and biting is supposed to appear, or so we expect it to appear, as dulled; a piece of history, its accusing finger cut off, blunted' (Azoulay 2015, p.195). Opening the archives concerning the making of race and unsettling the meanings made there in terms of knowledge produced around race equates to a burning down of the 'master's house' and using the remaining ashes to fertilise the soil so as to produce a liberated and fertile plot that grows out of its violent past to generate new meanings.

Burning down the house as a concept becomes representative of some of the key critical moments in modern history in which oppressed peoples have taken action towards ending the conditions of their domination. Meetings, protests, strikes, rebellions, revolutions and civil wars mark the paths to freedom. Looking back at the role of photography in these moments helps to expose the conditions in which anti-colonial, liberation and civil-rights movements were born. Reading photographs gives insight into how our present understandings of oppressed peoples' making in history have been constructed, often positioning them as victims of systems of state violence. For example, the photographs that Charles Moore took in 1963 in Birmingham, Alabama, that showed young civil rights protestors being attacked with police dogs and blasted with fire hoses, and the poignant archival retrieval work that Santu Mofokeng produced in building his 'Black Photo Album' project that redressed the lack of historical photographs of black middle-class South Africans from 1890 to 1950 (Mofokeng & Campbell 2013). Mofokeng used archival photographs as markers of absence of an indigenous black presence, locked out of civil society. As a photography slide show, the images helped Mofokeng and his audience to understand themselves differently. Photography, then, assists us in the continuous analyses of how these critical journeys towards freedom, modernity and equality for black people have been visualised, framed and represented. This is especially the case within the context of the global reconfigurations and the political failures that occurred throughout the first half of the twentieth century, which was devastated by imperialism, colonialism and wars. Reworking the history of photography explores the different temporalities of global conflicts that have European expansion at their core, and events such as the Second World War in particular may be understood as very different phenomena if read 'through the longer history of colonialism' and its visual regimes (Kruse & Tuck 2012, p.174).

'Cultures do not exist outside of how they are represented' (S. Hall 2008), and in the hands of the coloniser, photography has dominated how the Other has been portrayed. Europeans' photographic acts have played a leading role in the theatre of cultural violence against non-Europeans and, in representing the colonised and subjugated peoples of the world, the European camera can be read as constituting a 'decidedly ideologically positioned tool on the side of incursion' (Oguibe 2002, p.566). Historical photographs from within the colonial world or regimes that supported racial violence, such as those made during South Africa's system of Apartheid, or from the far-flung corners of the British empire that celebrate white dominance over the Others, now help us identify possible new entry points into the ideologies that produced racism in the West. Part of the work they can do in the present is to throw different light onto the history of these dark human chapters. Through the European dominance of photography, and the resulting massive overexposure of the Other, it could be argued that a condition in the West has been created within photography, where it has become difficult to see any photographs of black or subjugated people, let alone photographs of 'black people being abused (or caught in compromised circumstances such as famine, war or indeed the normal activities of their day-to-day life) as being wholly benign' (Berger 2011, p.52). The archive of the world image bank has built fortunes by trading in malign images of the Other.

The mass of photographs taken in Africa by Europeans, such as the one made in 1923 and sent back to England as a colonial Christmas card from the African Oil Nuts Company and Miller Brothers, based in Badagry, Nigeria, illustrates the debasing approach by colonials to taking photographs of Africans as a form of trophy image-making (Figure 5). The photograph's full caption reads:

> Christmas photograph of staff at the African Oil Nuts Company and Miller Brothers. Three rows of bare-chested African workers pose for the camera, each man's chest painted with a letter to spell out '1923, Badagry, Merry Xmas'. Four Europeans dressed in white sit on a makeshift bench up front beside three African children, possibly domestic servants. Badagry, Nigeria, circa 1923. Badagry, Lagos, Nigeria, Western Africa, Africa (Bristol Archives).

This seminal photograph now forms part of a permanent exhibition at Liverpool's Slavery Museum. It is on continuous public display, because it highlights the colonial cultural arrogance that was at work in visualising the black body in the early part of the twentieth century. In this instance, the European colonials use their 'staff' as human blackboards to convey the company's Christmas greeting. The black workers are positioned as if posing for a team sports photograph, but instead of celebrating the men as achievers their bodies are merely used to spell out the greeting for the intended recipients at home. In other words, the marking of the African men with white paint constructs the workers as being wholly devoid of any authority over their own bodies. Each painted letter is an absolute mark of domination by the colonial rulers. The company owners join the frame, positioning themselves for the camera in front of the marked black bodies that function as the backdrop to this colonial festive message. It is the complete objectification of the black men that makes the photograph so extreme.

Reading the photograph now allows us to connect the colonial mindset across space and time, observing how it creates a cultural affirmation of the racist attitudes that are so prevalent in the making of images of black subjects in Africa and within British imaginations. The colonisers are shown sitting dressed in their casual, bright white clothes. To add to the theatre of the image, two black children, also dressed in white, are positioned lying on the ground, pet-like, in front of the four seated Europeans. Additionally, a very small black boy, again dressed in white, sits centrally on the same bench as the Europeans. The caption informs us that the children are 'possibly domestic servants'. The smallest of the African boys is sandwiched in the middle of the four Europeans, between one of the men and the only woman in the photograph. The child folds his arms, mirroring the poses of the two men on the left. The placing of this African child visually constructs an abstracted colonial family, in which everything and everyone is owned. Despite the boy's position, it is not clear what his relationship was to the colonisers and at what age his induction into colonial service began. The presence of the small boy, although positioned on the same plane as the Europeans, can be seen as representing colonial infantilisation processes at work. Placing this child centre stage, and the other slightly older children on the ground in front of the Europeans, further emphasises the photograph's message of dominance; it communicates to the viewer the colonial pleasures of childlike African servitude and European rule.

Within this photograph, however, there is an engaging visual twist that emerges out of its 'oppressive' first reading. Time has fortunately diluted the colonial humour intended, especially when the photograph is read through the prism of a contemporary decolonial critique. The African man whose body was selected to carry the letter X in the Christmas message is head and shoulders above the rest of the men. Due to his large stature, the X is the most dominant sign in the photograph. He stands almost directly behind the European man seated on the right. The dominance of the letter X pulls the viewer's attention to it and marks, in a Barthesian sense, a punctive fault-line in the relationship between the colonisers and colonised. The X becomes a symbol of rejection that distorts the original jovial message. The towering black figure marked with the white X announces in the present that something is profoundly wrong within the politics of this frame, even beyond the objectification of the black men and beyond the politics of the time of the photograph's making. Reading the photograph from a twenty-first-century perspective aligns the black painted subject to a more recent political application of the letter X. X as a sign was used by black radical activists such as Michael and Malcolm X, among others, to mark the rejection of their European slave names and as a symbol of their awakened consciousness as black people. In reading this photograph today, and with the knowledge of how the letter X was used in black radical political contexts, the black central figure is transformed through time and political cultural appropriation to emerge as having the potential to challenge, from within this photograph, the colonial authority that is so evident in the production of it.

To understand the depth of black objectification in the transatlantic European psyche, one only needs to take a quick glance through the pages of James Allen's critically acclaimed *Without Sanctuary: Lynching Photography in America* (2000). The book places on display visual reminders of the intensity of race hatred at work in the US during the first half of the twentieth century and indeed beyond. The photographs in the book represent a pathology of race hatred. This pathology seems now to be illogical or abnormal, and yet as photographs of lynching they provide damning testimony to the perversity of violence and conditions of hate that were recognised by so many in the United States as being the natural order of things. When they were made, many of the photographs were transformed into postcards produced as memorabilia and, as such, they work within the long tradition of violent commodification of the black body in pain (Figure 6).

The photographs of lynching collected together within the context of the *Without Sanctuary* project were never produced as evidential documents in a court of law, where they might have assisted in the prosecutions of the perpetrators of such crimes. They were generated for wider appreciation and cultural affirmation of Jim Crow white violence, which was clearly sanctioned as normative evident from the fact that, although they portrayed graphic violence, they were allowed to be sent to family and friends through the US mail. What is shocking about these types of images, once we move beyond the obvious horrific depiction of the broken, brutalised and butchered black bodies, is the sheer sense of pleasure, cultural pride and excitement visible in many of the faces of the white participants at the lynching scenes. They gladly pose and in some instances jockey for the most prominent position in front of the camera, celebrating their presence or direct participation in a spectacle of unlawful human killing, confident in their knowledge that they would not be prosecuted. The photographs that make up the *Without Sanctuary* archive date from as late as the 1960s.

Representations of lynching in popular culture tend to locate it as a nineteenth-century practice, as seen in Steve McQueen's Oscar-winning 2013 film *12 Years a Slave* and subsequently the photograph he produced while scouting for locations for the film *Lynching Tree*, first displayed in Basel in 2013. As the title suggests, the latter focused on a large tree, which is located near New Orleans and was used for lynching slaves. The photograph, displayed as a colour transparency on a light-box, was shown as part of Tate Britain's *Fighting History* exhibition (2015). However, rather than being 'history', *Without Sanctuary* reminds us that, for many African Americans today, lynching forms part of living memory. Thus, some of the work that the photographs in *Without Sanctuary* do now is to close the temporal gap associated with race hate in the US, which, through the archive, is often represented as a phenomenon in the country's past. These photographs remind us that living with the threat of violence because of one's difference is real and potentially devastating, and that lynching remains, for many, a constant fact of life. This was highlighted by Isabel Wilkerson in her 2014 article for *The Guardian*: 'About twice a week, or every three or four days, an African American has been killed by a white police officer in the seven years ending in 2012'; this rate of killing black Americans 'is nearly the same as the rate of lynchings in the early decades of the twentieth century' (Wilkerson 2014).

Colonial and racist trophy photographs therefore serve as fragments and frames from within the grand narrative of white supremacist visual ideologies. They allow us to enter the catastrophic frames of violent colonial and racist times, and they become important articulations that signify the dark cultural codes constructed against people of African descent or Others classified as inferior (Young 1995).

Photographs such as the 1923 Christmas message from Nigeria haunt the old imperialists and segregationist regimes and, as images working on the present, they reanimate and reunite us with the violence of colonial time, a time when European values considered 'force ... a universal, simple, rapid, and easily understood method of communication', and a time when:

> cultural difference not only made the use of force helpful to the accomplishment of European objectives, but also made it easy for its employers to assume that the usual conventions of human relations could be partially abrogated in contact with members of alien and inferior cultures. (Cairns 1965, p.42)

Time also does its 'reconstruction work' on the *Without Sanctuary* lynching images (S. Hall 1984, p.106). Racist trophy photographs, like all photographs, have the capacity through time to mutate in meaning away from their original intended purpose. In the case of these images, they have become culturally recoded by their display as objects of shame that reveal the horror in the spectacle of lynching. This recoding becomes possible only through different modes of articulation, such as the museum, the gallery, publication and the internet, and by allowing a number of cultural perspectives into the archives. Reimagining the cultural work performed by violent images of black people has, in the case of the *Without Sanctuary* project, encouraged a recognition of the racist pleasure that was derived from lynching black people in the US. Photographs made from within the racist culture of Jim Crow-ism or colonialism now provide the space in which new articulations and political awareness of representations of the black subject in the Western world can emerge. If we look at photographic representations of acts of violence where race is the critical driver for their production, we can track back over time and ask pertinent questions about photography as an ideological tool concerning race, violence, Western visual pleasures and photography's role in the making of whiteness.

It is in the space and time of culture and politics that black trophy photographs such as the *Without Sanctuary* project and the 1923 'Merry Xmas' photograph can become transformative objects; they are referent, fragmented moments that evoke and invite a reworking of old formations and understandings of photography's work in racial time. With reference to Johannes Fabian's 1983 book *Time and the Other: How Anthropology Makes its Object*, I suggest that racial time is different from the linear progression of dominant time. Instead, racial time is a phenomenon where waiting forms the majority of the everyday. It is a time where progress is not charted through the prism of Western epistemologies. In racial time, slavery does not end, it merely evolves, changes shape and oppresses through different but equally violent regimes. Racial time also has its critical periods where progress is produced and reproduced through tangible events. For example, in the Second World War, racial time for the subaltern became the backdrop or opportunity for mounting a significant challenge against political dominance and the constructed time lags that framed it. The upheavals in Europe that were produced by war and conflict for the subaltern were moments in which the time for change could be seized, appropriated and sped up, in favour of liberation. Racial time is therefore not always slow. But as far as justice is concerned, racial time is probably the slowest of all and is best recognisable today in the US through the disproportionate amount of black men locked up in prisons and on death row. 'Time appropriation in racial politics', remarks Dilip Gaonkar:

> mostly occurs during periods of social upheaval and transformation, whether locally, nationally, or transnationally. Sometimes starting in relative isolation, as in the Montgomery bus boycott, time appropriation can launch a series of events, propelling a single act into a series of acts, within the same location or well beyond its geographical realm. (Gaonkar 2001, p.285)

Racial time does not tick along in a fashion that produces seconds, minutes, hours and days. It works more like a cultural pulse in which the political conditions around it cause it to quicken or slow down.

New formations of photography's previously orthodox history are indeed possible if we read photography through different political temporalities and cultural perspectives within the constructs of race and time. Race is a construct and photography has been mostly applied to aid the creation of a dominant Eurocentric symbolic order in which the subaltern has been condemned as an object, rendered and processed as a mute and inferior being. Given this, creating openings in which photographic epistemologies can surface from below allows different cultural readings and interpretations of photography to emerge. This resurfacing of the medium's history enables us to 'trace a larger journey of translation, from the disempowered to the empowered' (Young 2010, p.8). This was evidenced in the exhibition *Rise and Fall of Apartheid: Photography and the Bureaucracy of Everyday Life,* which opened at New York's International Center of Photography in January 2013. The organisers state in the accompanying media release that:

> A central premise of this exhibition is that South African photography, as we know it today, was essentially invented in 1948. The exhibition argues that the rise of the National Party to political power and the introduction of apartheid as the legal foundation of governance changed the pictorial perception of the country from a purely colonial space based on racial segregation to a highly contested space based on the ideals of equality, democracy, and civil rights. Photography was almost instantaneously aware of this change and responded by transforming its own visual language from a purely anthropological tool to a social instrument, and because of this, no one else photographed South Africa and the struggle against apartheid better, more critically and incisively, with deeper pictorial complexity, and more penetrating insight than South African photographers. (International Center of Photography 2012)

According to the curators of the exhibition, Okwui Enwezor and Rory Bester, photography in South Africa as visual language was altered within its core by the intensity of the Apartheid political regime. Here, I argue that it is not photography that is transformed by Apartheid; rather, it is the people on all sides of the racial divide. Under Apartheid, black photographers, trying to make their lives visible to the outside world, were under intense political pressure, often working in secret with concealed cameras. On being arrested by the police, Ernest Cole, the black South African photographer, was offered two options: join their ranks as an informer, or be sent to prison. He went instead into exile. His book *House of Bondage*, published in 1967, 'shows the Apartheid world within the world but also hints at a larger, yet unrealized world where black people could be seen or choose not to be seen, on their own terms' (Baer 2014, p.5). A statement from Cole's book reads: 'Three hundred years of white supremacy in South Africa has placed us in bondage, stripped us of dignity, robbed us of self-esteem, and surrounded us with hate' (Cole 1967). Reading photography from below, or from the south, opens the door for subaltern voices to address the impact of photography on the black body and mind, and enables them to recognise themselves as subjects in their own right. The making of photographs such as the one taken in 1923 at Badagry says nothing of any note or worth about the African and everything about the time and people of the photograph's making, when 'the Briton saw his world in terms of a broad three-stage hierarchy in which the white race, western civilization, and Christianity occupied the top rungs of the racial, cultural and religious ladders of mankind' (Cairns 1965, p.74). While this imperial northern perspective on the world has proved remarkably resilient, photographers such as Cole proved their revolutionary qualities – and those of photography; each time they released the shutters of their cameras, they chipped away at imperial systems of knowledge. They altered the frames of reference in which the subaltern subject had been located.

Likewise, the *Without Sanctuary* project, made possible through the collecting work of James Allen, a white American from Florida who describes himself as a 'picker', becomes a radical intervention in how we see race. He states:

I believe the photographer was more than a perceptive spectator at lynchings. The photographic art played as significant a role in the ritual as a torturer or souvenir grabbing – a sort of two-dimensional biblical swine, a receptacle for a collective sinful self. Lust propelled their commercial reproduction and distribution, facilitating the endless replay of anguish. Even dead, the victims were without sanctuary ... Studying these photos has engendered in me a caution of whites, of the majority, of the young, of religion, of the accepted. (Allen n.d.)

By bringing a corpus of lynching photographs together and positioning them within the public realm, where they perform critical and ongoing political work, social change becomes a reality. The *Without Sanctuary* photographs were cited as being a significant contributing factor for encouraging the US Senate finally to acknowledge its complicity in lynching. Senators George Allen and Mary Landrieu sought a formal apology from the state to be given to the victims of lynching, and, in this, they were partly motivated by seeing these images. The visual vocabulary of the book helped them to secure progress through the Senate of non-binding 'Resolution 39', which was passed by the Senate on 13 June 2005 (S. Res. 39 2005). On this historic date the US Senate issued a long-awaited formal apology to civil-rights political activists for not protecting people against lynching. The resolution reads as follows:

Now, therefore, be it *Resolved*, That the Senate –

(1) apologizes to the victims of lynching for the failure of the Senate to enact anti-lynching legislation;
(2) expresses the deepest sympathies and most solemn regrets of the Senate to the descendants of victims of lynching, the ancestors of whom were deprived of life, human dignity, and the constitutional protections accorded all citizens of the United States; and
(3) remembers the history of lynching, to ensure that these tragedies will be neither forgotten nor repeated. (S. Res. 39, 2005)

Over a hundred years after some of these photographs were taken, they still perform serious cultural and political work and caused change at the highest level of politics when re-introduced into the public realm. Here, we can point to a rare and direct moment when photographs have generated real social and political change. Resolution 39 is more than an apology for not prosecuting racist murderers and not protecting black lives. It is a symbolic moment of recognition and a significant moment of justice.

Such a journey across time to a form of justice for those black people executed for white pleasure is an example of racial time in operation. Racial time is exhausting for those whose lives have been historically managed and framed through the images and ideas of race, not because they are worn down by seeing images of violence against the Other, but because they are the Other so familiar with being framed in a violent totalitarian Eurocentric gaze. Homi Bhabha in his 1986 foreword to Frantz Fanon's seminal text, *Black Skin, White Masks*, states that:

> The black presence ruins the representative narrative of Western personhood: its past tethered to treacherous stereotypes of primitivism and degeneracy will not produce a history of civil progress, a space for the Socius; its present, dismembered and dislocated, will not contain the image of identity that is questioned in the dialectic of the mind/body and resolved in the 'epistemology of appearance and reality'. The White man's eyes break up the black man's body and in that act of epistemic violence its own frame of reference is transgressed, its field of vision disturbed. (Fanon & Bhabha 1986, p.12)

PART 2. RUPTURED IMAGE

Archives of images address the ebb and flow of the political realities through which colonised and African American subjects were brought into public focus by the Allied governments both during and immediately after the Second World War. Certain critical image positioning of the black subject was produced by the Allies, which sought to bring the black subject closer to whiteness at an unprecedented time of crisis. Images that addressed racism and colonialism were produced and put to work in various public realms within Britain and the US, and these public-service racialised images either aided or hindered the sociopolitical conditions of subaltern subjects under imperial rule during the war, and the question of race was managed through the photographic image at this critical juncture in global politics.

For colonised and subjugated peoples, the Second World War ruptured the established image of European dominance. With the experience of the war, as noted in the previous chapter, many from the colonies and those who had historically been subjected to racial, cultural and political violence, developed the conviction that they had the moral right to carry on the fight against European colonisation and against other oppressive practices of white racial superiority that had become widely accepted as norms across much of the 'developed' world. A steady process of political agitation against the hegemony of systematic colonial and racial oppression was unleashed during the war years. This represented a new kind of black cultural and political work from within the subaltern international body politic. For the subaltern, the war against the fascist threat seamlessly evolved into battles for equal rights, recognition and independence. This subaltern political work was staged on myriad cultural and ideological fronts, both from within the Allied states and throughout their colonial territories. Direct forms of agitation, effectively from below, produced a climate in which critical consideration of the subaltern had to be addressed by the Allied governments. In Britain and the US, the result was an attempt to produce an official visual shift in the perception of black people and their place in the fight against fascism. This desired shift in perceptions of race was consciously generated by state bodies to perform specific cultural work across the fault-lines of race that were opening up across the US and throughout the British empire. It became evident that the status quo around race could not be maintained as the Allied states faced the threat of the Axis powers.

During the Second World War the idolatry-like presence of the 'white, western, civilised male ... as the ultimate face of humanity was in crisis. It is this profile that monopolised the definition of humanity in mainstream western imagery' (Pieterse 1992, p.223). This was an imagery that would be profoundly challenged and altered as a key consequence of black participation in the war. 'The war diminished not only the power but also the self-confidence of Europeans to rule their colonial possessions. In so doing, moreover, it revolutionized the myth of white invincibility and superiority among indigenous peoples' (Lauren 1988, p.172).

For the European powers during and after the war, African nationalism and civil-rights movements became an unstoppable force for change. The great white nations in fighting themselves, effectively opened the door to freedom for the colonised and those who Fanon would later call *The Wretched of The Earth* in his inspiring 1961 revolutionary book. For African nationalist leaders, the Second World War was the point at which Europe's grip on Africa began to loosen:

> During the war the Allied powers taught the subject peoples (and millions of them!) that it was not right for Germany to dominate the other nations. They taught the subjugated peoples to fight and die for freedom rather than live and be subjugated by Hitler … Here then is the paradox of history, that the Allied Powers, by effectively liquidating the threat of Nazi domination, set in motion those powerful forces which are liquidating, with equal effectiveness, European domination in Africa … The emergence and the march of African nationalism are in reality a boomerang on the colonial powers. They fired the anti-domination bullet at Nazi Germany, but now the same bullet is being fired at them. (Sithole 1959, pp.19-23)

In the midst of the disasters of the Second World War, the image of black people in the Western world experienced a significant shift within and in relation to Western governments. This shift occurred not as a result of any great act of humanitarian Allied enlightened policies but because the Allied governments slowly began to recognise that the impact of the continuous promotion of cultural and political hostilities against black people was not beneficial to their wider objective of defeating the Axis powers. In the early 1940s, racial conflict in the US was absorbing vital resources and discouraging the much-needed labour power in the factories to defeat the Axis powers. In analysing some of the country's race riots, in the 'United States the War Department noted that 1,250,000 man hours of production were lost in the factories of Detroit' because of riots in 1943 (Menefee 1944, p.15).

Popular constructions of Second World War history, such as those produced by the BBC relating to Winston Churchill's famous morale-boosting speech to the House of Commons on 4 June 1940 after the great retreat from Dunkirk, tend to omit the fact that the empire was regarded as a vital element of survival should Britain be successfully invaded by the Germans. The designated role of the empire, according to Churchill, was to carry on the struggle against the Axis powers until the 'New World' (the US) could rescue, liberate and restore the old imperial world. Churchill stated, 'We shall fight on the beaches, we shall fight on the landing grounds, we shall fight in the fields and in the streets, we shall fight in the hills; we shall never surrender', but the final part of the speech is most revealing:

> and even if, which I do not for a moment believe, this island or a large part of it were subjugated and starving, then our Empire beyond the seas, armed and guarded by the British fleet, would carry on the struggle, until, in God's good time, the New World, with all its power and might, steps forth to the rescue and the liberation of the old. (Churchill 1940)

It was in this moment of Britain's most dire need that the idea of empire became a reassuring symbol of British freedom within the House of Commons and across the nation. The empire here is importantly framed by Churchill as a permanent entity, as much a part of Britain as Britain itself. He later stated that, 'We mean to hold our own. I have not become the King's first minister in order to preside over the liquidation of the British Empire' (Churchill 1942). Churchill understood clearly what was at stake in the war, and he insisted on distinguishing strategic and tactical war considerations, such as that of the Atlantic Charter (Kruse & Tuck 2012, p.174), over notions of decolonising the empire. Freedom for subject peoples was not, at this time, part of Britain's post-war agenda. Churchill's view of the empire's role during and after the war was profoundly different from that of the many anti-colonial and pro-independence groups:

> which had been formed in Britain before or during World War II ... The most important [of these groups] from an international perspective were the West African Students' Union (WASU), formed in London by Ladipo Solanke and Dr H. C. Bankole-Bright in 1925; the League of Coloured Peoples (LCP), formed in London by Harold Moody in 1931; and the International African Service Bureau (IASB), formed in London by George Padmore in 1937. (Adi 1995, p.12)

For political groups such as these 'the Second World War provided the opportunity to further develop their anti-colonial activities' (Adi 1995, p.12). It was therefore from within the body politic of the Allies that increasing political pressure was applied to the Allied leadership:

> to disclose their war aims, especially after the signing of the Atlantic Charter in 1941, to declare that self-determination was a principle that applied as much to colonies as to the occupied countries of Europe. British colonial administration came under the spotlight, as did the effects of racism in Britain, at a time when the Government was anxious to enlist support for the war effort, and to demonstrate how British imperialism was morally superior to Nazi fascism. (Adi 1995, p.12)

The Second World War was at a critical point in 1941, and Britain needed manpower. Across the colonies, appeals were made for colonial subjects to join the armed services and extensive propaganda campaigns against the Nazis were put to work to bolster manufacturing and recruits for the armed services (Sithole 1959, pp.19-23).

'The plan [as far as Britain was concerned] was to compete with Nazi Germany's highly efficient Ministry of Propaganda by promoting Britain's position both at home and abroad [as secure]. The Ministry of Information duly came into being on 4 September 1939' (Slocombe 2010, p.5). From that date, Britain's Ministry of Information produced images that attempted to construct a more intimate face of the colonial subject. This was done mainly through public poster campaigns seeking to reassure the British public that they were not alone in their fight against Axis aggression. The faces presented in these propaganda posters were designed to work as reassuring messages to the public that 'we' were not alone, as these Other loyal, British subjects were on hand to help; that they were fundamentally not separate subjects. Therefore these wartime posters, with the colonial subject in focus, represent a significant moment within Britain's imperial story. They are objects that function as critical visual markers in the perception of racial difference and racial time. The posters were aimed at a British nation that was perceived to be harbouring deep-seated anxieties and fears in relation to Germany's military might and grave concerns about Britain's readiness for war and fear of isolation as German forces swept across Europe. The posters were thus produced at a time when the British government was desperate to define a face of support, especially as the US was reluctant to enter the war. The distinctive message to the British public was that the colonies were the 'sinews of war' (Slocombe 2010, p.11), a resource that strengthened British resolve and would hold the muscle of Britain in place to resist any threat posed by German forces.

How effective the overall poster campaigns were in raising British morale is a matter of dispute, according to senior curators at the Imperial War Museum such as Richard Slocombe. In 1939, the same year as the posters entered the public domain, a survey was commissioned, which revealed that the British public felt patronised through a use of language that expressed 'lofty tones and abstract notions of "Freedom" and "Resolution"' (Slocombe 2010, p.5). These lofty 'abstract' notions that seemingly patronised the British public resonated differently throughout the empire, as thousands of colonial subjects rallied under the British flag to join the fight for freedom. The colonised subject identified in these posters a new sense of self that had not been widely displayed in public across the empire prior to the Second World War. In offering an image of closer cultural proximity between the coloniser and colonised, the posters visually articulated a people's aspirations for self-determination. 'WWII did not give birth to the spirit of independence, but rather gave expression to that spirit which was already there' (Sithole 1959, p.26).

As stated above, how successful the poster campaigns produced by the Ministry of Information in Britain may have been in raising British public morale is disputed. In his 2010 publication *British Posters of the Second World War*, Slocombe omits any analysis of race in presenting his interpretations of the cultural work the war posters performed. In fact, he references only one of the more popular posters that feature the colonial soldier or colonial war worker. Slocombe does, however, include four other posters from across the empire – from Canada, Australia, South Africa and New Zealand – but these present a rather anglicised vision of the colonial industrial workers' support for the war and are more textual than visual in nature. The single poster that references the colonial soldier that Slocombe chose to reproduce in his book is titled 'Together' and is credited to the British artist William Little. It was reproduced in various formats throughout the war and was used across colonial recruitment stations. Second World War public information posters, especially those that reference the colonies, warrant greater scrutiny than curators such as Slocombe have offered. Given the critical and contradictory nature of racial politics at work across both the Axis and Allied powers before, during and after the war, race should be a primary concern when exploring the archive of posters produced by the Ministry of Information.

In some of the posters, rarely seen in public after the war, the black subject is presented with a greater degree of parity and individuality, effectively singled out as visually honourable in their own right as either soldier or war worker. These images are radical, because they break with the tradition of portraying the colonised subject as merely the backdrop to white endeavours (Wood 2000). Prior to the outbreak of the Second World War, the dominant photographic images in circulation showed colonial or black soldiers or workers as an extension to the colonial mission or to white authority: the people were afforded no name, no rank, no worth. In the popular realm, black subjects were rarely portrayed as dignified fighting men in their own right. The normative mechanism and preferred visual message, when bringing the black subject into view, was to reproduce them as objects signifying the Allied army officers' superiority. In US print culture:

> the good black soldier remained conspicuous by his absence. *Life* magazine supported the war with gusto. But in seventy-eight glossy issues during the final year and a half of the war, when black (American) soldiers were at last in combat, *Life* published a mere ten pictures of black men in uniform – out of some 14,000 photographs. Most of these ten pictures were very small, and most of the soldiers were clearly service troops. One black soldier carried an accordion. None carried weapons. (Kruse & Tuck 2012, p.113)

However, in contrast to those posters and photographs discussed here, it is also the case that some of the lesser-known and now celebrated Second World War posters that are held at the Imperial War Museum and the United States National Archives can be read as attempts by the Allied forces to advance the publicly understood image of the black subject towards a more refined and human presence, a presence that opens up the possibilities of seeing the racialised subject not merely as a curiosity but as a professional participating soldier or as trained and skilled worker with a meaningful purpose, history and identity. These relatively rare images may have helped to close the cultural gap that surrounded the understanding of the black subject. In some cases the images were supported by informative and detailed texts relating to the black subjects' own personal journey in aiding the war effort.

PART 3. THE POSTERS

One of the posters produced in Britain, from the 1939 series titled 'Empire War Workers in Britain', which carries the subtitle 'A Tank Worker from Nigeria', participates in this more benevolent representation of the black subject (Figure 7). The full caption from the Imperial War Museum reads as follows:

Whole: the image occupies the majority, with a smaller image placed in the lower left, held within a blue circular inset. The title and text are separate and positioned in the lower fifth, in black. All set against a white background and held within a brown border.

Image: a half-length depiction of a Nigerian worker in a British factory. He is repairing a component of a tank. The smaller image is a Union Flag.

Text: EMPIRE WAR WORKERS IN BRITAIN: A TANK WORKER FROM NIGERIA This is Jack Smith, from Nigeria, who worked for the Secretariat there before coming to England to play saxophone in a dance band. When war broke out he, like many other West Africans, took a course in a Ministry of Labour training school, and now he is helping to repair engines of light tanks in a Ministry of Supply factory. Some of the tanks he has worked on were salvaged from France before the collapse. They were reconditioned in England and then sent out to his native Africa where they went into action against the enemy during the British advance into Libya. FOR VICTORY G.P.D. 365/67. (Imperial War Museum n.d.*a*)

'Jack Smith' is portrayed as a typical British factory worker. He is wearing standard navy blue workers' overalls and is at his position on the factory production line. There is no visual exchange between Jack Smith and the camera, as he is looking down at his work. The scene is reportage in style, and the poster has been produced as a colour lithograph. This gives the image a rich depth and texture, painterly in quality, as if it has been hand-tinted.

Through the text, Smith's individuality becomes an active agent in reading the image. His short story explains the conditions of his arrival in Britain, highlighting his skills and his place of origin. The dominant message is that he is here because Britain needs him, and he is fulfilling his sense of patriotic duty. We are told that he previously worked at the 'Secretariat', which suggests he has a high degree of literacy and administrative skill. He plays the saxophone, a complicated and expensive instrument, suggesting that he is a competent musician associated with jazz or an orchestrated big band of the time. We also learn that he has been retrained as a skilled engineer who now repairs the engines of tanks that are fit for purpose in front-line war manoeuvres. The African's transformation into a worthy war worker is completed through his anglicised naming: 'Jack Smith' is a very British name, and it serves to further trans-culturally locate him for the viewer. He has been made by Britain in Africa. In this guise, this colonial subject is an ideal contributor to the empire's war effort. Smith, here working in the 'Ministry of Supply Factory', through this poster, represents an African mirror, reflecting hope into the minds of the British while they are under siege. This poster has one other compelling factor. In the background another worker can be seen at his station. He also appears to be operating a machine. This man is white and he is out of focus, but his presence is critical to the message. The white man's framing within the image makes

Jack Smith a co-worker and generates in the audience the reality of racial equality within the industrial war effort.

Women from the colonies are also brought closer to their European colleagues through the cultural work they perform in a similar series of posters produced during the Second World War titled 'On War Work in Britain'. This series focuses on Asian women and men carrying out various highly skilled and trained tasks, such as the poster featuring 'Miss Dogdo Ardeshir Jilla' (Figure 8). The Imperial War Museum captions the poster as follows:

> Whole: the image occupies the majority, with a smaller image placed in the lower left, held within a blue circular inset. The title and text are separate and positioned in the lower fifth, in black. All set against a white background and held within a brown border.

> Image: a half-length depiction of an Indian nurse holding the back of a male patient's head as a doctor examines his nose. The smaller image is a Union Flag.

> Text: ON WAR WORK IN BRITAIN: No. 6: FROM INDIA TO PLAY HER PART IN BRITAIN'S MEDICAL SERVICE In the Prince of Wales' Hospital, Tottenham, London, twenty-year-old Miss Dogdo Ardeshir Jilla, a Parsee, is taking a four-year course as a probationer nurse. Now in her second year, Nurse Jilla lives in the nurses' quarters with the other nurses, takes part in the ordinary routine of the hospital, attends three lectures a week and studies in her off-duty time. In this photograph Nurse Jilla is seen adding to her experience by taking a turn of duty in the out-patients' department. She is assisting a doctor who is giving nasal treatment to a patient. FOR VICTORY G.P.D. 365/13/21/1. (Imperial War Museum, n.d.*b*)

'Nurse Jilla' is positioned in the centre of the poster gently supporting a young white man's head as he receives attention to his nose from a white doctor. Dressed in her immaculately clean, predominately white uniform, she looks down caringly at the patient. The poster is a colour lithographic print, the effect of which works to epidermally harmonise the range of skin tones of those portrayed. Racial differences between the three figures are diminished. The extended caption helps the viewer identify with the journey Nurse Jilla is making to becoming a nurse, and, by extension, becoming British. We are informed that 'Nurse Jilla lives in the nurses' quarters with the other nurses'. This implies that she has successfully integrated into living within the nursing institution. We are told that she takes part in the ordinary routine of the hospital, attends three lectures a week and studies in her off-duty time. Like Jack Smith, Nurse Jilla represents a much-needed colonial helping hand, framed as a real person doing valued wartime work. In caring for Britain's men in their hour of need, Nurse Jilla represents a saving angel from the colonies, as her dark right hand cradles the young soldier's blond head while he receives treatment from the doctor.

These posters help to shift the black body away from its historical debasing renderings produced across the history of Western visual culture. This new black face from the colonies is portrayed as committed to fighting and working for king and country, with both pride and an increased degree of cultural parity, but still bound by empire and loyal in the service of their colonial masters and as people allied in their collective purpose in defending Britain's interests. This juncture in the image production and presentation of the colonised subject at home and abroad marks a distinctive transfiguration in the portrayal of the colonised black body. It was out of political necessity and foreign invasion that the British propaganda machine produced the conditions in which 'the savage had turned subject, an image of mature colonialism' (Corbey & Leerssen 1991, p.192).

These wartime posters worked in different geographical and political conditions, and within the context of an empire on its knees, so, as forms of propaganda, they may have registered 'differently' within the colonies from how they appeared at home. In West Africa, the image of a dignified, respected black worker viewed from within the context of Africa's colonial reality could carry multiple different or transgressive meanings.

The British Ministry of Information further produced this sense of colonial coevalness within another series of posters that focuses directly on the colonial soldier. The series, produced in 1939, is titled

'Our Allies the Colonies'. One of these posters highlights the Royal West African Frontier Force, portraying an African soldier looking confidently at the viewer, as if staring them down (Figure 9). This series is also held in the archives of the Imperial War Museum and its object description reads as follows:

> Whole: the main image is positioned in the upper centre, with a smaller image placed in the lower centre. The title is separate and located in the lower half, in red. The text is separate and positioned across the top edge, in white cursive script, in the lower centre, in black, and down each edge, in black held within a brown and white design. Further text is integrated placed in the lower centre, in black outlined orange. All set against a grey background.

> Image: a portrait-length depiction of a soldier of the Royal West African Frontier Force. The smaller image is a depiction of the badge of the Royal West African Frontier Force.

> Text: The British Colonial Empire ADEN ANTIGUA BAHAMAS BARBADOS BASUTOLAND BECHUANALAND PROTECTORATE BERMUDA BRITISH HONDURAS BRITISH SOLOMON IS. BRITISH VIRGIN IS. CEYLON CYPRUS DOMINICA FALKLAND IS. FIJI GAMBIA GIBRALTAR GILBERT AND ELLICE IS. GOLD COAST GRENADA HONG KONG JAMAICA KENYA MALAYA MALTA MAURITIUS MONTSERRAT NEW HEBRIDES NIGERIA NORTH BORNEO NORTHERN RHODESIA NYASALAND PALESTINE ST. HELENA ST. KITTS ST. LUCIA ST. VINCENT SARAWAK SEYCHELLES SIERRA LEONE SOMALILAND SWAZILAND TANGANYIKA TONGA TRANSJORDAN TRINIDAD UGANDA ZANZIBAR Royal West African Frontier Force OUR ALLIES THE COLONIES R.W.A.F.F. Printed in England by A.C. Ltd. 51/2372. (Imperial War Museum, n.d.*c*)

The poster displays a head and shoulders portrait of a uniformed young African man with his regiment's name clearly stated just beneath him. The soldier looks resolute and proud. The signs of caricature or servitude, or exaggerated African props, are absent.

There are no indicators that support notions of the savage African Other. This is a portrait of a black man on the edge of modernity, a professional soldier bearing his British regimental regalia. It places him outside of racial time and into the contemporary condition of war. His only sign of servitude is the one that cannot be changed: his black skin, his Fanonian epidermal schematic marker, which holds him in a place of inherent cultural bondage. 'He is the object of information, never a subject in communication' (Foucault 1991, p.200).

The soldier wears a striking bright red fez on his head that carries his regimental crest. The fez is adorned with a long black tassel resting neatly down its left-hand side and stopping at the corner of the man's left eye. The gold braiding on the collar of his uniform frames his head in regal splendour. The braiding meets in the middle of his throat and surrounds the royal blue collar, separating it from the red fabric of the rest of his uniform. His image appears framed by a white halo that emphasises his black skin. It is as if his body heat bends the white light around him, creating a subtle suggestion of divine light. The white halo then fades to a sandy desert orange colour. Above his head in italics are the words 'The British Colonial Empire', and directly beneath his image, spelled out in small black letters, are the words, 'Royal West African Frontier Force'. In large red letters follows the most prominent text on the poster, which reads 'Our Allies the Colonies'. Below this is a simple graphic image of the regimental symbol of the RWAFF: a palm tree on a small mound. Either side of his image is an elaborate scroll, which lists the British colonies, starting with Aden in the top left corner and finishing with Zanzibar in the bottom right. In total, 49 colonial territories are represented through the face of this one West African soldier, who is rendered fit for purpose and is clearly portrayed as an asset.

Another poster from the same series portrays a young black soldier from the King's African Rifles. While he, too, is portrayed in a head and shoulders portrait style and also wears a tall bright red fez, he is shown looking attentively off to the right of the frame. His eyes do not meet those of the viewers. His uniform is more basic than his fellow African counterpart: it is a regular collarless khaki uniform. His regiment and its symbol are also named and positioned directly under his portrait. Similarly, this same text and overall compositional format are shared across the 1939 series of posters that includes colonial soldiers from Malta, Cyprus and Ceylon. However, it is the soldier from the Royal West African Frontier Force who stands out in the series, as only he is privileged with the right to project his gaze directly back at the viewer. The information available through the Imperial War Museum cites that all the posters are 'Subject Period: Second World War'.

To look directly into the eyes of the colonised soldier and for him to return the gaze of the viewer creates a more difficult and demanding exchange than the four other images. The other posters of soldiers with their gazes averted do not engage directly with the viewer, and thus might be read as losing a certain sense of authority. The construction of the other posters denies the viewer the task of looking directly into the face of the Other (Levinas 1987, p.74). Exploring the archive of this particular wartime campaign raises a critical question: was the direct face-to-face exchange with the colonial soldier rejected as an unacceptable public message and were the alternative, more passive images of colonial soldiers averting their gaze deemed more suitable by the British Ministry of Information?

For Africans who were among those colonial subjects that had been most viciously rendered as docile and dependent and in particular need of the British empire's civilising mission, these types of images would have represented revelatory moments in identification. Any visual communication that promoted African cultural worth would have been considered a major shift in European perceptions of African capabilities.

Many of the racialised recruitment posters and photographs produced by Britain during and in the lead-up to the Second World War can be read as representing a radical shift in the mindset of the colonisers. This shift clearly worked against dominant renderings of the black subject. It also served as a distinctive historical marker, exposing the hegemonic nature of the history of racial imagery in the West that constructed entire races of people as inferior. Once war with Germany appeared inevitable, the aim of Britain's national communications departments, as far as the empire was concerned, became to foster an image of equity among its subjects and to visually attempt to close the gap between the coloniser and colonised, at least for the duration of the war. 'It is not ethnicity, or "race" that governs imagery and discourse, but rather, the nature of the political relationships between peoples which cause a people to be viewed in a particular light' (Pieterse 1992, p.217). These particular Second World War posters now offer an opportunity to see the logic of racist imagery at work as attitudes in Britain shifted during the war and eased when it was deemed to be politically expedient.

This adoption of a sympathetic view of the colonies was not due to a concern with readjusting the archive of racist imagery that was so prominent across the field of perception. That field had been created by scores of photographers working within visual codes that had laid the foundation for the colonial view that Britain had of its subject peoples (Edwards 2001, p.139). Instead, this new inclination towards a more human view of the colonised subject was a matter of national survival. Across the British empire, and as far as this moment in the visual perception of the Other is concerned, the long-standing Eurocentric photographic and academic fascination with race, culture and religion was laid bare and rendered less significant. One hundred years after its invention in 1839, the racialised photographic discourse produced in Britain, due only to the possibility of its own destruction, was diverted away from its historical fixation with racial difference and European supremacy towards much-needed reassurance that the country was not alone. With the crisis of the Second World War, it became strategically important to move away from a stance of cultural ridicule towards a more unifying and humanitarian purpose. The European is 'fixed upon a certain variety of perception that favoured particular representational scales and could only follow on from the isolation, quantification, and homogenization of vision' (Gilroy 2004, p.35). The extreme conditions of war interrupted that Eurocentric visual homogenisation process.

These new wartime British state-sanctioned images carried a uniquely distinctive message that encouraged the British public and colonial subjects to see themselves as united, allied and equal, both in the workplace and the armed forces, in which they shared a common goal: to fight against Nazi tyranny and Japanese imperialism. These images, now only visible in the archives of the Imperial War Museum, were distributed throughout the British empire and carried the message that collectively the coloniser and the colonised were magnificent in their joint purpose: that of defending 'freedom'. Black subjects within the context of a modern world in conflict were thus no longer framed as dependent children or willing servants but as men and women with great potential and equal power to overcome the threat from the Axis powers. These more sympathetic images could be read as an early attempt by Britain to bring black cultures back to life (Gilroy 2004, p.31), and to awaken a sense of black cultural self-esteem, even if ideally this only represented another layer of colonial management to be prosecuted through the theatre of war: 'Visibility is a trap' (Foucault 1975, p.200).

PART 4. UNITED WE WIN

During the Second World War, race relations were a continuous problem across the US. 'By 1942, the federal government began investigating Negro morale in order to find out what could be done to improve it. The Office of Facts and Figures and its successor, the Office of War Information, undertook this project' (Hixson 2002, p.102). Walter Hixson goes on to inform us that:

> Surveys by these agencies indicated that the great amount of national publicity given to the defence program only served to increase the Negro's awareness that he was not participating fully in the program. Black Americans found it increasingly diffi-cult to reconcile their treatment with the announced war aims. (Hixson 2002, p.102)

The treatment of black servicemen was also a highly contentious issue, because:

> Urban Negroes were most resentful over defence discrimina-tion, particularly against the treatment accorded black members of the armed forces. Never before had Negroes been so united behind a cause: the war had served to focus their attention on their unequal status in American society. Black Americans were almost unanimous in wanting a show of good intention from

Figure 1: Alice Seeley Harris with Congolese children, c1905. *Anti-Slavery International, London.*

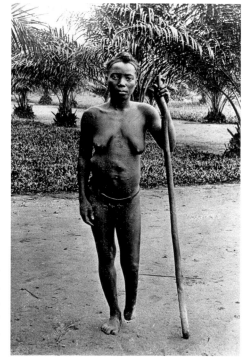

Figure 2: Original caption reads: 'Woman with amputated foot, mutilated by sentries from a rubber concession, 1905'. *Anti-Slavery International, London.*

Figure 3: Original caption reads: 'Nsongo District Nsala of Wala with severed hand and foot of his five-year-old daughter murdered by BAIR militia. This was all that remained of a cannibal feast following the murder of his wife, son and daughter, 1904'. *Anti-Slavery International, London.*

Figure 4: Original caption reads: 'Lokonal, three head sentries of the ABIR with a prisoner, 1905'. *Anti-Slavery International, London.*

Figure 5: Christmas photograph of staff at the African Oil Nuts Company and Miller Brothers, Badagry, Nigeria, c.1923. *Bristol Archives*.

The lynching of Thomas Shipp and Abram Smith, August 7, 1930, Marion, Indiana. Collected locks of the victims' hair framed under the glass. Written on matte, 'Klan 4th Joplin Mo. 33'. Second inscription, 'Bo Pointn to his Niga'.

Figure 6: Photographs and postcards of lynching, in James Allen, *Without sanctuary: Lynching photography in America*. Twin Palms: Santa Fe, NM, 2000. *National Center for Civil and Human Rights, Atlanta, Georgia.*

The lynching of L.W. Nelson, May 25, 1911, Okemah, Oklahoma.

The lynching of Laura Nelson, May 25, 1911, Okemah, Oklahoma.

The lynching of Laura Nelson and L.W. Nelson, May 25, 1911, Okemah, Oklahoma.

Figure 7: 'A tank worker from Nigeria', Empire War Workers in Britain series, 1939. © *Imperial War Museum.*

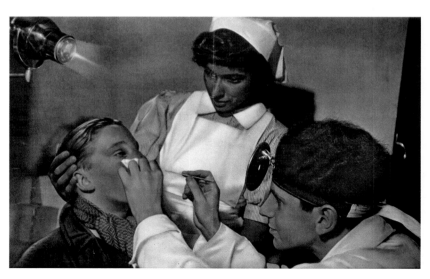

Figure 8: 'From India to play her part in Britain's medical service', On War Work in Britain series, no. 6. © *Imperial War Museum.*

Figure 9: Soldier of the Royal West African Frontier Force, Our Allies the Colonies series, 1939. © *Imperial War Museum.*

Figure 10: 'Together' poster, vertical and horizontal versions, the latter photographed on display at a recruiting centre in Accra. *Recruitment in British West Africa WWII collection* © *Imperial War Museum.*

The Abyssinian Delegate
Jomo Kenyatta asked for an Act of Parliament making discrimination by race or colour a criminal offence.

The Nigerian Trade Unionist
Chief A. S. Coker, represents unions with a membership of half a million workers. He demands full franchise for the negro worker.

The Liverpool Welfare Worker
Mr. E. J. Du Plau, is responsible for hostels and centres for negro seamen. "Negroes are social exiles in Britain," he maintains.

AFRICA SPEAKS IN MANCHESTER

Delegates from many parts of Africa and the United States to the first Pan-African Conference talk for a week— of freedom from the White Man, of the colour bar, of one great coloured nation, of force to gain their ends.

Photographed by JOHN DEAKIN

THE dance was a mixed affair—mixed in trade, from the stoker to the anthropologist; mixed in class, from the £3 a week labourer to the rich cocoa merchant; mixed in dress, from the baggy grey flannels to the suit of tails. But above all it was mixed in colour, from the blonde white to the midnight black. This dance, held at Edinburgh Hall, on the corner of one of Manchester's drab and soot-blackened streets, was the first gathering of delegates to the Pan-African Conference. They chose Manchester because its people have less curiosity or hostility to colour than the people of any other English city. Certainly, there was no self-consciousness among the white women who partnered their negro husbands or friends through "jive" to the last romantic waltz. Their attitudes varied. Some had approached the colour bar problem intellectually, others from a Christian viewpoint and others from simple human values.

Typical of the last attitude is the mixed marriage of Mary Brown to John Teah Brown, and before the conference got down to the more serious problems of the negro peoples, I went to their home to see a successful black and white marriage in its own domestic setting. Mary Brown was left stranded in Liverpool with her child when she met John Brown, a donkeyman on a merchant ship. He married her, gave her overwhelming affection, and saw that her child was properly educated.

I listened to John Teah Brown's story—a story which in many ways put in terms of one human being the resolutions and speeches of the whole week's conference. John Teah Brown was born in Sierre Leone and is a member of the Krou tribe. He was educated at a mission and brought up a Roman Catholic. He was devout and sincere in his religion until one day in a church at East London, South Africa. He went in to pray but a priest came up to him and told him it was a white man's church and he must get out. He has not been inside a church since, though he remains true to the Christian faith, practising it, he thinks, with rather more sincerity than the priest who turned him away from the altar.

He left Sierra Leone at the age of fifteen, for he
Continued overleaf

A Mixed Marriage That is a Success
Mr. John Teah Brown, with his white wife, Mrs. Mary Brown, in their Manchester home. He says the negro must earn the respect of the white man to merit full citizenship. **19**

Figure 11: 'Africa Speaks in Manchester', *Picture Post*, 10 November 1945, p.19. *All photographs John Deakin. Getty Images, Hulton Archive.*

In Conference: A White Man Urges the Negroes' Cause
John McNair, General Secretary of the I.L.P., addressing the delegates, says: "I object to the idea that the white people have anything to give to the black. There is, on the other hand, a debt which the white people owe to the coloured races: a debt which must and shall be paid."

But this is the extremist's view of the problem. There will be little sympathy with the overstated case put forward by Mr. J. E. Appiah, delegate for the West African Students Union. In a noisy, impassioned speech he declared: "The only language the Englishman understands is force. Others plead for more diplomatic negotiation but I am for firmer action. Only force will take us out of our disgraceful plight . . ." and so on and on.

More reasonable and more likely to succeed was the case put forward by the Labour and Trade Union leaders, the real strength of this Pan-African movement which seeks to unite all Negro Associations. They claim that the real force to be used is that of organised labour. They point out the success of the recent Nigerian strike, when thousands of negro workers came out to demand a minimum for all workers of 2s. 6d. a day. But for their constructive speeches, the conference would have produced merely a deluge of abuse and violent oratory.

On certain principles they are united. They demand strong representation on the legislative councils which govern the various territories. This already applies in certain areas but is restricted to negroes with an average income of £50 a year, which disfranchises the majority of coloured workers.

They ask for the principle of equal pay for equal work to be established, regardless of colour, race or creed. They ask for improved medical and educational services, for an end to the Uncle Tom shack, and the compound system of segregation.

Mr. Peter Abrahams, chief propagandist for the federation, told me that they did not intend to stop at merely organising the peoples of African descent. They planned to go on further and mobilise the whole of the Non-European nations, comprising over three-quarters of the world's population. Left Wing members of the Federation oppose this idea. "They accuse us of chauvinism," he said, "but the white workers of Europe have let us down and we must now all get together to fight for our rights and freedom." In other words, a reversed colour bar.

A few delegates admitted a positive side of our rule in Africa. There is a maternity hospital at Accra, capital of the Gold Coast, where a native woman can have a child for 1s. or nothing at all. In the Tanganyika sisal factories there have been established excellent factory welfare workers. In Uganda an enormous university, with mixed black and white staff, has been opened and negro students are helped with fees. A younger and more vigorous type of white civil servant has lately been sent out to the West Coast and their conscience and goodwill is showing results. On Britain's side we plead that six years of war has robbed us of much chance to put into operation White Paper proposals. It was Wallace Johnson, the negro Trade Union leader, who put the whole case most sanely.

"We turn," he said, "to the British Labour Movement to help us, and thereby help themselves. We do not want to be cheap labour, driven in competition against British workers.

To such reasoning, this country will not be unsympathetic. But to creating a black bloc, to the use of force advocated by hotheads of the Federation, there will be immediate white hostility.

HILDE MARCHANT.

felt that the discrimination, segregation and low standard of the negro's life there cramped his spirit. His escape was to the sea and for thirty years he has been in the Merchant Navy.

"The negro," he says, "must not only clamour for the help of the white man, he must also learn to help himself. The negro is not only exploited by white men—he is often exploited by the rich and wealthy negro traders. When we learn to help each other, then we shall merit citizenship and freedom from the white man."

The moral of his and similar stories was the motive force at the conference. George Padmore, leading negro journalist, maintained that a negro's skin is the passport to an oppression as violent as that of Nazi Germany's oppression of the Jews. "We don't need yellow armbands in Africa—just black skins," he maintained.

The American Red Cross Worker
He comes from Washington and cares for his own people in Britain. He suffers no colour humiliation.

The Barrister from Lagos
Mrs. Renner urges the need for a great raising of the standard of education and knowledge among African women.

The Founder of Pan Africanism
Dr. Du Bois is the head of the American Negro Association. He opposed the extremist idea of a new "nationalism of colour."

Figure 12: 'Africa Speaks in Manchester', *Picture Post*, 10 November 1945, p.20. *All photographs John Deakin. Getty Images, Hulton Archive.*

Figure 13: King Baudouin I and President Kasavubu standing in the back of their black open-top official car, Leopoldville, June 1960. Lebeck, R. (2008), p.88. *Photograph Robert Lebeck.*

Figure 14: ... the next photo in the sequence. Lebeck, R. (2008), p.89. *Photograph Robert Lebeck.*

Figure 15: A Congolese man snatches the king's sword. Lebeck, R. (2008), pp90-91. *Photograph Robert Lebeck.*

Figure 16: The sword thief under arrest. Lebeck, R. (2008), p.93. *Photograph Robert Lebeck.*

Figure 17: The sword thief handcuffed on the floor of a jeep. Lebeck, R. (2008), p.97. *Photograph Robert Lebeck.*

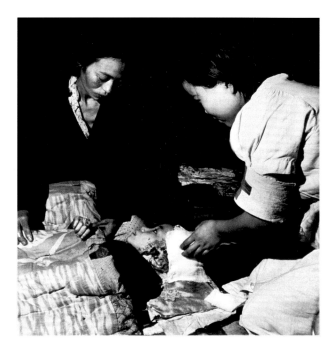

Figure 18: Hiroshima, Japan, 8 September 1945. A child being treated for a head wound in a fly-infested bank building, following the bomb. *Photograph Wayne Miller.*

Figure 19: Chicago, 1946. 'The type of housing for half of the city's black children'. *Photograph Wayne Miller.*

Figure 20: Chicago, December 1946. 'Royal Coterie of Snakes' debutante ball at the Parkway Ballroom. *Photograph Wayne Miller.*

Figure 21: Chicago, 1947. 'Father and son at Lake Michigan'. *Photograph Wayne Miller.*

Figure 22: Joy Gregory, 'Autoportraits: 1989-1990'.
Photographs by Joy Gregory.

Figure 23: Rotimi Fani-Kayode, 'Golden Phallus', c.1988-9. *Photograph Rotimi Fani-Kayode.*

the federal government that changes would be made in the racial status quo. (Hixson 2002, p.102)

The early 1940s in the US saw major racial unrest and cities explode with racial violence. 'In 1943 alone there were over 200 major disturbances across the country' (Kruse & Tuck 2012, p.109):

Riots in Los Angeles, Mobile, Alabama and Beaumont were all precursors to the massive 1943 riot in Detroit City, which lasted for four days and ended with the army having to protect black students trying to go to college. The city of Detroit was in the 1940s nicknamed the 'arsenal of democracy'. The days of rioting had been severe. Twenty-five black residents and nine white residents had been killed. Of the twenty-five African Americans, seventeen had been killed by white policemen. The number injured, including police, approached seven hundred while the property damage, including looted merchandise, destroyed stores, and burned automobiles, amounted to two million dollars. The Axis Powers grabbing the propaganda opportunity were quick to point out that the riot was symptomatic of a weak nation. The German-controlled Vichy radio broadcast on the riot revealed 'the internal disorganisation of a country torn by social injustice, race hatreds, regional disputes, the violence of an irritated proletariat, and the gangsterism of a capitalistic police'. (WGBH/PBS n.d.)

It is evident from the scale of racial unrest across the US during the Second World War that racial tension was damaging for the country's economy and that, as far as race was concerned, it could be described as being at war with itself.

One month after the outbreak in Detroit, another riot erupted in New York City's West Harlem. Again the U.S. Army had to intervene. Troops occupied Detroit for six months until Roosevelt felt it was safe to pull them out in January of 1944. Racial conflicts would not appear on such a visible and widespread scale again until the Civil Rights movement just one decade later. (WGBH/PBS n.d.)

As the Detroit riots of 1943 proved, African Americans were aware of the stark reality that they had to fight on two racialised fronts if they were to achieve the ultimate objective of the 'Double Victory', a term that the black press embraced in order to illustrate the paradox of being black in the US during the Second World War. Many of the African Americans participating in the war did so in full recognition that they were actually going to be fighting on two fronts: with the long-term aim of defeating fascism abroad in order to win freedoms at home. The contradiction and ironies of fighting a foreign enemy and not having equal rights at home were clearly evident to the black American workforce employed in the factories that built armaments. One of the core causes of the riots in Detroit was that whites were not prepared to work alongside blacks in the same factories:

> In 1942 James G. Thompson, a mere cafeteria worker in a Kansas aircraft manufacturing company, wrote to the *Pittsburgh Courier*, a black newspaper, stating that the 'V for victory sign is being displayed prominently in all so-called democratic countries, which are fighting for victory ... Let we colored Americans adopt the double VV for a double victory. The first V for victory over our enemies from without, the second V for victory over our enemies from within.' ('Hennessy History – Double Victory Campaign-1' n.d.)

Black Americans who entered the theatre of war were humiliated at every point of engagement: in the factory, in uniform and on return from front-line engagements. They bore this humiliation in exchange for some possible political domestic advantage in their fight for equality, which, as far as political reality was concerned, was still decades away. It is evident that old ingrained Jim Crow attitudes towards race were inherent within the body politic of the US government throughout, and indeed after, the war.

The American War Manpower Commission, which was formed by executive order from President Roosevelt in May 1942, was acutely aware of the negative impact that internal racism had on the US capacity to prosecute a war. As a move to counter the deeply ingrained hostile racial tensions in the US, the Manpower

Commission produced a key propaganda poster titled 'United We Win'. This poster represents a defining moment in the field of American racial and visual politics. It signifies a naïve and concerned critical point in state policy where race is visualised and acts as an indicator of that recognition sought by black Americans. This is despite the vast scale of the cultural distance that the 'United We Win' poster would have to cover in order to unify black and white citizens during the 1940s.

The purpose of the poster was to help overcome the damaging impact of racism on the American industrial war effort and workers' relationships. Since the onset of war, activists such as the black American Asa Philip Randolph had been prominent in highlighting the chronic extent of racism and discrimination in terms of the armed forces being segregated, the segregationist employment policies among America's employers and white workers' racist attitudes towards black workers. Randolph and several of his colleagues played an important role in the American civil rights campaign. He devised the systematic lobby of Roosevelt, to allow black people the right to fight as soldiers on an equal footing with white people, and the right to work for the US under the same terms and conditions as white workers. It was through this lobbying that, after the Second World War, the civil rights movement gained its powerful momentum and it was as a result of sustained pressure from these early campaigners that a new image of the US was attempted. The poster shows two young men, one black and one white, working together, constructing an aeroplane with the American flag as a backdrop. The photograph was taken by Alexander Lieberman, a skilled photographer, painter, sculptor and author who later went on to establish himself as an influential editor in the American popular magazines industry. The 'United We Win' poster was circulated across the US in 1943 and according to research undertaken at Bucknell University in the US, it became one of the best-known American propaganda posters of the Second World War. The researchers describe the poster in the context of its production and aspects of its interpretation and reception in the following way:

> The goal of the War Manpower Commission was to present an idealized view of race relations in America. However, the poster

may have been depicting racial inequality through the placement of the two main subjects. The white man stands above the black man. While this [placement] may have been unintentional, it could be interpreted as white superiority in the work force at a time when blacks still held lower positions, equality in the workforce was not actually occurring. The words 'united' and 'we' are significant. The government wanted the public to see that in order to unite the country individual differences must be put aside ... However, large numbers of employers refused to hire blacks for anything but unskilled work. (Anon. n.d.)

Further examination of the 'United We Win' poster reveals greater fault-lines in the desired message produced by the American War Manpower Commission in attempting to create an image/myth of American racial harmony. While the two men are working in the same space and on the same part of the aircraft, there is no sense of workers' solidarity between them, as they are engaged in disjointed autonomous work, although performing the same task. There is no empathy, solidarity or celebration in their shared mission in assembling the aircraft. Contact between the young men, both physical and ocular, is non-existent due to the positions of the subjects in the frame. The workers' focus is downwards, aimed at the job in hand rather than upwards or outwards towards the intended viewers, or to each other. As subjects in the frame they do not produce signs of coming together across racial and racist separation. Their shared space thus does not point towards a new, racially harmonious workplace. Instead, their division is made evident through their lack of engagement with each other, and the poster therefore inadvertently alludes to the extreme levels of racial intolerance in the factories of the US during the war. The image's framing throws into doubt that a single photograph of the two men in the same place at the same time was ever actually made; rather it suggests that the poster is a montage and, if so, it emphasises further the degree of racial distance active in the American workplace.

The 'United We Win' poster may well have been read by black Americans as a positive sign in the right direction towards some form of equal recognition in society. Given the extreme racial violence operating in factories at the time the poster was produced, it would likely have generated among white workers feelings of anger and anxiety that black workers were now seen by the state as being increasingly able to compete in the workplace for well-paid jobs. The poster represents a significant marker in the visualisation of racial politics in the US, during the crisis of the Second World War, when vital propaganda had to be employed by the state to advance the ways in which African Americans were literally seen and understood:

> While the UAW [United Automobile Workers] hierarchy outwardly supported integration of its work force, its rank and file did not. Whites didn't mind so much that blacks worked in the same plant, but they refused to work side by side with them. Three weeks before the riot, Packard promoted three blacks to work on the assembly line next to whites. The reaction was immediate and swift. A plant-wide hate strike resulted as 25,000 whites walked off the job, bringing critical war production to a screeching halt. A voice with a Southern accent barked over the loudspeaker, 'I'd rather see Hitler and Hirohito win than work next to a Nigger'. ('1943 – a race riot there will be' n.d.)

However, regardless of their failed impact, these posters from the Second World War suggest that it was a significant moment in which the production and promotion of images of black people by the Allies was seen as essential to national security, national morale and national confidence.

From a present-day perspective, these photographs and posters may be read as being a mild or minor attempt by the Allied governments to reconfigure public perception of the racialised subject through striving to build a sense of unity in a time of crisis. As images produced by official state agencies, they represent a few conscious steps in trying to reverse the historical tide of images that worked to negate black humanity in the West. However, rather than simply presenting an acceptable face of blackness for white consumption, these images may have created a space in which oppressed subjects saw themselves in a new independent light. The subaltern subject may have decoded these images as being a positive move by the Allied governments towards empathy, recognition and equality. As images placed in public spaces, their reception would always be in flux. Independence and civil rights movements were active agents working on the black subject, soldier and worker, and these images as frames for interpretation may have performed a task that aided further the awakening of black nationalist movements and claims for equality, especially as, in these images, black subjects are brought to more closely resemble Europeans and are therefore, by extension, brought much closer to the idea of self-determination and equality. The image of 'Jack Smith' could, for example, be read as that of the black subject being transformed into a man in a benevolent act of colonial coevalness or a more harmonious relationship across race. However, from a black nationalist perspective the image may also be read as that of black oppression: a man robbed of his name and African cultural identity, transformed into the complete subaltern colonial subject conditioned to serve the empire.

PART 5. TOGETHER

A photograph from the archives of the Imperial War Museum represents a rare instance in which we can see a colonial recruitment poster at work, articulating a new moment in black recognition within the context of empire, war and recruitment. The image is black and white, square in format and probably shot on a medium-format camera. It shows five young black African men all studying a rather weathered poster that has been put on the side of a wooden clapperboard colonial building (Figure 10). The white text of the poster's masthead reads 'The British Commonwealth of Nations' and is contained in dark borders. A larger text runs across the bottom of the poster. This is also framed in dark borders and reads 'Together'. According to information supplied by the Imperial War Museum, the horizontal central image of the poster shows seven representatives of the Commonwealth Armed Forces marching towards the right, with a Union Jack positioned behind the front four figures. We are informed that when 'reading the image left to right the men pictured in the poster are from India, East Africa, South Africa, New Zealand, a Canadian airman, an Australian soldier and a Royal Navy sailor'. This version of the 'Together' poster went into production in 1941 (there are several different versions, some of which incorporate representations of the Allied forces along with the Commonwealth forces). The five young African men appear to be engaged with the poster's message, as each of them stares directly at the Commonwealth soldiers marching off in unison. One of the young African men positioned nearest to the camera is dressed in long dark shabby-looking robes. His head is shaved around the back and sides leaving a small crown of hair on the top. His appearance suggests a rural or impoverished existence. Two of the other men are wearing shorts and loose-fitting shirts, while the fourth man also appears to wear only robes. The fifth man is mostly obscured but we can just manage to observe that he is wearing a checked shirt. The four men whose feet we can see are all bare-footed. The central figure with his robes and shaven head has raised his right arm and is pointing at the black East African soldier, although the actual tip of his finger appears to be resting on the shoulder of the white South African soldier. This suggests that the critical point of encounter for this particular group of young African men is the presence of the black African man in the poster. As a group, the young African men are presented in sharp contrast to the well-groomed soldiers. The caption informs us that the photograph was taken at a 'recruiting centre in Accra, Gold Coast [now Ghana], British West Africa' and that 'these men are joining up in the Royal West African Frontier Force' (in 'Recruitment in British West Africa WWII' collection, Imperial War Museum). In this instance, in Accra, if this photograph is to be believed, the 'Together' recruiting poster seems likely to have done its work in encouraging the young men to sign up to defend the Commonwealth. However, the purpose of this particular photograph and what its intended use may have been is also relevant; as a photograph of recruitment in progress, it supports the propaganda objectives of the empire by presenting 'real' documentary evidence of the interest and willingness of young Africans to join the armed services.

In studying the actual 'Together' poster, we can deduce that there is a racial hierarchy at work in its construction. White soldiers, from Britain, Australia and Canada, lead the parade and feature as a prominent presence framed by a flapping Union Jack. Indian and African soldiers are positioned to the outside of the flag and so appear to be forming the rearguard of the Commonwealth army. However, all the men carry rifles and the African presence is presumably intended, as is evident from the young African men seen viewing the poster, to stimulate the idea of recruitment to 'The British Commonwealth of Nations' armed forces, to become proud men in uniforms and march forth into the modern world and future freedom. Recruitment to the armed services is a moment of coming into being with the rest of humanity. It is thus represented in this photograph as a departure from the world of the primitives and into the world of Western modernity, with uniforms, regiments and technology signalling the potential exit from racial time.

These new, wartime constructions of black subjects were in effect complex strategic images that were put to work to close cultural gulfs that existed between black and white subjects. The question of race across Britain, its empire and the US is culturally and profoundly different, but is historically yoked together through the legacies of slavery and cultural Apartheid. Black Americans during the 1940s existed in their millions as a people separated by and within a culture of segregation, fear and violence. This, in theory, marks the 'United We Win' poster as a willing sign from the state that it wanted to take a degree of responsibility in easing racial tension rather than simply maintaining the status quo of oppression. Black American veterans from the First World War would not have been easily convinced by this type of message; they would have remembered the violence committed against them in lynchings when they returned home from the last war, and this legacy would still have resonance. The visual messages concerning the British empire and its colonial subjects, fighting or working for Britain, form part of a long process of cultural indoctrination that built on established racist hierarchies, dashed hopes, forced servitude and the British sense of imperial entitlement. All of these worked on the colonised subject through a false face of hospitality.

As images produced and sanctioned by Allied states' communication bureaus to serve a distinctive moral and immediately political/economic purpose, posters such as 'Together' and 'United We Win' can be read not simply as images that fostered black participation in the Second World War but also as images that subversively encouraged black involvement in the war as a route out of racial, geographical and economic oppression.

At the time of their making, black political activists would have also interpreted the images against the backdrop of the newly stated Allied principles of liberation, promised by the signing of the 1941 Atlantic Charter. During the war, subject peoples began to argue that 'self determination should be universally applied; that imperialism, as well as fascism, should be condemned and eradicated, as it was the basis of international inequality and the rivalry that led to wars' (Adi 1995, p.16). These state-sanctioned black images emerged in the context of other global forces that were gaining momentum during the Second World War, especially the Pan-African movement and the American civil rights movement. These two movements forcefully challenged the global dominance of colonial and racial politics, and both expressed desires for people from the subaltern world to be recognised as modern subjects with their own rights to freedom and rights to re-imagining their own political futures and cultural lives. These new wartime images of black humanity, released in the public realm across the colonies, the US and Britain can therefore be read as participants in resistance work, as images produced under pressure applied from within and without the Allied states. This meant that, as posters, they served multiple political purposes beyond and outside of their original intention, as they had the potential to be decoded as radical signs of black autonomy.

PART 6. SEEING THE PAN-AFRICAN MOVEMENT 1945

The Pan-African movement enabled connections throughout the colonies to be consolidated, to become a manifest reality. As an ideological platform, leaders from within the movement could form important alliances that hastened the liberation movement and intensified the demand to have a representational voice in the staging of a new world agenda subsequent to the Second World War. The Pan-African movement would give weight to the demand for a meaningful timetable that would see an end to European domination across the world. It would constitute its separate and critical demands through the production of its own resolutions, such as 'The Declaration to the Colonial Peoples of the World', which stated that freedom must be delivered to the colonised world and if necessary this would be claimed by force. The timing of these statements and the repeated references to force were politically critical, especially as Europe and much of the US was struggling with the moral dilemma of the atrocities committed in the German death camps. It was in this political moment, and with force being a real option, 'that black humanity takes its right to produce meaning, its freedom to choose a past from among the options that the (Western) culture offers it' (Mudimbe 1992, p.101).

Through the Second World War, 'third' world leadership envisioned a new postcolonial world. The liberation process represented an unstoppable quest for change, not just from the physical domination of colonial territorial occupation (the land) or structural domination in the form of governance (the order, through indirect or direct rule, assimilation or alienation) but perhaps most importantly from the psychology of the colonial mindset that had been ingrained in the black subject whenever the encounter with the European occurred. This concerned questions of power, whether on a micro level, through the basic tasks of servitude (the servant, or low-paid worker), or on a macro conflicted level, through ultimate resistance, represented by the form of force (the freedom fighter): the face of the well-trained black ex-serviceman, who, during and after the war, demanded equality.

Effectively, this postcolonial Pan-African vision added up to a modern concept of a new humanity that reconciled the past with a focus on traditional values, and called for justice through the creation of a different understanding of the universal man:

> It's a question of the Third World starting a new History of Man, a history which will have regard to the sometimes prodigious theses which Europe has put forward, but which will also not forget Europe's crimes, of which the most horrible was committed in the heart of man, and consisted of the pathological tearing away of his functions and the crumbling away of his unity. (Gilroy 2004, p.71)

From 15 to 20 October 1945 the Sixth Pan-African Conference was staged in Manchester. John Deakin photographed the conference for *Picture Post* magazine. His photographs represent a rare and defining visual legacy of the event, which, apart from Deakin's work, was not well photographed. The headline used by the magazine for its two-page article reads, 'Africa Speaks in Manchester', with a subheading that states, 'Delegates from many parts of Africa and the United States to the first Pan-African Conference talk for a week of freedom from the White Man, of the colour bar, of one great coloured nation, of force to gain their ends' (*Picture Post* 1945, p.19). The headline stating this to be the first Pan-African conference was, in fact, incorrect; similarly, it was cited by its primary organiser, George Padmore, as the fifth, although it was actually the sixth. He ignored the first Pan-African conference, held in London in 1900: 'it was at that first conference that Du Bois spoke his famous prophetic lines: "The problem of the twentieth century is the problem of the colour line – the relation of the darker to the lighter races of men in Asia and Africa, in America and the islands of the sea"' (Legum 1965, p.25).

Above the main headline for the 'Africa Speaks' article, three portraits of conference delegates are presented, run as single images across the top half of the page (Figure 11). Reading left to right the first photograph is captioned, 'The Abyssinian Delegate Jomo Kenyatta asked for an Act of Parliament making discrimination by race or colour a criminal offence' (*Picture Post* 1945, p.19). Kenyatta looks relaxed, confident but stern in his expression with his head leaning slightly to the left of the frame. He wears a heavy fur-collared coat over his formal suit, shirt and tie. His delegate's ribbon is clearly visible, pinned to the fur of his coat. The photograph suggests that the Chorlton-upon-Medlock town hall was a cold environment for the delegates. The background of the photograph of Kenyatta is one of the many handmade textual posters that were positioned throughout the conference hall and across the front of the raised stage. The poster states 'Ethiopia wants exit to the Sea'. Kenyatta's head blocks the word 'exit', but from another photograph on the following page we can clearly read the poster's slogan as it hangs high, decorating the front of the stage. The hard flash from Deakin's camera creates a strong shadow behind Kenyatta's head and brings his face into sharp focus as he returns the photographer's gaze, staring back directly into the lens of the camera. Kenyatta's left eye appears to be open wider than his right. This widened left eye creates a focal point for the portrait that is loaded now with a Barthesian punctive postcolonial charge. It appears as though Kenyatta, not the photographer, holds the ocular power to observe, and his eye is as much on the viewer as the viewer's eye is upon him. The portrait suggests defiance: a man confident in the context of his framing. When looking at Kenyatta's right eye, however, it has a different expression, a warmer one.

The second photograph, which is positioned centrally on the page, is captioned, 'The Nigerian Trade Unionist Chief, A. S. Coker, represents unions with a half a million workers. He demands full franchise for the negro worker'. Behind Coker is a poster that reads 'Freedom of the Press in the Colonies!' He wears a formal three-piece suit, shirt and tie. His smoker's pipe sticks out of the top pocket of his pinstriped jacket. Pinned on his lapel is his delegate's ribbon. He is framed looking over the lens, beyond the photographer, appearing to be a more reflective and friendly colonial delegate than Kenyatta.

The third photograph is captioned, 'The Liverpool Welfare Worker Mr. E. J. Du Plau, is responsible for hostels and centres for negro seamen. "Negroes are social exiles in Britain", he maintains' (*Picture Post* 1945, p.19). The photograph of 'Du Plau' mirrors the image of Kenyatta. His head, however, leans out towards the right of the frame. 'Du Plau', too, is photographed as a confident man, holding his own direct gaze back into the camera towards the viewer. He wears large rounded spectacles and sports a stylish pencil moustache. 'Du Plau' also sports a heavy coat over his formal suit. The poster behind him states, 'Down with Colour Bar'. His name in the caption – 'E. J. Du Plau' – is incorrect; his name is in fact E. J. Du Plan.

It is evident from the other photographs reproduced in the article and from Deakin's contact sheets and prints housed within the archives of Getty Images that the posters originally displayed at the conference were repositioned behind the three African men so as to provide a background for *Picture Post* readers, enabling them to fix the men within the context of simple one-line slogans. Through Deakin's image/text construction, the African men become synonymous with the messages that form their backdrops, rendering their physical presence as representing little more than human slogans. This act of visual elaboration effectively over-determines Kenyatta, Coker and 'Du Plau'.

Deakin's work thus creates an image of a Pan-African face that is clearly working against the grain of Britain's empire, and, as such, *Picture Post* suggests that these delegates' presence in Manchester is an act of political transgression. It is clear from analysis of the archive that Deakin effectively set up a makeshift studio at the front of the conference hall to provide a set in which to present the Pan-African delegates. The uncropped photographs in the Getty archives show the construction process of the image-making that Deakin performed, especially because the uncropped photographs portray the men in a much more relaxed conference environment. The vital elements of the photographs, when compared with their cropped usage, are made more distinctive. In the cropped photographs, the white backgrounds highlight the black subjects, as does the text behind them. It is evident that the men are being tightly framed. This framing device gives a police-mugshot-like quality to the photographs. This means that when these three African men speak, given how they are represented in the magazine, it is through a highly mediated code that visually works to negate the legitimacy of their political voice.

Another, and larger, photograph on the same page works in complete contrast to the three previous images of the Pan-African men. It fills around a third of the page and is positioned in the bottom right-hand corner. It shows a couple taking afternoon tea in their house. The caption reads, 'A Mixed Marriage That is a Success: Mr. John Teah Brown, with his white wife, Mrs Mary Brown, in their Manchester home. He says the negro must earn the respect of the white man to merit full citizenship' (*Picture Post* 1945, p.20). The photograph shows the couple seated in a bay window at a dining table, which is covered in a bright white tablecloth. In the centre of the table is a vase containing a bunch of flowers. An elegant tea is laid out across a very well-presented table. Mrs Brown smiles at her black African husband, who is smartly dressed in a suit, shirt and tie. The scene is framed through the genteel act of tea being served formally using a fine china tea set, which, along with the caption, suggests an ideal integration into British values.

This photograph is in sharp contrast to the more radical men pictured above it, who demand political change and equality. In the caption, John Teah Brown seems more concerned with earning respect from the white man, assuming inequality as something to be overcome, rather than an a priori equality that needs to be asserted. Deakin, however, in photographing John and Mary Brown seated directly in front of their bright sunlit bay window, has created an image so high in contrast that it renders John as an almost unrecognisable dense black form disrupted only by the whiteness of his teeth. As a portrait of a couple, the photograph is grossly inadequate. Its only redeeming quality is that the Browns are pictured exchanging smiles across the fabulously traditional display of English afternoon tea. The white teapot, placed so prominently on a stand directly in front of Mary, commands the attention of the viewer; it seems to symbolise the presence of the empire within the everyday life of this couple's British home. The Browns' 'Mixed Marriage That is a Success' is made more palatable for the presumably white British reader by the fact that they, as a mixed-race couple, are framed as subjects aspiring to traditional British life, represented in this photograph through the act of tea being served. This, in turn, becomes symbolic of the 'simple human values' the writer refers to in the first paragraph of the text that accompanies the photograph.

Hilde Marchant, a well-respected Fleet Street journalist, was sent by *Picture Post* to cover the Pan-African conference. Marchant's approach was to frame it through the 'mixing' that she discovered while in Manchester. Her opening sentences for the article are:

> The dance was a mixed affair – mixed in trade, from the stoker to the anthropologist; mixed in class, from the £3 a week labourer to the rich cocoa merchant; mixed in dress, from the baggy grey flannels to the suit of tails. But above all it was mixed in colour, from the blonde white to the midnight black. The dance, held at Edinburgh Hall, on the corner of one of Manchester's drab and soot-blackened streets, was the first gathering of the delegates to the Pan-African conference. (*Picture Post* 1945, p.19)

Marchant is clearly concerned with the myths, fears and the spectacle of witnessing miscegenation at work. In her text she draws on the hysteria and fears that were evident throughout the British empire of the white race being culturally contaminated as a result of sexual activity across the colour line. Marchant's mention of the blonde whites and midnight blacks 'mixing' potentially ignites the ultimate, ingrained, white males' fears of losing 'their' women to savage dark races if contact is allowed (Cairns 1965, p.59). In focusing on the fact of interracial mixing as seemingly a byproduct of Pan-African equality, Marchant creates a narrative that would be understood as subtly sinister by the readers of *Picture Post*, imagining that unnatural dark forces are at work in Manchester and that the sanctity and purity of British culture is being eroded and polluted. Manchester is constructed by Marchant as deviant, dark and 'soot-blackened' place with a unique breed of white people who have 'less curiosity or hostility to colour than the people of any other English city' (*Picture Post* 1945, p.19). The misery and drabness of industrial Manchester become synonymous with the presence of the Africans, as if their blackness has somehow infected the architecture and the indigenous population, causing them to act differently from the rest of the nation: this is a contamination so deep that it has darkened the atmosphere of the city.

Marchant's text further informs us that:

Certainly, there was no self-consciousness among the white women who partnered their negro husbands or friends through 'jive' to the last romantic waltz. Their attitudes varied. Some had approached the colour bar problem intellectually, others from a Christian viewpoint and others from simple human values. (*Picture Post* 1945, p.19)

She suggests that this display of interracial contact through jive and waltz is a bold and transgressive act. It is evidently socially problematic for Marchant that the white women show no signs of 'self-consciousness' in dancing with their black husbands and friends; her use of the word 'certainly' suggests that she is rather surprised by this lack of self-consciousness.

Marchant, as a concerned and experienced journalist, decides to investigate this matter of racial 'mixing' further. She states that:

Typical of the last attitude [shared human values] is the mixed marriage of Mary Brown to John Teah Brown, and before the conference got down to more serious problems of the negro peoples, I went to their home to see a successful black and white marriage in its own domestic setting. (*Picture Post* 1945, p.19)

The domestic space of Mary and John Brown becomes a critical site of journalistic enquiry for Marchant: a curious human zoo on which she can report. Marchant's moment of discovery of northern interracial mixing produces an editorial charge that overrides the core purpose of her article: to report on the Pan-African conference. The Browns' home becomes a metaphorical moment of concern regarding the issues of equality and rights raised at the conference. Coded within Marchant's report is a dangerous reawakening of the ghosts of forms of popular racism that had been so evident before the Second World War. Her obsession with 'mixing' pushes the readership of *Picture Post* to consider the notion of racial 'hygiene' and purity of race at home in Britain. For Marchant, something alien has settled in Manchester and it represents a disturbing presence.

Marchant goes on to describe in detail the circumstances of how Mary and John Teah Brown met. Mary was left stranded with her child in Liverpool when she met John, a donkeyman in the merchant navy: 'He married her, gave her overwhelming affection, and saw that her child was properly educated'. This subtly establishes the terms of the relationship, for Mary is implicitly portrayed as being morally suspect (she has had a child, she was abandoned, she is not married), and John as being solid, loyal and fully able to assume the mantle of paterfamilias. Marchant writes, 'I listened to John Teah Brown's story – a story which in many ways put in terms of one human being the resolutions and speeches of the whole conference' (*Picture Post* 1945, p.19). We learn that John was born in 'Sierre Leone' (sic) and that he is a member of the Kroo tribe. Throughout the early twentieth century the 'Kroomen' dominated dockyard employment in Sierra Leone. Tribal headmen from the Kroo were used as agents by the European shipping lines from 1916 onwards to recruit cheap labour on the docks (Mukonoweshuro 1991, p.108). We are informed that John was brought up in a mission to be a Roman Catholic and that, while in South Africa, he was ejected from a white church by a priest. 'He left Sierra Leone at the age of fifteen, for he felt the discrimination, segregation and low standards of the negro's life there cramped his spirit. His escape was to the sea and for thirty years he has been in the Merchant Navy' (*Picture Post* 1945, pp19-20). Through Marchant's text, John becomes the ideal colonial subject.

Alongside Marchant's fascination with 'mixing', the Browns' experience becomes the central narrative through which we enter the politics of the Pan-African Conference. Marchant finishes her focus on the Browns when she quotes John as saying, 'The negro is not only exploited by white men – he is often exploited by the rich and wealthy negro traders. When we learn to help each other, then we shall merit citizenship and freedom from the white man' (*Picture Post* 1945, p.20). Before she introduces any different voices into her article, and in quoting John Teah Brown, it is evident that Marchant is keen to highlight the notion of 'wealthy negro traders' as being one of the root causes of black exploitation. John is, of course, politically out of step with the conference, its delegates and its agenda. The conference organisers, George Padmore and W. E. B. Du Bois, do not regard independence and citizenship as something to be earned or merited from the 'white man': they regard them as their fundamental rights and not gifts to be bestowed by white people.

On page 20 of *Picture Post* are four more photographs (Figure 12). The main photograph positioned in the top left-hand third of the page shows the conference in full swing. The caption reads:

In Conference: A White Man Urges the Negroes' Cause. John McNair, General Secretary of the I.L.P., addressing the delegates, says: 'I object to the idea that the white people have anything to give to the black. There is, on the other hand, a debt which the white people owe to the coloured races: a debt which must and shall be paid'. (*Picture Post* 1945, p.20)

The photograph shows McNair, from the Independent Labour Party, standing with his hands clasped together. The distance of the photographer from the speaker and the low artificial lighting required Deakin to use a long exposure, so McNair appears as a blurred, soft and out-of-focus figure. His presence in this photograph as an identifiable white ally to the Pan-African movement is, therefore, rendered ghostly. Deakin's archived contact sheets show that the photograph has been heavily cropped to make it square in format. In so doing, critical visual information about the Pan-African movement's wider political alliances with other liberation struggles has been lost. Cropped out on the right-hand side is a slogan that simply reads 'Down with Anti-Semitism', and on the left in the original photograph is the slogan 'Arabs and Jews Unite Against British Imperialism'. Omitting these two slogans from the photograph of McNair for *Picture Post* neither enhances the visual impact of the image nor brings us closer to specific details of McNair's presence. What could be argued, therefore, is that there was a deliberate decision by the editors to omit from the photograph any visual links or political concerns that the Pan-African movement may have had in relation to the rising tensions in the Middle East at the time of the magazine's publication, or, indeed, to the recent horrors of Nazi anti-Semitism.

McNair, like John Teah Brown in Deakin's previous photograph, is almost unrecognisable. The lower third of the photograph is taken up by rows of delegates' backs and a small table at the front of the conference seated area, at which three white women appear to be working as note takers. The central, and most conspicuous, visual motif is the array of hand-painted slogans used to decorate the speaker's stage. The same posters and slogans that frame the delegates on the first page of the *Picture Post* article are clearly visible in the McNair photograph and have been repositioned for the rest of the duration of the conference. One of the slogans that can be seen behind the main speaker's podium reads 'Oppressed People of the Earth Unite'; another on the same rear wall reads 'Freedom for All Subject Peoples'. Others claim 'Africa for Africans', 'Freedom of Press in the Colonies' and 'Africa Arise'. High up on the left-hand side of the photograph we can see the words that form part of the coat of arms for Manchester – *'Concillo Et Labore'* – which translates as 'Wisdom and Effort'. The overall scene presented is one of a seedling African peoples' revolt.

Running across and filling the bottom of the page are three more portraits of delegates at the conference. These are square in format and appear to have been taken while the subjects were listening to the speakers. The first photograph is captioned 'The American Red Cross Worker. He comes from Washington and cares for his own people in Britain. He suffers no colour humiliation' (*Picture Post* 1945, p.20). It shows the side profile of a middle-aged African American man, unnamed in the caption, in a military-style service uniform. On his lapel we can see the letters 'ARC' (American Red Cross). He is well-groomed, wearing a shirt and tie, and his hair has been oiled back. His profile is illuminated by the daylight coming in from the window behind him. While there is no reference to his presence in the main body of the text, the caption negates black American servicepeople's experiences of the war and the deep-rooted racism that was so widespread. This included benevolent institutions such as the American Red Cross, which had, in 1942, been denounced by the *Pittsburgh Courier* for refusing to accept blood from black donors (Gates n.d.). The notion that this African American Red Cross serviceman 'suffers no colour humiliation' effectively ignores the harsh reality: all war service personnel and its support structures were racially segregated. The ARC racially segregated blood for transfusion throughout the Second World War. The tragedy of the ARC is that, in 1941, its racist practices led the great African American surgeon Charles Drew to resign from his post as Director of the American Red Cross Blood Programme. Drew's work was critical to medical science; he pioneered revolutionary methods of storing blood plasma for transfusion and his scientific work created the conditions for the first large-scale blood banks in the US and Britain to be developed. As a result of his endeavours, thousands of serving Allied lives were saved. Drew's argument was very simple: there was no scientific reason to segregate blood, and he duly resigned. The American Red Cross, however, carried on its policy of segregating blood until the 1960s.

The second portrait, in the centre of the page, shows a black woman in profile facing to the right. The caption states, 'The Barrister from Lagos: Mrs. Renner urges the need for a great raising of the standard of education and knowledge among African women' (*Picture Post* 1945, p.20). Mrs Renner strikes an attentive pose resting her chin on her raised hand. She wears a small hat and we can just glimpse the collar of her fur coat. Mrs Renner was in fact from the Gold

Coast (Ghana). She was attending the conference with her husband, Bankole Awoonor Renner, who had been championing the politics of a 'Federated West African State ... strong, and independent, free from feudalism since 1937' (Sherwood 2012, p.110), and who was a strong supporter of Kwame Nkrumah. The Renners were representing the Friends of African Freedom Society that was based in the Gold Coast. B. A. Renner was the conference secretary, while Mrs Renner sat on the entertainment committee. Marchant and Deakin appear once again to struggle with reporting accurately the story of the subjects present at the conference.

The third portrait shows an elderly black man with a receding silver hairline, facing left. He sports a waxed turned-up moustache and round spectacles, to complement his formal shirt and tie. He squints, and his mouth is raised slightly as if in a half-smile. In the bottom left-hand corner of the photograph, there is a white object. In the full, uncropped version of the photograph we can see that the man is seated with a small biracial girl sitting on his knee. He holds both her arms affectionately just above the elbows as she returns a smile directly back at Deakin's camera. The child's white puff-shouldered dress is just visible in the cropped frame used by *Picture Post*, and in the original version the man is facing the other way. The editors of *Picture Post* flipped the image so that it faces into the centre of the page rather than the central gutter of the magazine. The caption states 'The founder of Pan Africanism: Dr Du Bois is the head of the American Negro Association. He opposed the extremist idea of a "new nationalism of colour"' (*Picture Post* 1945, p.20). Du Bois's presence at the 1945 Manchester conference was hugely significant. It affirmed his intellectual and political relationship with George Padmore, the conference organiser, and cemented the continuity with the previous Pan-African conferences, which Du Bois had been central to organising.

However, the photograph used by *Picture Post*, although captioned as being a portrait of Du Bois, is clearly not him. The editors, writers, photographers and even current-day archivists at Getty Images have mistaken another delegate for Du Bois. Further research into Deakin's negatives shows that Du Bois was indeed photographed by Deakin while he was at the conference, and the image represents one of the stronger photographs taken there. However, the image reproduced in *Picture Post* is in fact that of Dr Peter Millard. Millard was instrumental in founding the Pan-African Federation in Manchester earlier in 1944. His political activity and, more importantly, his physical appearance were completely different from those of Du Bois. The only feature that Millard shared with Du Bois at the time of the conference was the fashionable handle-bar moustache. It seems that their moustaches were similar enough to have caused the editorial mistake.

In mistaking the photograph of Millard for Du Bois, *Picture Post* inadvertently raises the critical question relating to the reporting on and recognition of the black subject in European historical narratives. Given the significance of Du Bois being in the UK and the international standing he had as a leading political spokesman for black people, this misrecognition of him, together with the chain of other misinformation throughout the article, can be read as revealing a lack of both interest and due diligence in reporting black political presences in Britain. If we consider that the core premise of the conference in Manchester was that of black affirmation, political visibility and right to recognition, then Marchant and Deakin have done a journalistic disservice to these voices, choosing instead to focus disproportionately on the issue of 'mixing' couples. That the actual image of Du Bois, who at that time was the most important figure in Pan-African politics, has, through a lack of basic journalistic diligence, been rendered invisible, indicates a lack of concern for the politics of the day. Marchant and Deakin have therefore created a situation in which 'The Founder of Pan Africanism' has become the victim of a case of mistaken identity within the narrative of 'Africa Speak[ing]', from which he is absented. This misrecognition of Du Bois, along with the fact that he was never involved with an organising body known as the 'American Negro Association' and that no comment was sought from him by Marchant, illustrates, with a degree of irony, the attitude and lack of gravity this significant conference was given by the editors of *Picture Post*.

This editorial approach also, ironically, illustrates Du Bois's theory of 'the veil'. He formulated this theory over forty years before the events in Manchester, in his now classic 1903 book titled *The*

Souls of Black Folk, in which he describes that for black Americans a barrier exists, that a 'veil' stands between black Americans and white Americans' recognition of black people's humanity. Du Bois states that he was shut out from the white 'world by a vast veil'. This 'veil' serves to block the path to equality, black legitimacy and progress. The 'veil' silences and therefore makes the black subject invisible: 'It is a peculiar sensation, this double-consciousness, this sense of always looking at one's self through the eyes of others, measuring one's soul by the tape of a world that looks on in amused contempt and pity' (Du Bois & Gibson 1996, p.5). In absenting Du Bois, Marchant and Deakin undertake an incredible work of erasure in the context of reporting on the Pan-African conference in Manchester.

Marchant's text goes on to highlight that 'A few delegates admitted the positive side of our rule in Africa. There is a maternity hospital at Accra, capital of the Gold Coast, where a native woman can have a child for 1s. or nothing at all', and that 'a younger and more vigorous type of white civil servant has been sent to the West Coast and their conscience and good will is showing results. On Britain's side that six years of war has robbed us of much chance to put into operation White Paper proposals' (*Picture Post* 1945, p.20). Her reference to the war is also an early indicator of the way it would be framed historically as a white Allied victory.

Anne Sebba, in her book *Battling for News* (Sebba 1994), highlights that Marchant struggled in her later life: she became an alcoholic who suffered from ill health and a failed journalistic career. She eventually died destitute with no family to pay for her funeral (Sebba 1994, p.160).

Deakin was a war veteran:

> the war marks the moment when his career – and his legend – properly catches fire. Audrey Withers, editor of *Vogue*, was so impressed by his street photographs of Paris and Rome that she hired him as a staff photographer in 1947, and quickly regretted it. His offhand manner, his drinking, his indifference to 'fashion' and his propensity for losing valuable equipment damaged an already dubious reputation. (Quinn 2014)

Deakin is now posthumously celebrated for his portraits in Soho and his friendship with the artist Francis Bacon. His work has been marked by a book by Robin Muir (Muir & Deakin 2014) and an accompanying exhibition at the Photographer's Gallery in London of the same title, *Under the Influence: John Deakin, Photography and the Lure of Soho*. It is evident through the many omissions across the 'Africa Speaks in Manchester' report that Deakin and Marchant as a journalistic pairing may not have been best suited to the task of reporting on this significant event in post-war black British history. They, like John Teah Brown, are out of step with the new face of African politics: a face that will be determined as much by the emerging Cold War as by the politics and ideologies of colonial liberation struggles.

4

Decolonial Frames

The year 1960 was a landmark moment for the continent of Africa. It was the year in which the Belgian Congo and sixteen other African colonies gained independence from their European colonisers. According to Eugen Gerstenmaier, then president of the German Bundestag, 'Africa's entrance onto the stage of world history under the leadership of the Africans is probably the most important event of the year 1960' (Willenbrock 2008, p.4). It can also be regarded as the year in which the violent process of imagined disentanglement from Europe began in Africa, and in which the Cold War arrived on the continent in earnest. For the new African states, self-government was not going to be an easy task and increasingly, as the historian Paul Lauren has noted, the journey to independence was a complex political scenario. In the condition of post-independence, many African leaders 'found themselves confronting a bewildering array of complicated international problems, not the least of which was trying to chart a neutral course of nonalignment through the morass of the Cold War' (Lauren 1988, p.231). The relationships with the old colonisers across Africa were not settled affairs, as the economies and industrial wealth that underpinned Europe were still part of the fabric of many African societies. The face of leadership may have changed, but the ontology of 'empire and all of the violence that came from it' (Drabinski 2011, p.7) simply became less transparent but still present.

INDEPENDENCE CHA-CHA

In October 1958, just two years before Congo's independence, Patrice Lumumba, leader of the newly formed political party

Mouvement National Congolais, publicly demanded the immediate end of Belgium's colonial rule over the Congo. In Accra in Ghana two months later, as an invited guest speaker at the All Peoples African Conference, Lumumba located his case for the Congo's freedom firmly within the 1948 Universal Declaration of Human Rights. He stated at the conference that 'we base our action on the Universal Declaration of the Rights of Man – rights guaranteed to each and every citizen of humanity by the United Nations Charter – and we are of the opinion that the Congo, as a human society, has the right to join the ranks of free peoples' (Lumumba 1958).

Lumumba made a claim for international recognition of the Congolese cause and for this cause to be acknowledged within the global context of the humanitarian and decolonisation debates prevalent across international state relationships in the immediate aftermath of the Second World War. This was visible at events such as the Pan-African Congress in Manchester held in 1945 discussed earlier, and the 1955 Bandung Conference in Indonesia.

In 1956, Joseph Kasavubu's 'Abako' party also reiterated its demands for a fully independent state of Congo. This combined escalation of action by Lumumba, Kasavubu and a host of other political leaders ignited the historical smoulderings of political discontent that had existed for decades within the Congolese people. The presence of this long-harboured dissatisfaction was clearly evident in the unofficial speech that Lumumba delivered at the ceremony of proclamation of the Congo's independence on 30 June 1960. He stood, uninvited, on this day, and claimed his right to have a voice. He reminded the new nation of the huge indignities his people had had to bear during Belgium's eighty years of colonial rule. Through his speech, which was broadcast by radio across the country, he highlighted that he was determined not to negate the historical violence to which the Congolese had been subjected. Much to the discomfort of King Baudouin I and the other Belgians present, Lumumba evoked the nation's traumas when he stated that:

> morning, noon and night we were subjected to jeers, insults and blows because we were 'Negroes'. Who will ever forget that the black was addressed as 'tu', not because he was a friend, but because the polite 'vous' was reserved for the white man? ... Who will

ever forget the shootings which killed so many of our brothers, or the cells into which were mercilessly thrown those who no longer wished to submit to the regime of injustice, oppression and exploitation used by the colonialists as tool of their domination? (Lumumba 1960a)

The Congolese people's political discontent and fervour for independence had been earlier demonstrated when a bloody, riotous revolt erupted in Léopoldville on 4 January 1959 (Witte et al. 2009, p.394), sending shockwaves across Belgium. Today, this significant moment in the history of European colonial rule in Africa is marked throughout the Republic of Congo as Martyrs' Day. The riots occurred as a direct result of Kasavubu's Abako party being denied the right to hold a rally at its local offices, in the Kalamu district of Léopoldville. This was due to a minor administrative error in Abako's application to the Belgian authorities to hold a public meeting. Word was slow to reach the Abako supporters that the meeting had been cancelled. Once they began to gather at the place where the rally was due to be held, the supporters of Kasavubu and other nationalists were determined to go ahead with it; when ordered by the state soldiers to disband, they refused to do so. The conditions for confrontation with the authorities were heightened during the afternoon by a crowd of football supporters who emerged from the nearby stadium and joined the political gathering.

Reports from the day state that the rioters were quickly and bloodily repressed:

Official figures obtained from hospitals and burial services indicated only forty-nine people were dead, all were Congolese, and 116 were seriously injured including fifteen Europeans ... [other] estimates [of the number of] people killed were as high as 300. [This was because many of the] Africans killed on that day were buried by relatives and friends without any formalities, and not all the people injured [during the riots] sought hospital care. (Nzongola-Ntalaja 2002, p.85)

The riots 'had a major psychological impact on both the black and white populations' under Belgian rule (Vanthemsche 2012, p.89), leading to uncertainty, concern and an increased sense of urgency in both Brussels and throughout the Belgian Congo. Apprehension and fear were ultimately fuelled by the proximity, ferocity and violence of other liberation movements taking place across the African continent. The Mau Mau in Kenya and the intense violence during the French-Algerian war (Vanthemsche 2012, p.90), along with the growing influence of Pan-African political ideals, had the effect of destabilising Belgians at home and unsettling their sense of presence and dominance in the Congo. Belgium feared that the Congo was becoming part of a wider network of liberation movements in Africa.

Just a few weeks before the January riots, Lumumba had met, for the first time, Kwame Nkrumah, Frantz Fanon, Gamal Abdul Nasser, Ahmed Sékou Touré and many other African leaders at the conference in Accra. Contact with these highly influential Africans would prove significant, as all of them would later support Lumumba in his struggle to uphold the Congo's independence and territorial integrity (Nzongola-Ntalaja 2002, p.84). What occurred on this terrible day in 1959 was to some degree inevitable, given the historical violence inflicted for decades by Belgium on the peoples of the Congo.

The events articulate well the schema of Fanonian thought, as expressed in his writings on the psychology of violence under colonialism. Fanon's essay, 'Concerning Violence', was first published in 1961 in his seminal book titled *The Wretched of the Earth* (originally published in French as *Les Damnés de la Terre*). In it, Fanon describes violence as a necessary act that ultimately returns the oppressed subject back to his sense of humanity and human worth. He explores the psychological impact on, and damage to, the colonised mind through the prism of primary acts of violence that are perpetrated by the colonisers. This violence in turn and in time leads to intensive, spontaneous and cathartic acts of violence by the colonised subject. An example of these acts are those displayed in the riots in Léopoldville on 4 January 1959, during which Europeans and their property were attacked, burnt and looted. At this time in Léopoldville, and in the numerous other instances of anti-colonial resistance, we can recognise the dynamic trajectory and formulas of colonising to anticolonial violence that Fanon articulates so well. The power, violence and fear of the colonisers' regimes of terror in

the Congo came to a defining head that day. It was the moment when
the flow of violent colonial power was reversed through a profound
and unprecedented display of violence by the colonised. It is clear
from the reports that more Congolese subjects were killed during
the riots but these deaths, while individually tragic, also created a
liberating reality within the independence movement. As a result
of the riots, the Belgian state had to restructure its political and
economic objectives for the Congo as it became fully aware that the
direct colonising action, represented by eighty years of terror, had
entered the first phase of its eventual demise, and that in the future,
new modes and methods of control would have to be deployed if
they wished to maintain their colonial power.

With so much historical violence active on the psyche of the
Congolese people it is not surprising that the Belgians feared a
(Fanonian) backlash. Belgium's dread of Congolese nationalism
sought a specific representative, and this was found in Lumumba,
who was cast as a wide-eyed African Marxist, determined to bring
communism to the Congo. The code name given to Lumumba by
Col. Louis Marlière of the Belgian secret service was 'Satan', and he
stated that 'for us Lumumba was Satan and he did look like Satan.
You just have to look at those eyes' (Giefer [dir.] 2010). Constructing
Lumumba as non-human, a devil, an evil African brute, served
Belgian Catholic sensitivities well, because in killing Lumumba as
'Satan' they would be doing good Christian work. This ideological
formation goes to the very heart of the colonial justification for
the European enterprise in Africa. European modernity began in
Africa with slavery, and thus the European colonial sense of self and
progress in the 1950s and 1960s could not imagine itself outside
of Africa. As John E. Drabinski argues, 'The project of European
modernity begins at this moment; which is to say Europe begins in
what one might refer to as its elsewhere' (Drabinski 2011, p.7).

After the riots of 1959, Belgium had to acknowledge the effects
of its own cultural violence in the Congo over decades. Seeing
the Other manifest itself in the streets of Léopoldville as a violent
aggressor ruptured the assumed authority of the colonials, who
had previously imagined their violence as a form of historical
benevolence, as evidenced by the deluded speech given by King
Baudouin on independence day, of which more below. The

Belgian authorities, at this critical juncture, were traumatised by a Congolese sense of self that was unfamiliar to them. This sense of self rejected the myth of European superiority and ultimately smashed through the visible and invisible barriers of authority, domination and exploitation of the colonised subject. 'The root of this colonial trauma, however, emerged out of the utter Belgian unpreparedness for Congolese independence. From 1958 onwards, Belgium not only had to react to the rapid pace of events in the Congo; it was panicked and overtaken by them'. The loss of the colony also meant that Belgium had to face up to the reality that without the Congo it was just a small country in Europe dependent on its neighbours (Vogt 2014, p.26).

This new Congolese threat to its colonisers was reinforced by Belgium's military weakness and fear of a colonial war, for which it had neither the appetite nor the economic power. According to Roland Oliver and Anthony Atmore, Belgium's awareness of its size in relation to the rest of Europe had a strong bearing on the way it handled the decolonisation of the Congo. They state that, 'to a larger power than Belgium these disorders would not have appeared impossible to suppress. But to Belgium, in the words of a government spokesman, they presented a terrifying alternative' (Oliver & Atmore 2005, p.262). Fanon also states in 'Concerning Violence' that 'the naked truth of decolonisation evokes for us the searing bullets and the bloodstained knives which emanate from it. For if the last shall be first, this will only come to pass after a murderous and decisive struggle between the two protagonists' (Fanon 1963, p.28). The moment of decisive struggle for the Congo was the events of 4 January 1959, during which Belgium willingly turned away from its legacy of decades of direct physical, cultural and psychological violence over the Congolese. Belgium's fear of being consumed in violence was the critical condition that paved the way to the Congo's liberation. The moment can be described retrospectively as a decisive Fanonian twist, regarding the formulation of the country's independence. It was violence that lifted the veil of the assumed racial superiority of the Belgians, vigorously pushing aside decades of white authority. The Belgians were forced to recognise a new African reality that was defiant and willing to die for unconditional independence.

On independence day, in 1960, the outgoing Belgian colonisers were unwilling to admit their violent colonising past. In the transformative moment of liberation for the Congolese, this unwillingness became the ultimate instance of Belgian disavowal, in which violent colonialism was reinvented and presented as a glorious civilising gift to the Congo:

> On June 30, 1960, King Baudouin was still trapped in the Belgian colonialist state of mind as he tried to rationalise this paternalistic paradigm that his great-uncle Leopold II initiated in the Congo, appealing to the newly created Congolese independent government and the Congolese masses to work for its continuance. Baudouin's speech denoted either the monarch's utter loss of touch with the Congolese reality or his sheer lack of knowledge of the historical facts, and especially his lack of education about the empire that his great grand-uncle could have bequeathed him had it not been for the international outrage that forced Belgium to snatch the Congo from his deadly hands. (Frindéthié 2009, p.195)

In his official address at Congo's Proclamation of Independence ceremonies on 30 June 1960, in a speech full of delusional fantasy, King Baudouin stated that:

> For eighty years Belgium has sent the best of its sons to your soil, first to free the Congo Basin from the odious slave trade which was decimating the local population, and later to reconcile ethnic groups who, previously enemies, then worked together to create one of the greatest independent states in Africa ... When Leopold II undertook his great work which today reaches its crowning moment, he did not come to you as a conqueror but as a civiliser. (in original French at http://www.kongo-kinshasa.de/dokumente/lekture/disc_indep.pdf, accessed May 2010)

The speech revealed Belgium's fundamental denial of the extreme violence and cost in human life that shaped the Belgian Congo. This was the violence that had so outraged the likes of Alice Seeley Harris and other British missionaries that they campaigned for years internationally to raise awareness of the scale of forced labour, mutilation and murder taking place in the colony (see Chapter 1). Not a single hint of apology can be detected in Baudouin's words for the regime of terror that caused tens of thousands of deaths.

After the riots of 4 January 1959, nothing in the Belgian Congo was the same again. Reflecting on this through the later lens of Fanon's writing reveals that, in the necessary moment of grabbing power back – of rebellion and violence – self-recognition ultimately occurs from within the colonised subject and by the colonising powers. In effect, an act of anti-colonial violent rebellion enables a sense of human dignity to formulate within the mind of the subaltern. It is this clarity that charged Lumumba to speak directly to 'the hard facts of Congolese's daily lives from 1885 to 1960' on independence day (Frindéthié 2009, p.198).

Liberating acts of violence include mocking kings, snatching at freedom, destroying the totemistic presence of oppression, burning and smashing buildings, statues, flags and other symbols of power that are revered as sacred objects, worshipped and idolised by the colonial masters as marks of cultural authority and superiority. Acts such as these enable the colonised subject to see colonialism afresh for what it actually is: a pure form of 'violence in its natural state, and [in that natural state] it will only yield when confronted with greater violence' (Fanon 1963, p.48).

Patrice Lumumba was dangerous to the Belgians because he clearly understood the dynamics of liberation struggles for freedom and autonomy. Critically further than that, however, he also recognised that it was absolutely essential for the Congo, on political, cultural, historical and humanitarian levels, that the Belgians recognised the Congolese people and took responsibility for the violence perpetrated against them in the past. Lumumba would not accept independence as a benevolent gift because this, for Lumumba, would mean that he would always be in debt and subject to the myth of white superiority. He could not accept the rewriting of history, in which Belgium disavowed its genocidal past, as made manifest in the colonial fantasy of King Baudouin's speech in June 1960. Independence for the Congolese people was a long, hard, violent battle that was filled with decades of 'tears, fire and blood' (Lumumba 1960).

Events immediately prior to meetings on 20 January 1960 in

Brussels, which are now referred to as the Round Table Conference, saw Baudouin visit the Congo in December 1959 in a desperate attempt to defuse the ongoing political crisis.

> Lumumba, founder of the Congo National Movement Party, was in prison. The king, it was said, would establish concord between the whites and the negroes. The royal triumphal voyage was announced as though white men had never shed the blood of Negroes, as though the Congolese would fall down on their faces at the sight of the white king and chant his praise for his benefactions. Inwardly, the colonialists felt jittery. They were wondering whether it would not be the other way round, whether the king would not be hooted. They started cleverly spreading rumours among the Congolese. It was whispered into their ears that Baudouin I was a 'good white man', that he would have Patrice Lumumba released from prison into which the 'bad white men' had thrown him. (Laurent 1961)

The British historian Richard Tomlinson, when writing King Baudouin's obituary for the *Independent* newspaper, reminded readers of Baudouin's lack of political acumen when he stated that:

> against the advice of his ministers, [King Baudouin I] travelled to Léopoldville hoping to halt the Congo's slide into anarchy. Instead, he was met by jeering demonstrators along the twelve-mile route from the airport, and was accused of provoking by his presence the riots that soon followed. (Tomlinson 1993)

The humiliated Baudouin returned to Belgium, his attempt to restore the old status quo having failed. His imagined regal authority over the Congo had been ridiculed and rejected. Baudouin, even when confronted directly by the Congolese people, was clearly blinkered regarding the pace of political change and his own influence in the colony.

By January 1960, one year after the violent riots in Léopoldville, the song 'Independence Cha Cha' had been written and was being performed by the popular Congolese musician, 'Le Grand Kalle', in the heart of Brussels. 'Le Grand Kalle', whose real name was

Joseph Athanase Tchamala Kabaselleh, was part of the Congolese nationalist group that attended the Round Table Conference in Brussels. This crucial conference between Belgium's political leaders and the Congolese nationalists was where decisive discussions were held that led to the establishment of an independence date for the Congo: 30 June 1960. It was to be a fast transition from colony to independence:

> Several of the Africans who took part have stated that they went to Belgium expecting to settle for a five-year transition period leading up to independence. They would have been willing to accept this ... The Congolese negotiators at the Round Table Conference found no resistance against which they could bargain, no strength that would force them to unite. (Oliver & Atmore 2005, p.262)

It is evident from this statement that either the Congolese delegation had massively underestimated the scale of Belgium's collapse or they had failed to recognise the realignment of Belgium's political aspirations for the territories. After just one month of discussions the conference concluded, and it was Patrice Lumumba who was given the task of writing the closing statement on behalf of the Congolese delegation. The opening comments from the official statement dated 20 February 1960 read:

> At this moment when the Round Table Conference is closing down, we beg to be allowed to speak in the name of the Congolese National Movement and to express its thoughts and feelings. We are particularly satisfied with the results of the negotiations which have just been conducted with the representatives of the Belgian Government and Parliament. We demanded the immediate and unconditional independence of our country. We have just won it. (Lumumba 1960b)

In his acclaimed book *The Sixties Unplugged: A Kaleidoscopic History of a Disorderly Decade* (2013), Gerard DeGroot informs us that what had in fact occurred was that Belgium was planning a ruse for indirect rule by working with selected Belgium-friendly individuals 'that would give a semblance of self-government yet keep colonial interest intact. In order to increase the likelihood of this scenario, the Belgians intentionally quickened the pace of decolonization, while neglecting to prepare the Congolese for self rule' (DeGroot 2013, p.33).

THE IMAGE OF INDEPENDENCE

On 29 June 1960, the German photographer Robert Lebeck was in the Belgian Congo, along with many journalists, to record the historic events through which this vast colony would gain independence. He was a self-taught photographer, aged thirty-one, when he arrived in the Congo. He was working on assignment for one of Germany's leading editorial magazines, *Kristall*. He had travelled across the continent from March to June, to photograph its changing states. He had worked in Mali, Senegal, Guinea, Togo, Ghana, Rhodesia and South Africa. This arrival in the Belgian Congo was his final destination, where he planned to photograph the ceremonial handover of the country by the young Belgian King Baudouin I to the newly elected leaders of the country, President Kasavubu and Prime Minister Patrice Lumumba.

Lebeck later stated in an interview for the film *Boyamba Belgique* (2011) that he was 'just waiting like the others in Léopoldville, waiting for the king to come and the new president'. While he was waiting in Boulevard Albert, according to the film's narrator:

> Robert Lebeck would witness and capture on film a remarkable moment in the decolonisation of the Belgian Congo, a moment that is eternalised in a single frame taken around half past four in the afternoon, as the Belgian King Baudouin I was being driven through Léopoldville/Kinshasa, standing bolt upright next to the future president Kasavubu in a Cadillac convertible, he saluted the Belgian flag. At this very moment a young Congolese man steps from the crowd, steals the sabre of King Baudouin from behind, and runs away – Robert Lebeck eternalises the incident in a single shot. (Engels & Van Peel [dir.], 2011)

The events that unfolded over the next few months would have a profound impact on both Belgium and the future Republic of Congo. The fight for control of the old colony would reveal the massive ideological fault-lines that ran throughout the country, the manipulative covert strategies of Belgium's desire to hang on to the Congo by indirect rule and, ultimately, the political inadequacies of the United Nations to resolve conflicts in Africa. The struggle for power in the Congo would test and expose the United Nations as an ineffective forum of global diplomacy with regard to postcolonial states caught between old colonial desires and the theatre of Cold War politics. The event on 29 June provided Lebeck with a photographic opportunity that would make him world famous for capturing a unique and profoundly symbolic moment in colonial history and in the visual history of African liberation.

THE PHOTOGRAPHS

The photographs discussed here are reproduced in *Tokyo, Moscow, Léopoldville: Photographs by Robert Lebeck*, published as three separate books within one hard case by Steidl in 2008. The cover image of the Léopoldville book is a photograph taken in Ghana. It is captioned, as are all the photographs, at the rear of the book in a dedicated reference section. The photograph shows a well-built European man, wearing sunglasses, loafer-like shoes, long white socks, white shorts and a short-sleeved white open-neck shirt, being carried ashore by four muscular African men through the shallow tide waters in a sedan-like chair. The caption reads: 'Ghana 1960/ Port workers in Accra carrying a captain ashore'. The photograph illustrates well the nature of Europe's presence in its post-colonial states – a wealthy white man, supported on the shoulders of several black 'subjects'.

According to the inside jacket blurb, the book aims to be a 're-encounter' with Lebeck's 1962 exhibition, which was held in Hamburg at the Museum für Kunst und Gewerbe. The photographs that made Lebeck's reputation are reproduced across ten pages in the Léopoldville section of the book. The sequence is introduced by a brief white text on an all-black page that simply reads 'Leopoldville 30. JUNI 1960' (Lebeck 2008, p.86). This sequence of photographs is marked as being distinctive and special: they are the only photographs in the book that are reproduced on matte black varnished pages creating a separate portfolio within the volume.

Lebeck's first photograph from his Léopoldville series is captioned as a 'View through the window of the parliamentary building in Léopoldville. Military escort for the car of President Kasavubu and the King of Belgium. Independence for Congo' (Lebeck 2008, p.87). The photograph is divided into three sections by the window frames of the building through which it was taken. Lebeck's position provided an ideal platform from which he could observe the distant crowds and Congolese soldiers lining the wide Boulevard Albert. The sense of occasion is emphasised by a strong military presence, while crowds wait for King Baudouin and President Kasavubu to enter the scene. The top third of the photograph is dominated by the rear view of the massive equestrian statue of King Leopold II that occupied the centre of the boulevard in 1960. This focus allows space for a different narrative to be formed, one that can be read as an inverse to the actual events taking place. The crowds seem to be bearing witness to both the arrival of the new head of state, Kasavubu, but also to the departure of the historic, colonial ruler, King Leopold II. The huge, lone figure of Leopold riding out of the top of the frame, with his back turned on the parliamentary building and on the events that are about to unfold marks his departing, disinterested influence on the Congo. However, the visibility of this monument to Leopold II reproduces within the photograph particular 'cultural and political dispositions' with regard to how history continued to be perceived by the Belgians (Connerton 2009, p.34). So, the statue's ongoing presence, and visual dominance in the picture, also suggests that Leopold II's time and influence are not quite over. His retreat, at this moment, is not part of the post-colonial narrative. While the flags of both Belgium and the new Republic of Congo line the boulevard, creating a setting for the grand passing of Leopold's time, the Belgians' ongoing presence within this political change is emphasised further by the fact that the Belgian flag is the most visibly prominent national motif.

The central section of the photograph frames two shining Willys military jeeps, each bearing six seated Congolese soldiers with rifles. A black official car carrying dignitaries is in front of the jeeps.

The vehicles have just passed the monument to Leopold II. Three Congolese military motorcycle outriders accompany the jeeps and the car. On the right two soldiers are saluting the vehicles as they pass by. All of the pomp and ceremony of a European political spectacle is used to mark the day in which Léopoldville appears to be effectively transformed into Brussels.

The mid-section of the photograph shows another immaculate Willys jeep. This also carries five black Congolese soldiers and a white soldier in the front passenger seat. The latter is standing up looking back towards the other vehicles, and is pointing towards the parliamentary building from which the photograph was taken. He appears to be directing the vehicles behind to ensure that they follow his lead. His presence in this part of the photograph can be read as a subtle indicator as to who remains in charge of the military in the Congo.

In the bottom section of the photograph the heads of the spectators in the parliamentary building are shown in near silhouette. Framed in this manner they appear as dark shadowy figures lurking on the edge of the political proceedings, perhaps symbolically suggesting the European presence that, at this point in time, still maintained the most privileged vantage points.

The next photograph in the sequence shows King Baudouin I and President Kasavubu standing in the back of their black open-top official car (Figure 13, original in Lebeck 2008, p.88). The shot is taken with a wide lens, so the frame contains a lot of visual information from the scene. A Congolese chauffeur, dressed in a bright white military uniform that echoes Baudouin's attire, drives the car. The uniforms create a surprising sense of union between the two men, the only difference being that Baudouin's is decorated in the paraphernalia afforded by his status. Beside the black driver sits a highly decorated Belgian officer. He wears a khaki uniform, and his medals of honour are clearly visible on his chest. His authoritative gaze is firmly fixed directly back into Lebeck's lens as he rests his right arm informally on the passenger door of the car, suggesting his sense of control and ease in the situation. In the rear of the car, Baudouin stands upright and to attention. He faces the right side of the frame across Kasavubu. Baudouin wears a pair of dark glasses, although we can see from the lack of shadows in the photograph that it was not a particularly bright day, and few of the spectators watching the car pass by wear sunglasses. Kasavubu, dressed in a black suit, white shirt and black tie, seems to be enjoying the scene ahead of him. He smiles lightly and holds his right hand up to the crowd as if he is being sworn into power. In the distance, over Baudouin's right shoulder, the vast twin towers and statue that make up the monument to King Albert I of Belgium are clearly visible. Lebeck once again brings monuments dedicated to Belgium's colonial past into the frame, and brings them to bear on primary focus of the transition. This history, represented by the monument, is echoed in Baudouin as he becomes, in his white splendour, a living monument to his state's past.

The photograph introduces another critically important figure into the scene: a Congolese man who is running closely beside the state car and directly in front of one of the official motorcycle escorts. The man wears a pair of white trousers, a white shirt, a dark tie and a black jacket. A single medal is pinned on his jacket, signifying that he has been decorated by the state. The running man mirrors Kasavubu's gesture to the crowd. He holds up his left hand as if he too is acknowledging the presence of the spectators. His presence and his proximity to the open-top state car reflect the relatively relaxed attitude of the scene. Journalists with cameras and audio recording devices are also very close by, also chasing the official cavalcade. The pavements are lined mostly with white Belgians; parents can be seen holding their children and enthusiastically waving and cheering.

The next photograph in the sequence suggests that the cars have had to slow down (Figure 14, original in Lebeck 2008, p.88). It shows a few more journalists and photographers running ahead of the official car, jockeying for better positions from which to record the events. The scene photographed by Lebeck is of the rear of the car. Badouin's attention appears to be drawn towards two large Belgian flags and a small group of white men dressed in suits applauding the cavalcade, and has responded with a more formal stance. The Congolese man who was previously running beside the car is now walking with his left hand casually resting on it. By physically touching the car he becomes a point of focus in the photograph, encroaching into that focal space. It is the critical visual moment when he moves from being simply an enthusiastic spectator to being the main protagonist, and drawing attention away from the main participants, Baudouin and Kasavubu. Something in the car has caught the man's attention. His gaze is fixed on the back seat behind the standing dignitaries, who appear, at this point, not to have noticed the man. Across to the left of the frame, the mostly white crowd is happily cheering and waving. In the bottom right corner, a military motorcycle escort rider features prominently and is dutifully close behind the car. The rider must have had to alter his course to avoid Lebeck's position as his photograph appears to have been taken in the immediate slipstream of the Congolese man. The caption for these two photographs is a shared one and reads, 'Congo/A young Congolese running beside the open Cadillac carrying the King of Belgium in a white General's suit and the black president of the Congo in civil dress. The King's rapier is lying on the back seat' (Lebeck 2008, p.89).

The Sword 'Thief'? An Act in Three Parts Through One Photograph

PART 1. THE INTRODUCTION

As the Cadillac crawled down the wide boulevard, the 'young Congolese' man snatched the king's sword from the rear seat of the car. In the next photograph, he is visible then turning back with both arms raised, straight towards Lebeck and his anticipating camera (Figure 15, original in Lebeck 2008, pp.90-1). Lebeck, in an equally opportune moment, photographs one of the most spectacular incidents in Congo's colonial history. In this act of defiance, the Congolese man becomes a radical transformative figure across the space and time of the 'first, second and third world'. He is caught by Lebeck's photograph between the colonial and postcolonial moments. He becomes symbolic of 'both the country as a promised landscape and as a political body, both the ground and the figure of the Leviathan, his arms raised to exercise his sovereign authority with the twin powers of religion and war' (Mitchell 2012, p.118). The compulsion to grab the king's sword can be read as this colonial subject acting physically against the colonising authority, at the moment he recognises his release. The young Congolese man acts as if he is caught within an impulsive condition of cultural reclamation work in which, for a fleeting time, he is restored back to himself and, by extension, the nation is restored to an imagined freedom. In grabbing the sword this man is declaring, 'I am a human and I will be seen', and in stealing it directly from the king, he symbolically disarms or strips away the sovereign's power of authority over the Congo. European totemic power is imbued within this sword, and he reduces it to an object of ridicule that no longer threatens as its authority. Its power is defused in a fleeting and vengeful act of self-empowerment.

PART 2. *STUDIUM* (ROLAND BARTHES)

In discussing the wider narratives and cultural meaning contained within a given photograph, Roland Barthes presented the concept of these readings as the '*studium*', that is, the place where the wider meaning and reading of an image may be located by the reader:

> It is by *studium* that I am interested in so many photographs, whether I receive them as political testimony or enjoy them as good historical scenes: for it is culturally (this connotation is present in *studium*) that I participate in the figures, the faces, the gestures, the settings, the actions. (Barthes 1981, p.26)

The defining aspects of Lebeck's photograph are visible in the two opposing but distinctive gestures of the thief's left and right hands. His right hand, 'that has fingers that run straight to the soul of man' (Laughton [dir.] 1955), is clutching the stolen ceremonial sword of King Baudouin. It is caught not only in the act of stealing the sword but also, because of its angle at the moment the photograph was taken, it also appears to be making another and unwittingly symbolic sign of independence, freedom and love: the Black Power salute. The fist as a sign here is even more potent because the black Congolese hand is wrapped around the European king's historic symbol of power. The thief is therefore transformed into an iconic symbol of African liberation. The thief's black right fist is in contrast to the brilliant white of King Baudouin's royal uniform. The king salutes the Belgian flags on the left of the frame, which works as an ideological counter-narrative to the man stealing the sword behind the king's back, as both Kasavubu and Baudouin, oblivious to the incident, focus on their shared political vision ahead. Interpreting the picture retrospectively, the theft of the sword comes to represent Baudouin's obliviousness to the ways in which he would be undermined throughout the next day, and which would tarnish the future of the new state and open the door for covert Cold War politics to enter.

On the following day, during the independence ceremony, King Baudouin I received a second insult to his family's honour. It came from Lumumba, who broke the protocol, took the podium and made an uninvited speech, in which he condemned Belgian rule in the Congo. Such was King Baudouin I's anger, he had to be persuaded by his diplomats to stay for the rest of the ceremony. Lumumba's speech sealed his own fate, as from this point on, his life was under threat. Forty years after Lumumba's violent death in January 1961, a 2001 Belgian parliamentary report concluded that King Baudouin I was implicated in Lumumba's demise. Killing Lumumba was deemed necessary by Baudouin because, unlike Kasavubu and Mobutu, Lumumba was not willing to become a political pawn in Belgian plans for post-independence Congo.

Reading this photograph through Fanon's theory of the 'wretched ones' (Fanon 1963), and by building a context in which different knowledges can surface out of the past, brings forth numerous possible narratives in the present. These narratives make it possible to break with the burdens of tradition when we discuss the representation of African independence. The caption for Lebeck's photograph, which was produced for public consumption in a museum two years after the Congo's independence, reads 'Congo 1960/Drama on the eve of independence. Baudouin, King of the Belgians and Colonial ruler of the Congo, and Joseph Kasavubu, the President, travel together on the Boulevard Albert, Léopoldville. A young Congolese man steals the King's rapier' (Lebeck 2008, pp.90-1). The caption, in its traditionally reportage style, attempts to fix everything in a moment of absolute representational fact. This encourages us to read the photograph as a document displaying actual events, quite differently to what was previously hidden and politically suppressed when the photograph was first shown in Hamburg.

The sword thief image now performs a different function beyond the narrative that was presented at the time. The position of the sword visually and metaphorically cuts the torso of the king in half, and punctures the body of the newly elected president, Joseph Kasavubu. Because these two acts happen simultaneously in the image, the conservative Kasavubu is sutured to his old colonial masters forever. In the refracted reflection of the thief in the convex curves of the state car, the sword seems to be aimed at the compliant head of Kasavubu as he bows to the white crowds and the two Belgian flags being held high above him. In this pose, Kasavubu enters the dock of history charged with being a political puppet. Lebeck's photograph opens a historical visual trial in which all those present could be accused of delivering false new freedoms. The expression on the Congolese man's face as he grabs the sword is one of pained anxiety. This is not a jubilant moment for him. As he looks back down Boulevard Albert, the colonial/neocolonial transformation crystallises in front of him, in the form of the Congolese army soldiers still commanded by the white Belgian officers that are about to arrest him.

PART 3. THE *PUNCTUM* (ROLAND BARTHES)

In discussing the elements within a photograph that pull him in to a specific detail within it, Barthes states that 'A photograph's *punctum* is that accident which pricks me (but also bruises me, is poignant to me)' (Barthes 1981, p.27). Part of the turbulence that emanates from this photograph and causes its heightened sense of dis-ease is generated by the thief's empty left hand, 'the hand of hate' (Laughton [dir.] 1955), which he holds up to his face as if defending himself. In this moment the man appears to be fully acknowledging the futile nature of his rebellious act and, by holding both his hands in the air, seems to be surrendering. His left hand is open in a passive gesture, perhaps recalling a violent episode in the Congo's history, discussed in Chapter 1, in which King Leopold II's agents terrorised, mutilated and killed the Congolese people who failed to meet designated quotas for harvesting rubber. The agents collected the severed hands of their victims as evidence of the punishment meted out. The hand reaching out towards the viewer gives a visual reminder of Belgium's most violent past, which has to be reconciled even in this vital moment of Congo's independence. This is the violent past that Patrice Lumumba refused to put to rest and of which he would defiantly remind the Belgians during the official independence ceremonies the following day.

The next three photographs are captioned 'Congo 1960/The rapier thief did not have a chance. Belgian and local soldiers catch him a short time later at the monument to King Albert of Belgium, snatch the rapier from him and lead him away, a gun at his chin' (Lebeck 2008, p.93). On the left-hand page, two of the photographs are presented in half-page landscape format; on the opposite page the third is included in a full-page portrait format. In the first of the landscape photographs, the thief holds the sheath of the sword in his left hand and the drawn sword upright in his right hand. His focus is on the soldiers who are now beginning to close in on him. His expression and his movement forward suggest that the encircling soldiers do not intimidate him. His gesture is a direct challenge to the soldiers who now hold their rifles with a different sense of purpose: they are lowered for deployment rather than shouldered for ceremony. The soldiers that confront the thief are different from those who line the route taken by the king and Kasavubu. While their uniforms are adorned with the same white trimmings as seen on the soldiers riding in the official cavalcade, their armbands carry the bold letters 'PM', suggesting they are in the service of the military police. To the left of the frame a white Belgian soldier advances on the thief. The surrounded thief has held up the rest of the cars in the procession. The inevitable confrontation takes place in full view of the crowd that has gathered on the King Albert monument steps. The elevated statue surveys the spectacle before him.

The subsequent photograph begins a sequence in which the sword is taken from the man and he is arrested. The same white Belgian soldier is the main protagonist in this next photograph: he disarms the man and is supported by a Congolese 'PM' soldier. The thief's expression is pained as the sword is twisted out of his grasp. The ceremonial sword is, in fact, a blunt instrument of power; if it had been sharp, the three struggling men, with their hands on the blade, would have been badly wounded. The sword is purely symbolic, rather than a usable weapon, and therefore the man who has stolen it is not an immediate dangerous threat, despite his powerfully symbolic act of theft. Behind the man, two more Congolese soldiers are present, one of whom appears to be attacking him. As he recoils backwards we cannot see what this soldier is doing to him. This soldier's action is obscured from view and this symbolically represents a covert disarming of those that dissent against this authoritative body. The triangulation of violence against the thief renders his act of liberation hopeless: the old colonial forces close in on him, and the sword and its symbolic significance are restored.

The next photograph in the sequence shows the thief facing Lebeck's camera and being frog-marched by a group of soldiers (Figure 16). One soldier holds a pistol to the left-hand side of the thief's face while simultaneously holding the waistband of his trousers. Other soldiers grip his wrists and shoulders, pushing and pulling him towards the camera. The thief's hands are raised in clenched fists, signalling his defiant political body. His direct gaze toward the camera offers a mocking smile that seems to suggest mild indignation, and which belies the chaos of the scene. In contrast, the expressions on the soldiers' faces build a sense of urgency. One face, however, stands out: the out-of-focus Belgian soldier in the centre of the top third of the photograph. This soldier's ghostly face stares into Lebeck's lens, perhaps asserting his historical sense of privilege over the frenzied scene.

The last four photographs all appear as single images on the page and the sequence seems to show the thief still in defiant mood (Lebeck 2008, pp.94-7). His protest and efforts to resist arrest continue to require the attention of a group of soldiers. He is held from the back by the collar of his jacket by one Congolese soldier and from his front his arms are restrained by two Congolese soldiers holding his left arm and one white soldier holding his right. In the following frame, the thief is completely surrounded by soldiers once again. His arms are now raised as if pleading his case to a white soldier who stands directly in his path. From behind him another white soldier is attempting to grab his right hand to bring him under control once more. The thief is confronted from both the rear and the front by white Belgians, who are engaging directly with him. On the left a Congolese soldier with his pistol drawn raises the thief's jacket, as if searching for anything concealed by him. On the right, a Congolese soldier looks at the thief with an inquisitive gaze. The rest of the Congolese soldiers appear to await instructions. Only one soldier, on the far right, seems to be aware of Lebeck's position as he watches him take the photograph. Lebeck must have had to climb up onto something close by, as the image looks down on the scene. The height from which the photograph was taken and the use of a wide-angle lens create a sense of claustrophobia.

The final two photographs in the series show the man being pushed into and taken away in the back of one of the official jeeps. The penultimate shot captures the thief in mid-air, as soldiers throw him into the vehicle. A senior, flat-capped, white Belgian officer has emerged, to oversee matters. He stands, legs apart, with his arms braced behind his back. His own ceremonial sword hangs down his left-hand side, registering for the viewer that colonial order has now been restored. On the left, a ceremonial band provides an almost comical finale to the episode.

In the final image, the soldiers are back in their positions in the Willys jeep. Four soldiers sit in the back of the vehicle. We can see from the thief's raised hands that he has been handcuffed. He lies flat on his back between the four soldiers on the floor of the jeep, out of view of the crowds that line the streets (Figure 17). His hands are shown in an open gesture, and the two soldiers' faces that we can see look down on him. The thief's dialogue with the soldiers is clearly not finished. Although handcuffed and lying down he continues to speak, and, as this is the last photograph in the series, he thus appears to be having the final word, even in captivity. The caption for these last four images is again shared, and reads 'Congo 1960/The soldiers get a robust grip on the young rapier thief, push him into a jeep and put hand cuffs on him. Next Stop: Jail.'

Looking back from the perspective of the present day, across Lebeck's photographs taken on 29 June 1960, and through this unique sequence that follows the sword thief, they work as allegorical signs pointing towards the immediate future and the problematic politics of the emergent Congo state; this is a state that is not being transformed into a condition of full independence, as perceived by Lumumba and the people of the Congo, but is one that is, in reality, moving from one condition of oppression to another, in which the absolute power of neocolonialism will prevail.

CONCLUSION

The symbolic narrative in the images of the sword thief – the process of quickly snatching power (like seizing the sword), momentarily enjoying wielding it in direct confrontation with the old colonial forces (the soldiers, Congolese and Belgians) whose real presence in the colony is undisturbed and unyielding, then losing it (being physically overwhelmed) under the pressure and influence of Belgium's dark forces, and the final arrest – was echoed just a few months later when Lumumba was captured and returned to Léopoldville under the watchful eye of General Mobutu. Lumumba was tied up and thrown into the back of a military truck and driven off to jail. But before this last act of public humiliation and revenge, the soldiers guarding Lumumba in the truck attempted to force him to literally eat the paper on which his speech was written, in which he had restated his claim to be the Congo's rightful premier. This scene, like the final scene of the sword thief, was the last time Lumumba was seen in public.

The sword thief was later discovered to be Ambroise Boimbo. He was a Congolese patriot. Boimbo died in 1989 and remained in anonymity until, on the occasion of the fiftieth anniversary of independence, a team of Belgian journalists discovered his identity and found his grave. Lebeck later stated that, 'the rapier thief is until today my most frequently printed picture and my identity picture, almost like a trademark' (Lebeck, quoted in Böttger & Koetzle 1999, p.49).

5

Wayne Miller: 'Black Metropolis'

To think of humans as freedom loving, you must be ready to view
nearly all of history as a mistake.

John Gray, *The Silence of Animals*
(Gray 2013, p.57)

In Sean O'Hagan's obituary for photographer Wayne Miller, which
he wrote for *The Guardian* in May 2013, we are informed that,
'through his first-hand experience of the horrors of war, Miller came
to see photography as a medium that could effect social and political
change'. The obituary goes on to describe Miller's experiences of the
Second World War, quoting him as saying:

We didn't know the people we were fighting. They didn't know
us … maybe if we knew each other better, the war would be a
different kind of a war … there would be less carnage. I thought
that after the war, if I could get involved in some kind of a project
that was related to that thinking, it would be my way as a photographer of participating in maybe slowing down the next war.
(O'Hagan 2013)

The quote above from Miller used by O'Hagan is taken from an
eight-minute film about his life, which borrows its title from Miller's
1958 book *The World is Young*. The film was made in 2009 by a
young San Francisco-based documentary film-maker named Theo
Rigby (Rigby [dir.] 2009). From these reflective comments made
by Miller towards the end of his life we can infer that, for him, the
Second World War had failed in much the same way as the First
World War had failed: it had failed to be a war that would end all

wars (Wells 1914). It is evident in his comments that Miller was completing his career as a war photographer pessimistically: 'I could have attended the surrender ceremonies, but I didn't. I was just tired of it all' (Light & Tremain 2010, p.47).

However, when Miller left the navy in 1945, there was a growing political desire among many nations to create an international forum that would protect the world from future wars and protect individual lives. That year marked the end of the old pre-war League of Nations and saw the emergence of the United Nations, which theoretically had at its core an inclusive, rights-based, universal approach to humanity and humanitarian matters. The formation of the United Nations was based on a renewed focus on the protection of civilians, and on making new conventions as a direct response to the suffering of civilians during the Second World War (Oberleitner 2015, p.49). Miller's words suggest he experienced a very real sense of humanitarian responsibility and felt that with the aid of his camera he would endeavour to make the world a more humane place.

At this point in Miller's thought process, the idea of working on a photography project in the heart of the US's black metropolis, Chicago, had not yet been fully formed. He was a mainly self-taught photographer fresh from art school when he enlisted in the navy in 1942. There, he spent four years photographing American servicemen under the direction of Edward Steichen, who was in charge of the Naval Aviation Photographic Unit.

The tragedies of war clearly had an impact on Miller: he was one of the few photographers that had directly 'witnessed and recorded the horror and immediate aftermath of Hiroshima', an experience that he would later refer to as, 'the ultimate denial of sanity' (Miller 2000, p.13). At Hiroshima, he photographed the epicentre of the bomb blast and the plight of people suffering from radiation burns who were being treated in the most basic of conditions. The burned Japanese subjects of his photographs – the emaciated women, children and men – are portrayed looking forlorn, covered with flies. Observing these people today, they appear to share the familiar characteristics of refugees caught by the documentary photographer's lens, but, in this case, they did not get the chance to flee the scene of disaster. In his large-format retrospective monograph, titled *Wayne F. Miller: Photographs 1942-1958*, published in 2008, these images show the subjects against a backdrop of deep black tones that create around them a *mise-en-scène* of utter dejection.

One of the photographs is of a small group of Japanese men and women at prayer (Miller & Daiter 2008, p.90). They are shown literally emerging from the dark, on their knees, waiting for salvation. With an empathy not usually expressed for former enemies, one of these dark photographs shows a Japanese child lying down while being treated for a serious head wound (Figure 18, original in Miller & Daiter 2008, p.88). He is being attended by two Japanese women. One of the women wears a Red Cross armband, and can thus be identified as a nurse; the other woman, due to the intimate exchange of looks between her and the boy, is probably his mother. The child looks helplessly up at his mother who appears dramatically out of the dark, her face turned down towards the tragic sight of the injured child. Her face is framed by light. On the face of the nurse in the foreground we can just glimpse the hint of a smile, as she leans to dress the child's wounded head with a clean bandage. The scene Miller has photographed is a stark reminder to his audience of the cost to innocent civilian life of the dropping of the bomb. The caption for the image simply reads 'Victims of the atomic blast are treated in primitive conditions for radiation burns and shock: Kangyo Ginko Bank'.

Miller also photographed Japanese soldiers on their way to being demobilised (Miller & Daiter 2008, pp. 82-3). The focus of his attention for this sequence appears to be the hopelessness, but also the intimacy, shared by a defeated people. For example, the soldiers are shown gently lighting each other's cigarettes as if leaning forward to exchange a tender kiss, the tips of their cigarettes as they touch becoming an extension of their lips (p. 82 Miller & Daiter 2008). Other soldiers waiting for a train to depart lean out of the carriage windows and gaze into Miller's camera in a shy, inquisitive manner. The men appear simultaneously young and old, as if war has aged them. It is an image in which everyone is a loser, both the observer and the observed. The soldiers are clearly a spent force and Miller, who we now know was sickened by his experiences as an observer, does not take a photograph that demonises those who are now directly facing him. It is as if, when photographing the Japanese soldiers, Miller remembers his early instruction from

Edward Steichen: to photograph the 'little guys' (Light & Tremain 2010, p.46). Steichen was referring to non-commissioned sailors, but here, in Miller's photographs, the 'little guys' emerge as the defeated Japanese infantrymen. The final image published from this section of photographs is a bombed-out barren cityscape (Miller & Daiter 2008, p.93). Its caption reads 'Destruction caused by atomic bomb blast'. It shows the remains of a burnt tree and the ruins of a church-like building. Here, Miller creates a scene in which both nature and religion are dead, and evokes the presence of something distinctively evil and unnatural.

Miller's photographs in Hiroshima are melancholic, detailed, quiet studies of the effects of war rather than grand or dramatic documentary moments. They attempt to relay the personal experiences of the individuals who suffered when the new atomic weapon was detonated. These images, then, are not 'decisive moments'; instead, they amount to a series of unexpected intimate exchanges across the lines of conflict. For those steeped in the documentary tradition, such as Kerry Tremain, the principal author of Miller's book, Miller's work in Hiroshima fails to satisfy a need to see more details of the horror. Tremain states that, 'Indeed, his photographs, some of the first taken after the bomb, can feel unsatisfying, unequal to writer John Hersey's searing descriptions of extreme suffering or to the moral significance of the new weapon' (Miller & Daiter 2008, p.12).

Hersey's essay on Hiroshima was first published in *The New Yorker* magazine in 1946. He described in graphic detail the injuries to some of the survivors of the bomb. He cleverly employed the style of fiction to write up his journalistic accounts of the victims. We can see from the following quotation that Hersey's text sought to bring his reader as close as possible to understanding the experience of surviving an atomic bomb blast and its actual impact on an enemy body:

He saw a uniform. Thinking there was just one soldier, he approached with the water. When he had penetrated the bushes, he saw there were about twenty men, and they were all in exactly the same nightmarish state: their faces were wholly burned, their eye-sockets were hollow, the fluid from their melted eyes had run down their cheeks. (They must have had their faces upturned when the bomb went off; perhaps they were anti-aircraft personnel.) Their mouths were mere swollen, pus-covered wounds, which they could not bear to stretch enough to admit the spout of the teapot. (Hersey 1946a)

The edition of *The New Yorker* that included Hersey's text sold out in days, and his essay was quickly published as a book (Hersey 1946b). It became a bestseller and is now recognised as a landmark piece of writing on the horror of nuclear war (Green 1946). This sales success also represented a clear indication of the American appetite for understanding what happened at Hiroshima in the previous year. Miller, in contrast to Hersey, decided on a less forensic or anatomical approach to narrating the aftermath of the bomb. Hersey's work takes the stories of the individuals he worked with and narrates them in intimate and potentially invasive detail; it could be argued that his main task seems to be to seek to prolong his enemies' suffering for the entertainment of readers at home. His approach risks dangerously sliding into a form of pornographic detail and obliterating the potential for human empathy (Scarry 1985, p.65), especially as we focus on the injuries rather than the wider political causes of the individuals' conditions.

In Miller's work at Hiroshima, he appeared to be looking for a shared symbolic order out of the chaos, reaching beyond the scene of conflict. While in Japan, he did not fuel the public imagination by photographing the pure physical horror created by the atomic blast. He also did not, however, avoid the violence that he encountered. However, the critical question that his photographs invite is: how much of the results of the dropping of the atomic bomb on actual people do we need to see, or indeed imagine, to understand the bomb's devastating nature? Culturally and politically, within conventional Western thought, 'Hiroshima' by Hersey might work best as a narrative of the Hiroshima trauma, because photographs alone may not have had the capacity to fully satisfy the imaginations of those seeking information about such a significant global event. The work that Miller's photographs perform as an after-image of the event could be read as disappointingly 'real', rather than fulfilling viewers' desire for the anticipated spectacular violence they could have portrayed – as is suggested by Tremain's analysis. This may be why Hersey's work on Hiroshima was so immediately popular with American audiences: he filled a cultural gap in the articulation of this new type of violence.

Miller's photographs of Hiroshima were produced in a single day, and, as he told an interviewer, he had not anticipated the trauma he would face (Light & Tremain 2010, p.47). His primary focus, even at Hiroshima, was to record the more human moments. Even here, right in the face of his wartime 'enemy', he appears to feel a sense of responsibility toward the people he photographs. He manages to bridge a gap in the depiction of the 'enemy'; it is hard within his work to locate the menace of the racist fears of Asian expansionism, which were historically constructed as the 'yellow peril'. First and foremost, he sees the Japanese as people, and secondly as victims of circumstances now beyond their individual control.

For Miller, Hiroshima did not stand out from the carnage he had seen elsewhere; it merely consolidated 'his hard-won humanist convictions' (Miller & Daiter 2008 p.12). His state of mind as the war was coming to an end was not one of victorious celebration: he was not interested in documenting the Japanese surrender, nor was he deluded by a sense of national pride in being part of the Allied forces' victory in the South Pacific (Light & Tremain 2010, p.47). Miller was already reflecting, while still on board his racially segregated US navy aircraft carrier, on how to use his camera to construct a photographic project that would bring people closer together. His theory that photographs could, in the future, make a difference to global human understanding, was formed in his mind out of the chaos of war. Like the celebrated British photographer George Rodger, Miller would never photograph war again after seeing so much devastation. Through witnessing such violence, he became critically concerned with mediating and defusing aggressive intolerance, and, in his later life, his family would become the primary focus for his photographic work. Miller believed that it was cultural distance, along with ignorance and a lack of empathy towards those we do not understand, that ultimately resulted in violence and war. It may well be logical to assume that his presence on board a racially divided ship and his daily close proximity to those Others, in this case black Americans, whom he did not understand, caused him to feel a profound sense of unease about his own place and privileges in the world.

On speaking about his photographing of the aftermath of Hiroshima, Miller exclaimed, 'Christ almighty! I just spent four years with them as the enemy and then it was like changing a channel' (Miller & Daiter 2008, p.251). At this critical juncture in Miller's experience of the war, and through his close proximity to the 'enemy' at Hiroshima, he was able to unlock the dominant frames through which he had been conditioned to see Japanese alterity. His reference to 'changing a channel' shows how he reconfigured his point of view when considering how the Japanese were to be framed. Radically then, his photographs of the Japanese soldiers are images of 'brotherhood, not only between the soldiers but also with the viewer' (Miller & Daiter 2008, p.12).

Miller's war helped him to identify how his future photographic work might evolve. By the end of the conflict in 1945, he understood that how we see each other has a profound impact on how we relate to each other, and he came to recognise the role that photography could play in lifting the 'veil' of race (see discussion of W. E. B. Du Bois in Chapter 3). In portraying the Japanese in a way that brought viewers closer to their plight and suffering, he built a dialogue with his audience that produced a counter-narrative to the war's propaganda machine against the Japanese. His tender photograph of a man having his hair cut outside by a young Japanese woman, amid the ruins of Tokyo (Miller & Daiter 2008, p.91), is a testament to his desire to build an image of the Japanese beyond the conflict and the old 'yellow peril' stereotypes (Dower 1986, p.176). The photograph resonates with dignity for both the man and the woman. She is dressed in traditional Japanese clothes, and she attentively cuts the seated man's hair from behind him. The man sits covered in a white robe, which protects him from the cut hair that is falling from his head. His eyes are closed and his pose seems reflective. This act, photographed in the midst of the surrounding devastation, becomes readable as a small resilient moment, suggesting this man's desire to preserve his dignity and to pursue life's routine acts of existence. Miller's work in Japan indicates well his self-designated Herculean task at the end of the war, which was to begin to roll back the forms of visual 'opacity that prevents peoples from seeing and understanding each other' (Mitchell 2012, p.89).

Miller's future as a photographer was not only shaped by his past relationship with the influential Edward Steichen, it was also profoundly altered through his encounters with his fellow servicemen. It was with them that he had a transformative exchange near the end of the war that helped to mould his thoughts. Miller recalled a key moment on board his ship:

> One evening toward the end of the war I drifted out on deck and joined a group of my shipmates. We swapped jokes and gossip for a while, but then our mood shifted, and we began to discuss the blind futility of war. Many of us felt we were fighting in the dark, by instinct, against enemies we didn't know and who didn't know us. Guns and bombs might win the war, but ignorance and suspicion would surely lose the peace. Only through awareness and understanding, we agreed, could foes ever become friends and friends become neighbours. I never forgot that conversation. It convinced me that after the war, with a camera, I might be able to document the things that make this human race of ours a family. We may differ in race, color, language, wealth, and politics. But look at what we all have in common – dreams, laughter, tears, pride, the comfort of home, the hunger for love. If I could photograph these universal truths, I thought that might help us better understand the strangers on the other side of the world – and on the other side of town. (Miller 2000, p.13)

After the Second World War, Miller had set himself the utopian task of photographing the 'universal truths' that for him and his mentor Steichen bind mankind together. In this mode of thought, Miller would, a few years later, prove to be a willing and able assistant to Steichen as the latter worked on his landmark and much-celebrated 1955 photography exhibition, *The Family of Man*, for the Museum of Modern Art in New York (Mauro 2014).

GOING HOME

After completing his embedded service with the Naval Aviation Photographic Unit, Miller returned home with his wife and two children to the city in which he grew up, with the intention of photographing Chicago's South Side African American communities. He had the financial support of two successive Guggenheim Fellowships in 1946 and in 1948, and was therefore able to spend extended periods developing relationships with and photographing Chicago's African American communities. He wanted to work where his photographs would make a difference and, for this reason, he chose Chicago, his hometown, as the place in which to exercise his humanitarian photographic vision, a vision that was aimed at opening up new perspectives and dialogues relating to race relations in the US. For Miller, the global conflicts of the Second World War and his humanitarian acts of making photography had now shifted focus, and become a local concern mediated through the prism of race. Mark D. Faram, author of *Faces of War: The Untold Story of Edward Steichen's WWII Photographers* (2009), comments in a short film made by the Smithsonian Institution in 2009, that at the 'end of the war he [Wayne Miller] had such a touch with people that he was allowed access into a lot of the segregated parts of the ship by the people in those areas' (Wolly & Burke n.d.). The aircraft carrier that Miller worked on was clearly a microcosm of life back home: a racially segregated space.

The black strangers encountered by Miller both when he was growing up in Chicago and while he served in the navy were close to him physically but distant culturally. Miller's parents still lived on the North Side of Chicago and his mother did not approve of his new photographic project. In an argument over a family dinner she asked, 'so do you want Jeanette [his daughter] to marry a negro?' (Miller & Daiter 2008, p.13). Such was his mother's racism that she feared his project would influence her young granddaughter to break a fierce social taboo in the US, which was to marry across the 'colour line'.

Having been born in 1918, Miller grew up in a Chicago infected by racist violence. The summer of 1919 in the US became known as the 'Red Summer', due to the number of race riots in major cities that year. As a young white woman in Chicago, Miller's mother would have directly experienced the riots, the most violent of which occurred in Chicago, Washington, DC and Elaine, Arkansas. The riots represented a landmark moment in American racial history and are recognised as being the first time that black citizens fought back against white violence in significant numbers and across different cities. One of the key reasons identified by white Americans for this change in black American attitudes, that is, having the audacity to fight back against white aggression and oppression, was that during the First World War the French had 'put ideas of equality in African American [soldiers'] heads' (McWhirter 2011, p.71). The 1919 riots in Chicago shook all of the US: they 'showed ... that large-scale white violence would be met by large-scale black violence. [It signalled profoundly] that black Americans had no intention of abandoning their place [within the heartland of] industrial America' (McWhirter 2011, p.148). Miller's mother's racist attitudes are a poignant reminder of the depth of fear and prejudice that existed within Chicago's North Side white community. It was against this historical context of deep-seated racism and hostility that Miller began his photographic work within the city's black South Side community.

STRANGERS ON THE OTHER SIDE

Chicago was a culturally contested city even before the early- to mid-twentieth century, but the city was dramatically transformed epidermally by mass black migration north. It became known across the US as the 'black capital of the Midwest' (McWhirter 2011, p.15). Historically, white immigrants had:

> thronged to the city from all parts of Europe for decades. Irish, Swedes, Germans, Italians, Russians, Jews, Poles, Hungarians, Serbs, Croats, Greeks, Bohemians, and others transformed Chicago into a network of cramped insular neighbourhoods set apart by language and religion. (McWhirter 2011, p.115)

The continuous flow of southern black Americans in vast numbers to Chicago during this period was seen by many of the city's white communities as a major threat. The perceived potential for social problems caused by black mass migration, especially in relation to the competition for housing and jobs, had prompted the *Chicago Tribune* as early as 1917 to state in an editorial that 'a new problem, demanding early solution, is facing Chicago ... the sudden and unprecedented influx of southern Negro Laborers' (McWhirter 2011, p.118).

The number of black people moving northwards increased dramatically before, during and after both the First World War and the Second World War, partly because northern industries solicited the cheap labour that the black workers from the south offered, and partly because, as a non-unionised workforce, these new arrivals were easy to exploit. That meant that the tense, racialised urban space that Chicago represented in 1917, as suggested by the *Tribune*, remained similarly fraught in 1945, when it remained a racially segregated and intolerant city. The harsh reality was that, since the turn of the twentieth century, very little had changed culturally, politically and economically for black people across the US with regard to their overall social wellbeing, and this was very apparent in Chicago.

Black workers operating outside the unions was a major contributory factor in the ongoing conflict between black and white workforces across the industrial north of the US:

> Between 1940 and 1944, 60,000 new Negro migrants arrived in the Mid-West Metropolis. There were plenty of jobs, but already troublesome problems of inadequate housing, conges- tion and inferior recreational facilities, and overcrowded schools in the Black Belt were aggravated by the influx. Half-forgotten memories of the Great Migration and the race riot [of 1919] were revived among both Negroes and whites. The Negro was once more becoming a 'problem' and racial conflict seemed to loom in the offing. (Drake & Cayton 1945, p.91)

Black urban workforces were particularly vulnerable in 1945, at a time when soldiers – and especially white soldiers – were returning home and demanding employment. The National Urban League predicted that:

> 400,000 Negro war workers would lose jobs between V-E Day and V-J Day ... this spectre of widespread unemployment and poverty hovered over the community and exacerbated the housing and health care issues laying siege to the African American ... this was a national phenomenon. (Anderson 2003, p.66)

The dire condition of the African Americans prompted a major detailed academic study of black life in Chicago. This groundbreaking work, published in 1945, was entitled *Black Metropolis: A Study of Negro Life in a Northern City* and was written by two leading African American scholars, St Clair Drake and Horace R. Cayton. Cayton would go on to play a significant role in helping Miller obtain access to Chicago's South Side, and helped to develop his understanding of it. Miller later stated that,

> I had good luck from the start. Guided by some angel, one of my early stops was at the Parkway Community House. It was a gold mine. Horace Cayton the director, and co-author with St Clair Drake of the sociological study *Black Metropolis*, knew everyone and, without question, was most generous in sharing his immense knowledge and contacts with me. (Miller 2000, p.13)

Without the work and generosity of these remarkable black academics, Cayton and Drake, Miller's project may well not have got off the ground. Miller's 'gold mine' was, in part, the discovery of their key sociological work. In the acknowledgements that accompany his book *Chicago's South Side 1946-1948*, published in 2000, Miller states that without Cayton he could not have taken the photographs. One could therefore argue that his project represents a collaborative dialogue, facilitated, and participated in, by the authors of *Black Metropolis*. This remarkable academic study was the key that opened the door for Miller's project.

Drake and Cayton's book contained an insightful foreword by the author Richard Wright. Wright's text is politically melancholic and damning concerning the progress and quality of black life in Chicago, and by extension across the US, as he describes the unbearable ennui of the black American experience. This was a position he would reaffirm a few years later in an article for *Ebony* magazine, in which his own critical account of the city was linked with Miller's photographs to dramatic effect (Ward & Butler 2008, p.192).

In his foreword, Wright draws on the philosophy of William James to articulate what a 'man would feel if he were completely socially excluded'. He goes on to quote James: 'No more fiendish punishment could be devised were such a thing physically possible' (Wright 1945, p.32). Wright continues his theory of how damaging complete social racial exclusion can be claiming that:

> the American Negro has come as near to being the victim of a complete rejection as our society has been able to work out, for the dehumanized image of the Negro which white Americans carry in their minds, the anti Negro epithets continuously on their lips, exclude the contemporary Negro as truly as though he were kept in a steel prison and doom even those Negroes who are as yet unborn. (Wright 1945, p.33)

This text by Wright may well have gone on to influence his friend and fellow writer Ralph Ellison, who began working on his seminal book, *Invisible Man*, in 1945. The critically acclaimed novel was finally published in 1952 and was constructed from the same theoretical premise concerning the condition of cultural violence on black people made invisible within white US society.

In the late 1940s and early 1950s, how to make black life more visible was a critical point of concern for black writers and photographers alike. *Ebony* used Miller's photographs in December 1951 to illustrate an essay that they had previously commissioned from Richard Wright in September 1950, entitled 'The Shame of Chicago'. The editors of *Ebony* had wanted the magazine to focus on the upward social mobility of black people in Chicago, and strongly disagreed with Wright's perspective on the development of black people in the city (Ward & Butler 2008, p.192). His text highlighted the 'bleak façades of the slum hovels' that stretched 'endlessly across the South Side' (Ward & Butler 2008, p.348). For Wright, by the end of the 1940s, there had been no improvement in the quality of life for black people in Chicago since he had left the city in 1937.

Miller's photographs accompanied Wright's sombre textual analysis of Chicago as a city that never 'became the promised land, the longed for Mecca which Wright so eagerly sought when he left the South [Mississippi] and headed North [to Chicago] in search of freedom in 1927' (Ward & Butler 2008, p.348). On the pages of *Ebony*, Miller's photographs of the South Side entered the public realm for the first time, illustrating and supporting a damning critique of the city, and the place of race within it. Wright's grim view led to a permanent falling out between himself and the owners of *Ebony*. He never worked for the magazine again, and Miller's photographs of Chicago appear to have been set aside, apart from just two images that were selected for inclusion in Steichen's 1955 exhibition, *The Family of Man*. Surprisingly, as a body of work, Miller's photographs from Chicago were then not seen for another fifty years. That the photographs were linked to Wright's text may well have had an adverse effect on the reception of Miller's project for many years. Through Wright's words, Miller's work became exclusively an indictment of the city's racial problems rather than also a celebration of black humanity, as he had intended.

The intensity of violence and injustice against African Americans immediately after the Second World War was not just articulated by black academics, creative writers, photographers and white humanitarians. The black subject was in a dire state across the US; by 1946, due to the increase in the number of lynchings, murders and vicious attacks on black war veterans and their families, President Truman had to admit 'that he was deeply troubled' that, 'in this country' there was 'disturbing evidence of intolerance and prejudice, similar in kind, though perhaps not in degree' to that of the Nazis. He lamented that the 'better world we fought for' was not here yet (Anderson 2003, p.68).

Founded in 1945, *Ebony*'s primary focus was on the lives of black celebrities and the US's upwardly mobile black middle class. The magazine's denial of the vulnerability of African Americans, as highlighted by Richard Wright, was politically out of step even with President Truman's concerns. Miller commented on the outrage within the South Side community when black war veterans were specifically targeted for lynching. One of his photographs from the project is captioned 'Anti-lynching demonstration'. It portrays an apparently warm evening, in which a young bare-chested black boy, aged around ten years old, is seen on the edge of a crowd holding a placard in the air that states, 'Negro Vets Dared Vote They Were Lynched'. By focusing on the young child demonstrating against the lynchings, Miller delivers a critical message about the serious nature of the community's distress surrounding the issues of rights and violence.

THE PHOTOGRAPHS

Miller's Chicago project for his Guggenheim Fellowships was formally titled 'The Way of Life of the Northern Negro', drawing on St Clair Drake and Horace R. Cayton's title *Black Metropolis: A Study of Negro Life in a Northern City*. The specific use of the word 'Northern' in Miller's title helped to define the parameters of his photography culturally and politically. It also signified an important characteristic in Miller's approach to the project: he, like Drake and Cayton, recognised that in 1946 black Americans living in the north were distinctly different. These people, who had established themselves in Chicago, could no longer be framed as being culturally from elsewhere, transient Others, from a generic, southern-US, alien space. They were not migrants but were rather individuals within a large, settled, permanent community that was now fundamentally ingrained within the social fabric of Chicago and other northern cities. Black citizens of Chicago had contributed fully through the workplace to the industrial success of the city. The riots of 1919 played an important part in anchoring the black presence in the north: 'Anchorage in a space is an economic-political form which needs to be studied in detail' (Foucault & Gordon 1980, p.149). Miller's use of the term 'Northern' effectively closed the gap in relation to the hierarchy of migratory claims over Chicago and demanded parity for the black presence within the city's migrant story.

Miller's photographic intentions in 1946 echoed the historic photographs commissioned by W. E. B. Du Bois in 1900 for his 'American Negro' project, which won a gold medal at the 1900 Paris Exposition. Du Bois organised over 350 images into albums entitled the 'Types of American Negroes, Georgia, USA and Negro Life in Georgia, USA'. The central idea behind his project was to visually unlock black US citizens from the burden of scientific racism that, at this time, dominated perceptions of black people, suggesting that they were inferior human subjects. There is a correlation between Miller's and Du Bois' projects in their shared intention to use photography as a tool to disrupt ingrained cultural hostilities towards black Americans. This moment of international acclaim for Du Bois (who should also be recognised as probably the first curator of a black photography exhibition) at the Paris Exposition acted as a significant cultural and visual indicator. It announced the possibility that France could be a place where black Americans might receive the recognition they sought and which was absent from their lives in the US. As the French Revolution proved, liberty, equality and fraternity are infectious political ideals when used to mobilise the disenfranchised. This potential for rebellion and revolution, as previously mentioned, was acknowledged by white American racists, who aggressively employed lynching in an effort to re-establish the old racial, and racist, order. Richard Wright also used his experience of being in Paris from 1946 onwards as a cultural barometer of how far behind the US was, as a place in which to live and work as a black person. His essay that was commissioned in 1949 by *Ebony* about his experience of Paris was entitled 'I Choose Exile', and was part of a trilogy of commissioned texts that included 'The Shame of Chicago', discussed above. In 'I Choose Exile' 'Wright argued that he experienced in France the freedom, equality and human dignity which was denied him in his native land, there was more freedom in one square block of Paris than there was in the entire United States' (Ward & Butler 2008, p.192). *Ebony* never published the essay.

It is now apparent that Miller's Chicago project was part of a longer radical tradition within the US to mobilise photography in an attempt to humanise the black American subject for the wider, racist public. His images were an important visual channel constructed out of the core body politic produced by those such as Du Bois, Cayton and Wright, which sought to alleviate the social forces and forms of violence that were at work on the black American subject. Miller effectively opened up a critical visual site of recognition across the question of race and place within Chicago, and, by extension, across the US. Importantly, this work is not a simplistic set of humanitarian moments, but is culturally complex. On the one hand, Miller wanted to bring the humanity of the South Side into focus but, on the other and in order to do that, he himself literally begged for what his subjects likely feared most: the condition of invisibility. He required this, so that he could take his photographs: '"Please", I said, "pay no attention to me just keep doing what you're doing". Believe it or not they usually did' (Miller 2000, p.14). In desiring and being allowed by his subjects to acquire the state of invisibility, while taking photographs, Miller may well have been evoking, consciously or unconsciously, a degree of white privilege that has historically allowed white constructions of black life to become manifest. Indeed, having the choice to become invisible or visible becomes an important indicator of power, when documentary photographs are being taken. Miller believed that, through the coat of invisibility that he was able to wear whenever he chose, he could make more tangible the realities of the everyday black subject in Chicago. Miller's project invites the question: who sees whom, and where? 'Somehow or other, they understood that my motives were sympathetic and uncritical. They sensed I was not looking for good or for evil. My search was for the everyday realities of life – *their* view of the world, *their* feeling, *their* attitudes, their stories' (Miller 2000, p.14). What Miller naively did not recognise was that, as a white man with a camera, he may well have been considered by the South Side black community as a figure of authority that would be difficult to challenge and that, if they ignored him, did not trouble him, he might simply go away.

Capturing the everyday moments of black American life was by no means a new concept. This mission was also central to the work of several less celebrated African American photographers, such as Robert H. McNeill, for example. Almost the same age as Miller, McNeill was born in 1917 in Washington, DC, a city that was also traumatised by the intense racial violence of 1919. His photographs of the lives of black Americans were:

> frequently published in black newspapers such as the *Pittsburgh Courier*, *Washington Afro-American* and the *Chicago Defender*. McNeill's photographs showed that African Americans living in a segregated city survived – even thrived – by creating their own social and community organisations. (Willis-Thomas 2002, p.88)

What was important about McNeill's images, however, was that they 'suggested the dimension seldom acknowledged in illustrated American studies ... of the 1930s-1940s: [that they represented the] non-monolithic nature of black experience' (Natanson 1997). McNeill's experience of taking photographs of people was very different from that of Miller. In an interview with the historian Nicolas Natanson he recalled an experience he had had in a small town called Pocahontas:

> I was driving this Ford black coupe, with 'USA' on the license plate. As I pulled into town, this sheriff with a long gun going practically to his knee, stopped me and started in with, 'Boy, what are you doing with this USA car?' He emphasized the 'boy' and the 'USA'. I gave him the logical explanation, and he was still suspicious. 'Well, I got to check into that!' So I was taken to the sheriff's office, and they telegraphed the [headquarters] office to investigate. Found out I was telling the truth … but they never did let me photograph in the mines. Only the show mine. (Sullivan 2005)

As this illustrates, black photographers working outside of familiar spaces did not have the privilege of simply requesting to be ignored. A black man with a camera clearly represented a visible threat to the local Southern authorities, as this instance proves, to the point where McNeill was not allowed to work.

Whiteness was also a critical factor in photographing the civil rights movement. The Southern American authorities wrongly assumed in the early days of the development of the civil rights movement that all white photographers were sympathetic to the state authority's position. In contrast, a black photographer working for the civil rights movement was an easy and obvious opposition target. When challenged by police, white pro-civil rights photographers Matt Herron and Bob Fitch would simply adopt Southern accents or slip away into the crowd. Their whiteness enabled them to float across both sides of racial conflict. It protected them against state violence and gave them access to black spaces. In a filmed interview for Ryerson University, Fitch says that he was informed by leaders of the civil rights campaign that they 'could not send black photographers and writers in the field, they get beat up and they get killed' (Sealy 2010).

CALIFORNIA FIFTY YEARS LATER

By 1946, Miller had been able to manoeuvre himself into a position where he could imagine, through his photographs, that he might speak for Chicago's African American community. He sought to bring these black lives into view from behind both the visible and invisible barriers that oppressed them, and this made Miller's photographs readable as part of a dynamic political conjuncture aimed at producing resistance work against the culture of American racism. Had they surfaced in the public realm at the time of their taking, then the photographs might have been effective in lifting, however momentarily, the weight of historical oppression that burdened Chicago's black population.

Plate 3 from Miller's Chicago's South Side book is captioned 'A tenement on South Indiana Avenue, the type of housing for half the city's black children' and is one of only two photographs in the book that do not include people (Figure 19, original in Miller 2000). It shows a four-storey housing project surrounded by litter and rubble: an image of depressing urban squalor that reflects the desperate daily lives of its residents. While the actual image is devoid of any black children, the wording of the caption causes the viewer to reflect on the terrible conditions endured by black American families. Plate 10 is captioned 'An alley between overcrowded tenements, with garbage thrown over the railings of the back porches. Most of the area's tenants were transient' (Miller 2000). The photograph shows a lone figure walking through piles of garbage. It is a wet day, and his reflection is caught in the stagnant pools of rainwater. The man wears a long overcoat and a wide-brimmed hat and walks towards the camera with his hands pushed firmly into his pockets. He is positioned in the middle of the frame, slowly walking through the scenes of chaos all around him. The background to the photograph is a steaming, smouldering atmosphere that obscures the buildings lying beyond, hinting that the rubbish there is alive with fermentation. The photograph complements Plate 3 well, as it suggests that behind the squalor presented earlier things are actually even more desperate.

In examining Miller's 'The Way of Life of the Northern Negro' project today, we are able to observe, through his depiction of such abject poverty, the stark reality of the violence present in the post-war US and the social politic at work on the black body even when it is absent from the frame.

Chicago's South Side was home to several large, environmentally damaging steel mills and other forms of heavy industry that needed human labour power. It is not surprising, then, that the majority of Miller's photographs examine the black subject in the workplace, doing hard manual labour, taking breaks from their work, on strike or just waiting in public spaces.

However, one photograph, Plate 46, stands out, bucking this trend of depicting black labourers. Miller's caption reads, 'Debutante ball sponsored by the "Royal Coterie of Snakes", an exclusive gentlemen's club, at the Parkway Ballroom, December 1946' (Figure 20, original in Miller 2000). Here we are presented with many black men and women packed tightly together, all dancing formally hand-in-hand as if doing a gentle slow waltz (none of the dancers have any signs of sweat or physical exertion). The men are dressed in dinner suits, bow ties and white shirts, many of them with white carnations. The women wear fine evening gowns. Smiles are exchanged between couples as well as being directed towards the camera. This is not an impoverished group of people. The 'Royal Coterie of Snakes' according to *Jet* magazine was established in 1922 as an organisation, 'dedicated to the betterment of social standards of Chicago's business and professional leaders' (Major 1973). The smiles suggest that Miller's presence was welcome on this elaborate occasion, when Chicago's black middle-class elite was on display. From the angle the photograph is taken, it is clear that Miller has found a high place from which to work, presumably making him clearly visible to his subjects. This photograph is a rare celebratory moment within the book, recording black wealth and black subjects enjoying themselves as an affluent and confident group, while being watched by a white observer. It can also be read as a moment that smiles back in the face of the oppressor. As a photograph from Chicago's South Side, it changes the perception of the community presented in the previous published images. It stands alone because it interjects a visual dynamic of the black middle class across Miller's project. Apart from celebrities such as Paul Robeson and Lena Horne who visited Chicago, and other than this photograph, the black middle class who resided in the southern section of the South Side are absent from Miller's project.

In Miller's photographs from Chicago, even through the image of the 'Royal Coterie of Snakes', we see a people historically trapped, a people fixed culturally and temporally through race, despite their profession or social aspirations. Only two photographs in the book portray black and white people sharing a physical space, and both are of manual workers at the Harvester Tractor works. One of the photographs, Plate 29, shows two men, one black and one white, and its caption reads, 'Black safety worker, the supervisor of his white coworker at International Harvester' (Miller 2000). The two men, both covered in coal dust from their tasks, stand shoulder to shoulder; the white worker places his arm around the shoulder of the slightly larger black worker. They both return full broad smiles back at Miller's camera. The black man proudly displays his Safety Inspector's badge. The image represents a rare moment of official black superiority over a white colleague. It is indicative of a cultural turning point in the place of race in the workplace, where the presence of the black subject is traditionally nearly always subordinate (see the wartime posters discussed in Chapter 3, for example).

Miller's project attempted to radically recast black people as fully-fledged human subjects, making up an undeniable community, fused together by all the ordinariness and complexities that occur when people are simply allowed to go about their everyday lives despite social forces working against them. Street sweepers, female impersonators, policemen, debutantes, celebrities and ordinary black men and women form these black communities, who go to church, party, flirt, bring up families, mourn the dead and celebrate the new born. They are all part of Miller's 'Negro' story. His project can therefore now be read as grounded in a form of cultural 'reconstruction work' (S. Hall 1992), with the aim of seeing others not through the prism of epidermal judgement but through photographic moments of familiarity, hospitality and possible identification with a people beyond the confines of race. Miller's sympathetic eye shifts the black subject out from the historical frames of reference in the US that sign them as an alien or object Other, and into the realm of the collective 'us', rather than the distant 'them'.

However, it took fifty years for the work to surface publicly in any meaningful way, either as an exhibition or a publication. This seems astonishing, given Miller's support from the Guggenheim Foundation and his direct connection to Edward Steichen. The question, then, for Miller's work, and indeed for the history of American photography is: was the US politically and culturally ready for the challenges that this body of photographs might have invited if they had been shown closer to the time of their taking? And, indeed, were Miller and his core sponsors really prepared for them to be seen? We recognise that 'the past cannot speak except through the archive' (S. Hall 1992, p.106). With this work appearing so late after its making, when looking at the images we now have to resist nostalgia in viewing and interpreting them.

Reading Miller's photographs from the perspective of the present means that this specific body of work can be considered a rare and significant, self-assigned post-war act by a white American photographer, to take responsibility for the Other. It could therefore represent a direct attempt to use photography as a tool, to cut through the Gordian knot of historical racism and violence in the US.

Miller's act of taking responsibility pre-dates many of the white photographers who would later record black American daily and political life. Miller's photographs from 'The Way of Life of the Northern Negro' can also be read as a form of cultural investment in African American life not just in terms of race, but also with regard to class, gender and age. It was an investment that would not yield any significant return until at least fifty years later, when, after lying dormant at his home in California for decades, Miller's work was the inaugural exhibition curated by Ken Light for the newly formed Center of Photography, which was housed at the University of California, Berkeley. A 1998 Public Affairs news release from Berkeley informs us that 'Miller has handpicked 70 black and white photos for exhibition' (UC Berkeley 1998).

After the exhibition, the University of California published the project retitled as *Wayne F. Miller: Chicago's South Side 1946-1948*. Time and shifts in the politics of race and language render titling a book 'The Way of Life of the Northern Negro' in the year 2000 a backward cultural step in the dynamic discourse of race and authorship. The new title disperses the seeds of problematic anthropology that attach themselves to the author's old title, and it

WAYNE MILLER: 'BLACK METROPOLIS'

lays open a path for a different discussion about the work performed by the photographs. The back cover of the book reiterates the desire for a new conversation on race, by featuring an endorsement by Gordon Parks, who, at the time of publication, was the US's most celebrated African American documentary photographer. Parks's testimony is embellished with the myth of the divine photographer on a mission. He states that 'Wayne [Miller] went to wherever his conscience called him, and his camera's eye baptized whatever confronted him' (Miller 2000, p.x). The image accompanying the Parks text on the back of the book is also reproduced inside the book as Plate 43, where it is captioned 'Western Union telegram messenger' (Miller 2000). No caption appears on the back cover, so its meaning is therefore much looser and less fixed when read in the context of Parks's comment.

The photograph portrays a black woman in uniform, wearing a cap and heavy wool double-breasted coat. On the buttons of the coat are the letters 'WU'. Her shirt is neat and buttoned to the top. Under her arm is tucked a clipboard with documents and dollar bills attached. Just visible at the bottom of the photograph are the two bars that run in a circular pattern around her coat's sleeves. On her head, she wears a typical postal service peaked cap with what looks like a bold metal badge on the front. The woman, however, is photographed out of focus, blurring the detail of her features. Despite this, we can see that her mouth is open and her teeth are visible as she moves her head sideways while laughing. She her eyes half closed as she leans slightly back. However, in reading the photograph through the context of Gordon Parks's symbolism, the image becomes loaded with religious baggage. The blurring of the black woman's face gives the photograph the sense of a spiritual encounter with the Other. The choice of image here suggests that it is not so much a photograph of a black woman worker with whom we are being invited to engage; it is her spiritual essence beyond the physicality of her racialised body and being that we are encouraged to see.

The image selected for the front cover of the book is taken in a pool hall and captioned 'Afternoon game at Table 2'. The room is lined with black men stylishly dressed in hats, coats, shirts and bow ties, observing the action. It is clearly a cold environment as nearly all the subjects wear big heavy coats. One player is leaning over 'Table 2', about to strike the white pool ball with his cue. His opponent looks on in anticipation as to where the balls might go after the strike. He stoops slightly to get a better view. The lights hanging above the pool tables add to the ambience of the photograph. All the men in the room seem locked in contemplation of the players at the tables. It is a serene, intimate, tight space in which the men are shown calmly engaged with time and leisure. Alcohol or any form of exuberance is markedly absent and as a cover photograph it signals well the visual intention behind Miller's project.

THE LAST PHOTOGRAPH

The last photograph in Miller's *Chicago's South Side* book, captioned 'Father and son at Lake Michigan', is highly significant in his depiction of African American males (Figure 21, original in Miller 2000). The photograph is taken from behind the subjects: a black man is sitting quietly with his young son, who looks around three or four years old, on the beach at Lake Michigan. The backs of the father and son are caught in bright sunlight. The man's back is broad, straight and strong, and contrasts to the vulnerability of the small child. On the surface, the photograph seems to be merely a record of an intimate moment between father and son, but the dominance of the man's back in the frame invites a number of interpretations. By focusing on the black backs, but in approaching it in a different way, and with different intent, Miller breaks the hegemony of images throughout history that portray the black male body by focusing on the subject's back. These black backs photographed by Miller are not marked with the violence of the whip or stressed by toil. They carry no signs of the burden of racism and are not loaded with an erotic or exotic charge. The father's back could be read as representing a solid place of security, like a rock on the shore of the lake, and is emulated by his son's back, suggesting a statement of genealogy, and thus permanence.

Because the photograph is taken on the lake shore and the urban context of the city has been removed from the black subject, we focus instead on the close relationship between the father and son. The backs of the black man and the young boy carry a 'punctive' charge

(Barthes 1981). The image could also be read as evoking a darker moment from the history of Chicago, namely the violent incident that triggered the 1919 riots, which occurred at the same beach. A young black boy swam across an invisible racial line in the lake, and was wounded by a rock thrown by a white man standing on the shore, which hit the boy directly on the head. He drowned. This photograph, which appears to be an image of escape and relaxation away from the pressures of Chicago, becomes a potential site of contested space and the violent imposition of racial boundaries. When reading the photograph with the knowledge of the race riots in 1919, the man's gaze across to the right of the frame away from the horizon of the lake becomes an act of vigilance rather than of reflection or contemplation.

The radical nature of Miller's project lies in the fact that he refused to acknowledge the extreme edges that may have been photographable across Chicago's black community. Looking through this body of work we can see that no matter what the circumstances of the situation focused on by Miller, his photographs do not indicate that the subjects here have fallen 'apart' or been broken by racism. What they are doing, as a people, is hanging on. Miller's project gives a sense of the complexity of threads that bind them together as a people and to us as observers of historical conditions of race at work. They remind us that we can read photographs either through the specific history of the medium itself and the romance of authorship or we can choose to untangle them through different historical moments relevant to the time of their making.

6

Rights and Recognition in the Late Twentieth Century

Article 6 of the Universal Declaration of Human Rights 1948 states that, 'Everyone has the right to recognition everywhere as a person before the law'. If the concept of 'recognition' as a 'human right' is so clearly enshrined within the Declaration, then by extension this has to include a right to recognition of one's cultural identity. This is especially the case with regard to those cultural identities that concern the historically oppressed, the victimised, the marginalised, the migrant, the refugee, the stateless and all other subalterns. Cultural difference and questions of identity within 'the right to recognition' have, for many of the disenfranchised people of the world, been front-line battles in establishing their dignity and human worth. They have been faced with forces of oppression, as they have been systematically excluded from being able to articulate or take control of the means of cultural production, through which their lives have been made visible.

In 1948, alongside the proclamation of the Declaration of Human Rights, another significant event in Britain's relationship to its colonies took place: the 1948 British Nationality Act. This Act paved the way for workers to arrive in Britain to help with the post-Second World War reconstruction work in the 'motherland'. The merchant ship *Empire Windrush* arrived at Tilbury Docks, in Essex, on 22 June 1948. On board were 492 workers from the Caribbean, and their arrival, along with many others later from across the empire, marked a significant chapter in modern British history, one that transformed the very fabric of British society and notions of Britishness. W. E. B. Du Bois famously claimed in 1903 that 'the problem of the twentieth century is the problem of the colour line' (Du Bois 1996, p.1). Echoing this when addressing the challenges of the twentieth century, Stuart Hall rearticulated the problems with race not just through the prism of the colour line but through the question of cultural identity and ethnicity, when he claimed that:

> the issue of cultural identity as a political quest now constitutes one of the most serious global problems as we go into the twenty-first century. The re-emergence of questions of ethnicity, of nationalism – the obduracy, the dangers and the pleasures of the rediscovery of identity in the modern world, inside and outside Europe – places the question of cultural identity at the very centre of the contemporary political agenda. (S. Hall 1995, p.4)

The politics of photography, and the role that photography played in helping to shape debates concerning identity, were seen by Hall as a critical front on which to engage the issue that he called 'secondariness'. This was especially the case as Britain's black communities came under increasing attack from both the state and the media who, in their respective ways, demonised and terrorised black communities (S. Hall 1978, p. 339).

MAKING THE RIGHT TO RECOGNITION POSSIBLE

The genealogy of many of Britain's black photographic practices can be found in the radical, left-wing cultural policy-making corridors of the Greater London Council (GLC) and, to a lesser degree, its regional equivalents in the 1980s. From 1981 to 1986, the GLC had a profound influence on London's black artists. It could be argued that, through direct forms of social engineering specifically targeted at marginalised groups and individuals that it wanted to support, the GLC created the conditions out of which the concept of (B)lack British photography could grow. Capitalising the 'B' in the word 'black' came to signify that works produced under this label would have a direct political and social focus on black experiences and questions of black identity. Financial support through the GLC's Ethnic Arts Sub-Committee, which was dominated by black artists and activists such as Parminder Vir, meant that black photographic practitioners based in London had access to funding streams for the first time in a meaningful way and over a sustained and intense period of time. The impact of this shift was dynamic and profound. 'In terms of cultural policy', writes Franco Bianchini, 'this meant going beyond Labour's traditional concentration on centralised planning and even beyond existing forms of decentralisation' (Bianchini 1987, p.108).

It was recognised at the highest levels within the GLC, and in light of the 1981 riots in Brixton and beyond, that 'new alliances could be built only by devolving power and resources to the constituencies represented on the Ethnic and Community Arts Sub-Committees. The concept of representation was central to this policy'. For Alan Tomkins, an influential and leading policy advisor at the GLC during the 1980s, 'representation is not just a matter of parliamentary democracy: it is one of the principal means through which the cultural and political configurations of a social formation are historically produced'. In order to promote the 'production, the celebration of working class, women's, black and youth histories' (Bianchini 1987, p.108), one of Tomkins's principal objectives, the GLC began to fund contemporary cultural forms like photography, collectives working in film and video, pop music studios and community radio, which had traditionally been neglected by the state. As a GLC report on black arts pointed out, this was a precondition for creating:

> a new aesthetics which is not "traditional", "ethnic", "folk", "exotica", but which is appropriate for what needs to be expressed here and now. It was probably in the area of Black arts that the Arts and Recreation Committee's social engineering strategy worked most successfully. (Bianchini 1987, p.109)

It is clear from the objectives laid out by political activists such as Tomkins that the arts were to be used by the GLC to maximum political effect across the left's agenda for social change, and black practitioners took full advantage of this unique opportunity. Most importantly, however, the astute among the black artists and activists began to understand the politics in arts funding. As a strategy to gain access to funding a simple equation was employed: if 4 per cent of the population in the 1980s were labelled 'ethnic' then surely those 'ethnic subjects' had the right to at least 4 per cent of the nation's arts funding budgets.

THE FIRST WAVE

The first wave of what can now be described as a form of black photographic resistance work is evident in the photographs produced by a generation of mostly self-taught black British, Caribbean-born, male photographers who had grown up in metropolitan cities in the 1950s. The most prominent of these were the London-based Armet Francis, Neil Kenlock and Charlie Phillips. Their collective retrospective exhibition titled *Roots to Reckoning*, held at the Museum of London in 2005, consolidated their historical significance in the city's photographic history. This was further evidenced when the organisers of the exhibition dramatically stated in the catalogue that 'if the black British community can be said to have a soul, these images are a reflection of what it is' (Philips 2005, p.4). It was naively romantic in 2005 for the organisers to argue that Francis, Kenlock, Phillips or indeed any other photographer is capable of reflecting the soul of an individual or a whole community through their photography. Further, their work excludes the important regional differences that make up the black British presence. However, such inflated statements are often induced by a sense of nostalgia that is generated by these types of exhibitions, wherein a community is retrospectively re-imagined to be wholly and definitively representable through the frames of the documentary photograph. This community re-imaging work may well be because, historically, these communities have been denied the opportunities and the spaces through which they can visually render themselves. However, when these moments of exchange are offered through a museum, the work is in danger of becoming fixed and susceptible to a programming and contextualising process that locks the work within the 'steel pan syndrome' (McGuigan 1996, p.137), meaning that it is reduced in spectacle to a mini carnival experience.

What can be claimed, however, regarding these three photographers' working methods, is that, during the 1970s and early 1980s in London's black communities, they sought to take responsibility for recording accurately the different forms of social pressures under which these communities existed, such as inadequate housing, disproportionate unemployment and aggressive policing. They independently made important photographic, often quiet, records of black people's presences in the UK, the results of which now constitute collectively a rare archive, with intimacy at its heart. Intimacy in these photographers' works is important. For them, the houses, churches and public houses that they attended were part of their own, personal social make-up.

Crucially, if we look through these three bodies of work, we can see clearly that as documentary photographers Francis, Kenlock and Phillips collectively rejected making work through the prism of racial conflict, nor did they draw out clichéd moments of alterity when photographing the black subject. Their contribution within the field of black representation effectively comes from a place of cultural familiarity, affinity and reflection. They aimed to be at the service of their community rather than simply observers of it. They were separately but simultaneously documenting the black subject, trying to capture tenderly, through photography, the unobtainable essence of black Britain's humanity. They were attempting to create a new image of black life that would work to reframe their communities' affectionately and make these communities visible on the terms of their own individual perspectives or ideas of what constituted a black life.

In practice, these communities were, to some degree, romanticised through photographs. People are shown, for example, in their Sunday-best clothes, or at work, smiling at the camera, masking the realities of their hardships through a willingness to participate in the recording of their lives. On reflection, within this type of essentialist documentary focus it is evident that a rather conservative construction of a homogenous black subject is at work. So, for example, across this generation of photographers' works the more transgressive, queer or counter-cultural side of black cultural life in London is absent. Roles within these communities are defined along nuclear and normative family lines, with the result that the photographic archive of black life in London becomes a very straight, traditional and patriarchal affair. Nonetheless, without their intervention that straight, black, patriarchal image would also be absent. The photographs produced in this period, then, served not only as an expression of black life from within, but also worked as a way of presenting black life in forms in which 'normal' white society might also recognise themselves. When read in this capacity, the photographs can be seen as producing a visual dynamic that offers parity of experience. By making visible shared social narratives, such as weddings and funerals, to a white British public, the photographs open up the possibility for a greater sense of empathy and connectivity to the black strangers in their midst.

What Francis, Kenlock and Phillips shared as photographers was primarily the desire to represent and record the missing stories of what they deemed to be 'normal' daily black London life. These social gatherings – weddings and funerals, but also attending church and going to parties, family gatherings and carnivals – during the 1970s and early 1980s, were central to their focus as photographers, as were the moments of black celebrity, fashion shows and protest. This kind of reportage and positive image affirmation work drew attention from audiences within the communities they portrayed. The photographs were often exhibited within local, community-orientated spaces that were supported by small amounts of local authority funding, drip-fed to practitioners from diminishing budgets. Libraries, town halls and foyers of civic centres were primary places of encounter for their audiences, with wider distribution for the work being rarely achieved beyond these points of display.

The recognition on a local level that this type of work received should not be underestimated, however, as it represents a radical turn in race and image translation. The early 1970s in particular marked a low point in media representations of black communities, as a wave of hysteria was generated across the nation concerning rising crime rates among black youths and incidents of violent muggings (S. Hall 1978). As a result, black youths were widely regarded as a dangerous criminal element, terrorising white society. The new wave of image-making facilitated by the availability of public funding is important, because in many instances black people could see their own lives framed for the first time in these photographs, in a way with which they could identify in a positive light. At the moment of their photographic making, the critical and aesthetic qualities of the work are not a primary concern; the radical nature that underpins their aesthetic fault-lines is the fact that these photographers picked up a camera and acted to arrest the waves of negative images that bombarded black British communities.

The work produced by practitioners such as Armet Francis belongs to a radical form of engagement, an engagement that works on its black audience through a form of aesthesis. In this context, the (B)lack British photographer must be seen as a uniquely insightful chronicler of black people's experiences. In discussing the act of taking a photograph from within the places and spaces defined as 'the black community', the core theoretical dialectic at work was whether the epidermal schema of the photographer made a difference to the making and reception of the work. The preferred politically-correct answer during the late 1970s and early 1980s was an essentialist and defining 'yes'.

Vanley Burke, the Birmingham-based photographer who is of the same generation as Francis, Kenlock and Phillips, claims that his work is a form of 'histograph':

> A histograph, capturing the personal, social and economic life of black people as they arrived, settled and became established in British society ... The 'histograph' metaphor makes the camera and the photographer appear to be a sensitive recording machine, making a template to the life being lived in black communities. It throws the emphasis away from the photographing process itself – the practice of representation which the photograph always represents – onto the photographed subject. It is the people and their lives, it seems to be saying which are important. (S. Hall 1993, p.13)

This mode of positive template-imaging photographic practice was typical of the work that attracted support from the GLC. This is illustrated most effectively by one of the last photographic exhibitions that the GLC supported in 1986, which opened just a few days before the GLC itself was finally shut down by Margaret Thatcher's government. The exhibition was shown at the Brixton Art Gallery and was titled *Reflections of the Black Experience*. It showed the works of nine photographers operating across the documentary tradition: Marc Boothe, Vanley Burke, Sunil Gupta, Mumtaz Karimjee, Dave Lewis, Zak Ove, Ingrid Pollard, Suzanne

Roden and Madahi Sharak. The exhibition also included a tribute to Armet Francis with a modest selection of his work. His presence marked a generational gap as he was cast as an established and authoritative black photographer. In 1983, Francis had had a solo exhibition at the Photographers' Gallery in London and had self-published his book titled *The Black Triangle: the People of the African Diaspora* in 1985. These two events marked him as the most significant black photographer working within the UK during the 1980s.

The key organiser of the Brixton Art Gallery exhibition was Monika Baker and in the accompanying publication she stated:

> We are proud to present the specially commissioned works of nine black photographers, as part of the GLC Race Equality Unit's Black Experience Programme ... *Reflections of the Black Experience* marks a milestone for Black photographers in this country ... The strength of the final work presented was achieved through the sensitivity that comes from an identification with the subject ... It is through the medium of photography that this exhibition has chosen to express the mood of and feeling of black people's presence in contemporary Britain. (Baker 1986, p.5)

The primary act of focus, even within the last few days of the GLC, was to endorse, in the heart of London's black community, a political agenda relating to self-affirmation in the making of images. In reading the work produced for the exhibition, it is clear that the objective was to try to bring a more human face to images of black subjects caught up in the pressures of daily metropolitan life and to highlight the urban spaces they occupied. This project then, via the GLC, was a direct attempt to bring new ways of seeing and understanding to blackness.

On analysis, as documentary moments that reflect black life, the commissions suffer from being far too generic, with no one project being fully developed beyond a series of single images of black people's daily existence. The lack of photographic narration makes it difficult to locate 'the mood of and feeling of black people's presence' in the UK within the works. When compared with the images that the African American photographer Dawoud Bey produced in the

1970s in Harlem, for example, the GLC initiative unfortunately resonates poorly. In discussing his project Bey later stated:

> As I got to know the shopkeepers and others in the neighborhood, I became a permanent fixture at the public events taking place in the community, such as block parties, tent revival meetings, and anyplace else where people gathered. The relationships and exchanges that I had with some of these people are experiences I will never forget. It is in those relationships and the lives of the people that these pictures recall that the deeper meaning of these photographs can be found. (Bey 1979)

However, in the British context and as photographs, the works in the *Reflections of the Black Experience* exhibition are different mainly because they stand outside of, and are away from, the debasing media representations of black subjects that were so prolific here in the 1970s and 1980s. These documentary moments are not made with news media as their primary purpose. No one black person in any of the photographs in the exhibition could be read as constituting a threat. When we look at work of this nature, it is not its formal qualities alone that need to be assessed, it is the social and political world in which they were made that needs to be considered. It is their rawness as images and their early articulations of framing race in this period that mark them as culturally relevant and historically significant. This goes some way to explaining the recent drives from major cultural institutions such the Museum of London and the Victoria and Albert Museum to purchase images with support from the Heritage Lottery Fund from this unique aspect of Britain's photographic history, acknowledging now that these works fill vital missing chapters in their collections, regarding Britain's visual culture.

Reflections of the Black Experience marks the desire for popular and mainstream media representations of blackness to be made something else. In this black photographic moment, the black radical imagination is at work. This type of work suggests a pursuit of an image of blackness that could be made real photographically, theoretically, politically and emotionally, and that should ideally and exclusively be articulated through those black subjects such as Francis, who occupy the physical and psychological space of race. Therefore, the 1980s marked the moment of the arrival of the epidermal schema in photography in Britain where the photographer's cultural identity, as being black, was considered to be a transgressive, political act within the politics of black recognition. This was because taking ownership of the means to re-present blackness back at those in society that negated black presences, was recognised as an empowering and positive step.

There was no privileged decisive moment in black British photography; what was at work was a black photographic call and response that wanted to change the hearts and minds of the nation's people. The British population had been permeated by stereotypical, debasing images of blackness through, for example, popular television shows such as the 'Black and White Minstrel Show', which was seen at its height by up to 18 million viewers a week. The programme was aired on British television from 1958 to 1978 despite several campaigns against it for being racist (Newcomb 2014, p.271). Black photography was a call that was visually aimed at the centre of the nation's psychological state and, in particular, its limbic system; in other words, the work wanted to affect the emotional condition of the nation. But this took place against the backdrop of state-run institutions such as the BBC, which encouraged the public to seek pleasure from ridiculing the image of the black subject. Black photographic work was, in many respects, an early attempt to help people on both sides of the colour line see race holistically differently.

The *studium* (Barthes 1981) at work within the photographic image to which Barthes famously refers – that is, its overall conventionalised meaning – is in black photography created within different racialised zones of experience and encounter. These early black British documentary photographs represent a bold attempt to offer the viewer new perspectives on race, and the opportunity to consider the work that the images carry out from a position where race is not only central to the reading of the photograph but is also central to the making of the photograph. This demands that different criteria be applied to reading the work and that the work is assessed through different cultural codifications from those that traditionally dominate the making and curating of photography.

The critical question here is: how would the *studium* or *punctum* of an image be addressed through the optics of racialised ways of seeing? Early black documentary work is therefore an attempt to find a new language, a subaltern visual presence from within the burden of the old photographic discourses. In those old (and still ongoing) discourses, black cultures have been predominantly framed against a blinding white cultural backdrop, which works pervasively to misrepresent black people and suggests that their lives can only come into existence through the space of whiteness. Historically, the vast range of images that bring black life into focus have been produced by white photographers. Wayne Miller in the 1940s, Bruce Davidson in the 1960s, Eugenie Richards in the 1990s and Pieter Hugo in the 2000s, are among the many ranks of celebrated white photographers who have built their careers on framing black subjects. Burke and his peers' work in this context says more about the quest for black authority and a desire for the impossible condition of authenticity than anything else. What these photographers have been attempting to do, through their documentary work, is to make the black gaze the dominant feature within the framing of the racialised subject. Black documentary photography from this period is, in essence, an offer to share a wider view of marginalised lives, this time authored by the marginalised. This is what was being developed, culturally and politically, through the display and funding of these types of photographic translations or conversations. Therefore, the possibility of a black way of seeing was being constructed, one that disrupted the homogeneity of photography's past and acknowledged that photography in and of itself is not the sole domain of the European eye.

The black gaze is a radical oppositional act that has its location in many different origins associated with power. For example, black slaves were punished for looking too hard at their white owners. How this informed black spectatorship is investigated at length by the scholar bell hooks in *Black Looks: Race and Representation*. Here, hooks reminds us that:

all attempts to repress our/black people's right to gaze had produced in us an overwhelming longing to look, a rebellious desire, an oppositional gaze. By courageously looking, we defiantly declared: 'Not only will I stare. I want my look to change reality'. (hooks 1992, p.116)

Black photographers working with the tradition of the documentary genre looked through their lenses and, as they did so, they believed they would be contributing to changing black people's realities. The GLC was instrumental in creating a framework within which these photographers could come together, facilitating a collective dialogue across the work they were producing. As Sunil Gupta, one of the photographers commissioned to make work for the *Reflections of the Black Experience* exhibition, later stated, 'the process brought a bunch of people together all interested in the idea of black photography. The research [funded by the GLC Race Equality Unit] had unearthed this elusive creature, the black photographer' (Gupta 2007, p.2).

Something 'other' had happened to photography in Britain through the support of left-wing institutions such as the GLC. Something new emerged and came into visibility in the 1980s that had been ignored, overlooked or never imagined. This was the moment when black British people 'enter their own subjectivity … and put themselves in the frame' (S. Hall 1992). As Hall states, entering the 'frame', by which he means engaging with society, visually, culturally and politically, in this case through the act of making a photographic image, has been possible to a degree. However, managing the institutional dialogues and the positionality that determine where the frames of race sit, within the wider cultural-institutional context of British life, has proved to be far more difficult to achieve. Resisting the cultural ghettoisation that informs the ways in which black photographers' works are seen and read is an ongoing process. These historical black images, even when entering the domain of white cultural institutions, appear as reluctant guests within the museum or art gallery, as often they are merely corralled into corners. This was epitomised by a recent small photographic 'display' at the Victoria and Albert Museum, titled *Staying Power: Photographs of Black British Experience 1950s-1990s* and described as 'a project to increase the number of black British photographers and images of black Britain in the V&A collection. It aims to raise awareness of the contribution of black Britons to

British culture and society, as well as to the art of photography' (Victoria and Albert Museum 2013). This project was produced in 'partnership' with the Black Cultural Archives and the fact that it was not staged until 2015, nearly thirty years after the GLC's final photographic initiative, illustrates the depth of cultural time-lag at work concerning black photographic practices within the state's archives.

ENTERING THE FRAME

The theoretical work produced by academics such as Stuart Hall and Kobena Mercer, coupled with the visual work of black photographers and artists, challenged the dominant ideologies and distribution networks that produced the knowledge and popular cultural frames of meaning, which made up the problematic image of the racialised British subject. This work opened up the conditions of black existence and demystified the representational fields of their reception and the power structures that disenfranchised black lives. Both in theory and in images, this political work comes together to create a new epistemic front that challenged the history of the racially inscribed black body. It is important that this challenge to the racial insignia on the black body was recognised through the visual. In one of his key emotive speeches delivered in 1986 at the launch of the GLC's 'Black Experiences' programme at the Commonwealth Institute, London, Stuart Hall addressed the politics of race, culture and their relationship to state funding:

> We [black migrants] are here to stay. We are the centre of creative cultural life of this society and we require the jobs, the training, the opportunities [and] the funding. We want the path open, especially for the young black people of this society who have created in their myriad art forms – writing, poetry, dance music, right through to rap – a new culture which in its variety and power astonishes now the eyes of young white people. It is a mark, a sign, that they are the people of the future. (S. Hall 2012)

This theoretical and visual race work was grounded in the recognition that post-war:

black experiences in British culture [were] not fortuitously occurring at the margins [of society], but placed, positioned at the
margins, as the consequence of a set of quite specific political and
cultural practices which regulated, governed and "normalized"
the representational and discursive spaces of English society.
(S. Hall 1992, p.252)

Therefore, especially in the 1980s, the 'issue of black [British]
cultural identity, based on the deconstruction of established
stereotypes, presents itself as one of the most serious problems in
the definition and defence of black identity' (Sarikaya 2011, p.165).
The phenomenon or idea of black British photography as a kind of
'shooting back' was effectively forged within the heat and tension of
the contested social formations surrounding the politics of race and
the nation state that characterised the 1980s.

As the 1980s progressed, a typical example of the contestations
over this difficult political and cultural terrain, which were
unfolding within photography in Britain, was the verbal mauling by
black delegates that the feminist photographer Jo Spence received in
1987 at the National Photography Conference, in Salford, Greater
Manchester. This was the city in which, just a year before, a thirteen-
year-old Bangladeshi boy named Ahmed Iqbal Ullah was stabbed to
death in the school playground by a white pupil.

After Spence's keynote speech titled 'Questioning Documentary
Practice? The Sign as a Site of Struggle', arguments within the
conference raged. She had infuriated some of the black delegates
by not addressing the question of race. George Shire, a young
Zimbabwean scholar, led the outrage that split the conference for
the rest of its duration along the lines of gender and race. According
to Sunil Gupta, a photographer and gay activist who was present at
the event, Spence had 'skirted around the issues of race and there
was an uproar, she finally left the conference'. Gupta puts the politics
at work during the conference into a wider context when he states
that, 'in retrospect, those were also the days when folks were pretty
territorial about work, women did women and blacks did blacks etc'
(Gupta 2015). It was at this conference in Salford, funded by the
Arts Council of Great Britain, that black British photographers came
politically into full view on the national stage of photography for the

first time. The year 1987 therefore marks a critical turning point for the question of race and photographic practices in Britain: a turn that the funding bodies present at the conference had to recognise as a growing and vocal presence that was demanding, militant and not easily appeased – even within its own body politic, which was itself also fragile and fractured. After the conference, several of those present were invited to the Arts Council of Great Britain's offices in London to discuss future state funding possibilities for black British photographers. It was at the invitation of the state that black British photography moved out of the local and into the national cultural field, with the Arts Council attempting to pick up on some of the social engineering the GLC had seeded.

1987 also saw another opening of an important group exhibition of young black British photographers. It was a touring exhibition, first shown at the Ikon gallery in Birmingham in July and August under the title *D-Max*. It then travelled to the Photographers' Gallery in London in January 1988. The exhibition included the works of David A. Bailey, Marc Boothe, Gilbert John, David Lewis, Zak Ove and Ingrid Pollard, all of whom, at that time, were working at the edges of documentary practices. Also, as they were all based in London, they were aware of the cultural debates and economic initiatives behind the production of a new black aesthetic, which had previously been at work through the GLC (four of them had taken part in the *Reflections of the Black Experience* exhibition).

D-Max was curated by Eddie Chambers, who stated in the introduction text that accompanied the exhibition that, 'In terms of aesthetics, our second objective is to contribute to the development of something which could be referred to as a black aesthetics in British photography' (Araeen & Chambers 1988, p.69). The new black British aesthetic that was being generated throughout this exhibition was a clear echo of what had been articulated by the GLC. However, the concept of a black aesthetic within photographic practice was easier to claim than to actually theoretically identify, especially through the form of documentary works. In a tetchy and important exchange between the artist and activist Rasheed Araeen and Eddie Chambers for *Third Text* journal in 1988, we witness the critical fragility of such a notion. On discussing black aesthetics with Chambers, Araeen states that:

the ambition to create black aesthetics is of course laudable, and I'm very interested in the idea of a new visual language with its own distinguishable features. But I'm still not clear what it is. I know what it is in relation to jazz, but when I look at those contemporary art works which claim to be concerned with black aesthetics, I don't find anything there which could convince me of its presence or development ... My understanding had been that these photographs had been selected and legitimized as 'Black Photography' not only because they were taken by black photographers but also their contents were about black life or experiences. It seems common sense to say that in the end we will have to look at the work, whatever it is meant to be about or say ... What worries me, personally, is that we are making claims on a basis which does not yet exist and we would perhaps end up promoting mediocre works – which is not an unusual situation in the black arts scene today. And to tell you the truth, I was very disappointed by the *D-Max* exhibition. It's time we pay some attention to the question of quality. (Araeen & Chambers 1988, p.69)

The black aesthetic as far as Araeen was concerned had not yet arrived within photography. In the exchange between the artist and the curator we witness the opening of a major and unresolved critical fault-line in the articulation of race and photographic practices. Araeen, in his challenge to Chambers, is primarily concerned with issues of quality within the actual photographic work. He is clearly 'disappointed' that some of the works have not engaged with what he constitutes as quality, and he cannot locate a definable black aesthetic in the work.

However, Araeen failed to recognise that one of the major critiques of (B)lack photographic work was that it was too didactic in nature. The *D-Max* exhibition attempted to free the black photographer from the burden of representation but at the same time allow the question of race to be present within the work. *D-Max* was effectively a break with the first generation of black photographers, by viewing blackness as being polysemic and fluid in nature. This, however, created tension within the positioning of black photographic works among black practitioners. Some, for example Dave Lewis and Franklyn Rodgers, became unanchored from the documentary genre and the cultural expectations concerning positive representations of race, opening a critical fault-line in attitudes within black photographic practices. One side of the fault-line claimed responsibility for representation in the comfort of a black essentialist paradigm, the other desired to be free from representational burdens. As Tanya Barson points out, it is evident when we look back that 'feminists and black artists and filmmakers during ... [the] 1980s used, and frequently subverted, documentary modes and conventions in order to address, respectively, the role of women in society and the construction of a multicultural image of Britain' (Barson 2006, p.17). Barson is correct in her analysis of the strategies of subversion in respective documentary practices, but what linked these practices together across the politics of their individual difference was not so much a readable aesthetic but a shared contempt for the ideologies of social exclusion epitomised through Thatcherism. What unified people who had been relegated to the margins of society was an equally complex deep desire to enter 'the domain of representation' (S. Hall 1992).

THE AUTO-PORTRAIT

> Photographic practices are always historically specific, they belong to particular conjunctures. Black self-portraiture, in this historical moment, has broken many of its links with the dominant 'western' humanist celebration of self and has become more the staking of a claim, a wager. Here, the black self-image is, in a double sense, an exposure, a coming out. The self is caught emerging. (S. Hall 1990, p. 3)

It is evident within Britain's photographic history that the 1980s represented a seismic shift in the cultural landscapes of photography politics, race and representation. It is a narrative that is well encapsulated in the last edition of Birmingham-based, Arts Council of England-funded photo-journal *Ten 8*, published in 1992, titled 'Critical Decade: Black British Photography in the 80s'. The introduction to the magazine was written by Stuart Hall and states that the editors intended the reader to gain:

a clear understanding of the complex debates which have taken place ... [and understand that] the photographers and writers [published in this edition] offer an insight into a range of key issues, [such as] the meaning of blackness, gender and sexuality in a discourse of racial difference, the role of racial representations in popular culture, documentary and its relation to realism and authority, [and] the politics of the constructed image. Set against a background of debates around post colonial theory and its critical questions of hybridity, marginalisation essence and identity, Critical Decade seeks to provide the ground for new critical responses in the 1990s. (S. Hall 1992, p.4)

The editors' intentions are clearly complex. When read now, they can be seen as an attempt to present a strong theoretical hand of different discursive tools, offering the early-1990s reader of photography politics an opportunity to engage culturally with a different kind of photographic discourse. That discourse represented a chance to interrogate the space of visual marginality and to examine the recent role photography had played across the critical space of identity politics, particularly when we consider the legacy of colonial encounters inherent within the grand narratives that surround the making of photography's history. What is essentially and uniquely on offer in these few pages of *Ten 8*, is an ideological place in which to reflect on the myriad different voices that are absent or ghosted from the narration and making of photography. The publication represents a small example of the difficult cultural turning points that occurred within a decade of turns, which collectively added up to a series of complex but incisive cultural incursions into the hegemonic body politic of British photography and its cultural institutions. It is an undeniable fact that, by the end of the 1980s, very few people working within cultural institutions and managing photographic collections were aware of the work being produced by black photographers and artists based in Britain. This issue of *Ten 8* aimed to address that lack of knowledge in the field of photography.

The ideas presented in the *Ten 8* editorial crashed theoretically and directly into the master narratives that comprised the established canon surrounding photography in Britain. In this form of politically conscious photographic and theoretical work, there was the possibility and recognition of new, racially charged heterogeneous photographic moments that were emerging forcefully from the margins and disrupting the institutional centre by making race in photography a major issue. Black photography in this racialised condition is a productive and radical moment, which visually moves the question of race onto and into the wider socio-political cultural field. The act of picking up the camera from within a condition of oppression becomes an act of transgressive liberation, almost as important as the making of the photograph itself, because it creates the possibility for something new to be seen, something different to emerge.

The 1980s uniquely signify the formation of a new photographic epistemology concerning race and photographic practice in Britain. The pages of *Ten 8* marked the signs of a cultural rupture across the 'normal' flow of images that relate to the cultural business and image exchanges that have historically and temporally fixed black subjects in spaces that are not of their own photographic making. In considering the surrounding politics and ideology of photography's dominant histories, we can begin to recognise through *Ten 8* the signs that point towards the end of a white monocultural perspective on photography in Britain, and the uncoupling of how its black subjects are rendered, framed and articulated from the dominant discourses of the medium.

Typically, this moment of disrupting the old imperial ways of seeing race is articulated through the early photographs produced by Joy Gregory. Her work is reproduced on pages 28 and 29 of this edition of *Ten 8*. Gregory's series titled 'Autoportraits 1989-1990' was shown at Camerawork in the East End of London for the first time in 1990 (Figure 22). This series of nine separate multiple selves was produced as a direct response to the lack of visibility of black women in popular culture, and in particular within the fashion industry. This radical intervention into how black women have been historically framed offered a direct challenge to the reader to locate the 'real' black woman subject as she moves cinematically through the frames of her own auto-photographic moment. As a subject, Gregory occupies different locations within the actual photographic frame; it is as if she is physically and temporally moving through the laboured positionality of the camera's long, historical, racist resting place. It is an act stating that she refuses to be fixed as a subject. Gregory slides across the frame, entering it and presenting herself to it however she so chooses. The making of the self-portrait here is a mark of control that extends across the actual exposure and focal length of the photographic moment.

This auto-photographic moment also marks, for Gregory, the end of absence and pacificity. This is done in what appears to be a double act of playfulness and challenge. Nothing in this work is stable. The reading is uncertain because it is Gregory who controls the camera and the junctures of release and capture. She is simultaneously in your face while covering hers. Her eyes, lips, ears and hair, as well as hands, which in one of the frames cover her face, all play a central role in the abstracted notion of the multiple framed selves that she presents to the camera. Within this sequence of images it is as much the object of the camera as a mechanism for recording that comes under scrutiny, as the subject that is positioned in front of its lens. The subtle interchange between the subject as photographer and camera as recorder becomes confused for the reader because these images lead ultimately to a subversion of the traditional role that the black woman plays within photography. As representations, these images become markers of the individual survival strategies employed by the photographer to disrupt the indexicality of the photographic medium. The subject in this 'Autoportrait' series wilfully refuses, in an unruly but playful manner, to behave in front of the cameras lens. What is ruptured formally here is the unspoken conservative code that demands the subject is positioned centrally when presented in front of the camera, and the visual comfort that this offers.

This photography breaks the orthodoxies of anthropology and fashion photography. In the making of a single portrait through a series of nine fragmented works, all the traditional rules of photography portraiture are subverted. Therefore, as photographs they are a politically and culturally defiant act; they place the questions of gender and race centre stage in the contested field of representational politics in the 1990s. They break with tradition, as nothing of what is presented within the sequence of images offers the reader the chance to settle on the idea of a definitive black woman. Within this unsettling process, the viewer's subject position is 'under threat' (Burgin 1982, p.150). This photographic work invites the viewer to consider and deconstruct the actual act of seeing the black woman. Gregory consciously 'deconstructed [the self, in order to produce] a conception of seeing [gender and race] as a site of work' (Tagg 1989, p.23).

ENTER 'ESU' (THE TRICKSTER IN BRIXTON)

At the vanguard of these marginalised and newly forming anti-essentialist and reconstructive photographic practices within the UK was the Nigerian, gay, Brixton-based photographer Rotimi Fani-Kayode. Fani-Kayode was born in Lagos, Nigeria, in 1955. After the military coup of 1966, the Kayode family moved to the UK. Fani-Kayode went on to study at Georgetown University, Washington, DC, and the Pratt Institute, New York, where he completed an MA in Fine Art/Photography in 1983. He returned to the UK that same year (Bishton 1991). He emerged from his studies as an openly gay African photographer; his work was charged with hybrid visual motifs that positioned the black male body as a central figure in transgressive moments of desire, fantasy and memory. These images were infused with imaginative visualisations of Yoruba deities, constructed within frames of deep saturated colour or dense black and white photographic tones, and they announced a new moment in representations of the black male body. To fully understand this work, one would need to access a different epistemological sphere of reference, because they lie outside the usual discourses of Western photography. Rotimi Fani-Kayode's work is produced within the ideology of 'the diasporic attitude [that] often finds itself compelled to look back to something – a ground, a beginning – which may never have existed, exist only in remembered form or is now embedded in fantasy, memory, or desire' (Hall & Sealy 2001, p.42). The black men in his frames perform difference both theatrically and culturally, and he stages constructions that enquire into the nature of desire, fantasy and ecstasy. Fani-Kayode wanted to position the black male subject beyond being an object of Eurocentric enquiry; he offers the black male nude as the key to unlock a different set of African cultural codes. Fani-Kayode's black male bodies are not translocated out of their racialised reality and placed in a studio to become a mere backdrop to someone else's visual story, real or imagined. These bodies are active agents that seek 'to emulate the "technique of ecstasy" of Yoruba priests' (Doy 2000, p.157). As images they become a direct conversation with the Orisha.

Fani-Kayode's photograph titled *Golden Phallus*, taken sometime around 1988-89, helps with decoding the transgressive qualities of his project (Figure 23). Within the image, an athletic-looking black man is seen seated. He is positioned as if he is about to rise from his pose. The distribution of his weight passing through the right side of his body provides the resistance required for the muscular torso to become active. The subject wears a bright white *commedia dell'arte* mask that has a long pointed protruding nose. The mask emphasises his rich deep brown skin and critically the fact that this moment is symbolically not real: it is an enactment, a moment of a masquerade. The tone of his skin is almost perfectly matched in the lighting used for the backdrop in which he is framed. This merging of the backdrop with the sitter's skin colour flattens the space in which we read his body and creates an ambiguous warm but dark Rubensesque non-place, in which the figure is lavishly located. The figure is literally stripped of any signs of modernity and time. The skin-toned backdrop used by Fani-Kayode allows the majority of the subject's body to be present but not overly dominant in the frame. He is simultaneously from the dark, merging out of the dark and comfortable in the dark. It is as if we are in an unconscious visual register of race and desire. The subject looks directly back at the viewer from behind his white mask, directly referencing the psychological work of Frantz Fanon in his book *Black Skin, White Masks*, in which he 'investigates the way in which black men, in particular, internalize myths of blackness invented by the colonial society and damage their psyche in the process' (Doy 2000, p.158). Critically, through the presentation of the white mask, the work becomes a grotesque reflection of whiteness and desire. The mask presented as an object through which to look becomes both a shield and a mirror that reflects back a caricatured, racialised and distorted Eurocentric gaze.

The golden phallus referred to in the title of the work is the penis of the seated subject, painted gold. His penis is suspended by a white cord that runs diagonally down the frame, left to right, under his penis and over his knee. His right hand is out of view but from the position of the cord and of his arm we can deduce that he is holding the cord in his left hand, which is just glimpsed in the photograph. The weight of his penis could therefore be lowered or raised at will by the subject's movement of the string. It is positioned as neither fully erect nor fully flaccid; it protrudes at a 45-degree angle from his body. The golden phallus hanging here by a white thread becomes representative of the trickster Yoruba god Esu. The trick here is in allowing the viewer to reduce the image of the black man to that of his penis but at the same time reminding the viewer of the workings of the veil of race at play within this exchange, through the symbolic use of the mask. Kobena Mercer and Fani-Kayode himself both write that his work is immersed in Yoruba traditions and that within this photograph Esu is indeed represented. Esu 'is the Trickster, the lord of the crossroads, sometimes changing the sign posts to lead you astray' (Fani-Kayode et al. 1996, p.119). Therefore, nothing within this photograph can be read at face value, and its radical nature is formed through being an invitation and a wager to see the world of black masculinity through the prism of a different cosmos. The golden glow of the subject's penis lights up everything within the frame. It exposes the phallocentric obsessions ingrained in racial myths concerning the black male body, and it playfully constructs the penis as a drawbridge to a new place, perhaps hinting that in this different world desire and fantasy can roam freely, unfixed from the burden of culture and history, and hinting at an uncharted terrain of ecstasy.

Fani-Kayode's work is progressive in nature, hybrid in construction and thoroughly Yoruba in creation. It is made in a world that is inherently and ideologically different. Maybe it is here, within the photographs of Fani-Kayode, that we can begin to see or read the black or African aesthetic at work that Rasheed Araeen found so difficult to locate in the documentary photographs of black artists. Fani-Kayode's cultural heritage ran deep, and his family were rooted in Yoruba culture; towards the end of his life this became the bedrock of his practice and symbolised a return from a diasporic place. In his work, though far away from his family and home, he is able to stay located and connected to his place of origin. Fani-Kayode's family holds the ancestral title Akire, and they are the keepers of the Shrine of Yoruba Deities and Priests of Ife. The Yoruba-isation of making photography was the critical point at which Fani-Kayode was able to enter into a process of self-fashioning. This ultimately created the conditions in which he could expose the constructed nature of identities, discover himself and, by extension, the world around him:

> In his artistic project he found the freedom to use the complexity of his experience as a resource with which to embark upon a journey into emotional states of being where it is hard to tell where sexuality ends and where spirituality begins. What he brought back from his travels into such nocturnal spaces are glimpses into a world illuminated by the ancient enigma of something so violent, so marvellous and so tragic as to be un-representable: the human experience of ecstasy. (Mercer 1996, p.108)

Within his work we can read the announcement of something distinctively new within photography; this was a moment when black African gay imagination is made visible. It is an articulation of a hybrid identity that builds race, migration, sexuality and indigenous religion into a complex form of photographic staging.

The complex nature of Fani-Kayode's work and its potential to be read primarily through its homoerotic currents would have carried with it a stigma, especially for his middle-class exiled family living in London. Though different in degrees of acceptance of gay life, neither London nor Lagos was an easy environment in which to discuss or display different masculinities or desires publicly in the 1980s. Fani-Kayode stated that, 'As for Africa itself, if I ever managed to get an exhibition in, say, Lagos, I suspect riots would break out. I would certainly be charged with being a purveyor of corrupt and decadent Western values' (Fani-Kayode 1992, p.70).

Even today, more than twenty-five years after the publication of his 1988 essay titled 'Traces of Ecstasy', and with Lagos now recognised as a throbbing Afropolitan city, it would be almost impossible to stage an exhibition of Fani-Kayode's photographs there. Perhaps this marginalisation created a wider sense of dislocation for Fani-Kayode, which may have pushed him deeper and deeper into new transgressive, imaginative and spiritual paradigms in his photographic work. Ironically, much of this work was produced within the tight confines of his small one-bedroom housing association flat on Railton Road in Brixton, which he shared with his white partner, Alex Hirst. As a flat transformed into a studio, his home became a space of limitless horizons for his photographic work, where a new cosmos could be imagined. It was also an ambitious undertaking in the mid-1980s to engage Western conservative galleries with this particular form of 'African' photography; it was simply too early for it to be recognised by the cultural gate-keepers of the time. This was distinctively new work, and few in positions of authority had the capacity to decode or unlock its points of reference beyond false or simplistic comparisons to Robert Mapplethorpe's phallocentric images of black male nudes, which had caused a wave of criticism and debate from black critics in 1983 when they were shown at the Institute of Contemporary Arts in London. This criticism tended to fix Mapplethorpe's work within what Hall describes as the 'tropes of fetishization [and] fragmentation of the black image' (S. Hall 1992, p.256), and negated the difficult question of gay desire within black identity politics into which Fani-Kayode enquired.

Railton Road in Brixton was not only Fani-Kayode's home, it was also a frontline for riots in 1981 and 1985. The critical journal *Race Today* was also located here, and it was where the historian and journalist C.L.R. James lived until his death in 1989. Fani-Kayode's local environment was one of the most politicised and policed areas in Britain as far as race was concerned. His sense of being an outsider in this radical black British space and beyond is evident from his own words in 'Traces of Ecstasy': 'On three counts I am an outsider: in terms of sexuality; in terms of geographical and cultural dislocation; and in the sense of not having become the sort of respectably married professional my parents might have hoped for' (Fani-Kayode, 1992, p.64). He was aware both of the external and internal pressures in what constituted the traditional representational fields of the 'black experience' in Britain and beyond, and what it meant to be a black, gay, African man in exile politically, sexually and artistically. Being an outsider 'on three counts' suggests he fitted in nowhere, but we might consider that, to some degree, this may well have released him from the burdens of black representational politics that were grounded in the theories of 'us an dem' (Chambers 1994), and from the responsibility of his Yoruba traditional family heritage.

> While many were beguiled by the multiple adjectives that sought to name his identity – a modern African artist, a metropolitan black gay man, a key figure in Black British photography, the irony is that Rotimi's life and work were never about the comforts or security of mere identity. (Mercer 1996, p.109)

When we read Fani-Kayode's work through the prism of Hall's 1988 essay titled 'New Ethnicities', we can recognise that what it did was bring:

> to the surface the unwelcome fact that a great deal of black politics, constructed, addressed and developed directly in relation to questions of race and ethnicity, has been predicated on the assumption that the categories of gender and sexuality would stay the same, remain fixed and secured. (S. Hall 1992, p. 256)

We could also add to Hall's statement here that, until the emergence of Fani-Kayode, the majority of black photographers working in Britain prior to the 1980s were concerned mainly with and subscribed to the idea of a documentary truth, which was wedded to the notion of recording, through photography, a 'real' life rather than imagining a different narrative. By the late 1980s, Fani-Kayode's work was at the forefront of blowing apart the stereotypical image of the black male body. He resisted categorisation and labelling on a least two fronts. Firstly, he resisted a traditional black political narrative that focused on a counter-perspective of the black subject and functioned primarily as a direct response and rebuff to the tide of negative imagery produced throughout the history of Western photography, which was continuously pulling the black subject into focus as a mere simpleton wherever his location may be. And secondly, Fani-Kayode also resisted being cast as an essential African subject. Critically, then, Kayode's work operated as a direct challenge to the established idea that the essential black male subject existed, and through his work we can begin to unpick the threads of that mythical construction from both within and outside of black cultural politics.

Rotimi Fani-Kayode's untimely death in 1989 meant that he did not enjoy the accolades he was soon to receive throughout the 1990s. If the 1980s signalled the arrival of the black British postmodernist photographer in the guise of Joy Gregory, Rotimi Fani-Kayode, Sunil Gupta and many others, then the 1990s can be defined as the 'definitive decade' that introduced the contemporary African photographer to the mainstream, Western art world. It would be the period in which the African photographer would emerge as a significant new 'discovery' within the theatre of Western photography, and in which African photography would break free from the condition of Eurocentric mimesis. The 1990s can therefore be read as the decade that permanently changed the epistemologies of photography and fine art. The 1990s tilted enquiries into the discourses of photography towards the south, with African practitioners such as Rotimi Fani-Kayode being recognised for entering the field of the visual through forging new possibilities with the camera. However, it was not Lagos that provided the catalyst for a different type of enquiry into the black subject; it was Bamako.

THE BAMAKO TWO-STEP

In the summer of 1991, two of New York's cultural institutions – the Museum of African Art and The New Museum – co-organised an exhibition titled *Africa Explores: 20th Century African Art*. It was organised by Susan Vogel who was then the executive director of the Museum of African Art. The exhibition's stated aims were to 'focus on Africa, its concerns, and its art and artists in their own contexts and in their own voices' (Museum for African Art and New Museum 1991). The event was relatively well reviewed in the mainstream press. For example, the *New York Times* art critic Michael Brenson wrote that, 'As a result of this show all contemporary African art in New York will make sense in a new way' (Brenson 1991). According to the *New York Times* this exhibition was transformative.

The exhibition clearly followed in the curatorial footsteps of the producers of *The Magicians of the Earth*, which was staged in Paris in 1989. Controversially, non-European contemporary artists from across the globe were invited to show their work in this latter exhibition, alongside that of European and North American artists for the first time, across two significant cultural spaces: the Georges Pompidou Centre and the Grande Halle de la Villete. The curator and main architect of *The Magicians of the Earth* was the now-celebrated Jean-Hubert Martin, and he was assisted by Mark Francis, Aline Luque and André Magnin. Magnin's research for the exhibition mainly took place in Africa. He chose to work there for personal reasons that went back to his childhood, and he states that his 'travels through the end of 1988 took [him] just about everywhere in Africa' (Magnin n.d.). However, while travelling extensively and carrying out his research, Magnin had crucially not visited the old French colony now known as Mali.

On show in New York as part of the *Africa Explores: 20th Century African Art* exhibition was a series of small photographs in various styles and formats and from different African locations, which were all captioned as being taken by 'unknown photographers'. Three of the photographs were studio portraits, approximately 18x13cm in size, and credited as being taken in the 1950s in Bamako, Mali. The first photograph shows a young couple posing in a studio, the second is a portrait of a young man dressed half-way between European styling and traditional African clothes, as if on arrival at the studio he decided to don a jacket, hat and shoes from the props closet of the photographer. The third photograph is a portrait of two young men. They wear traditional long white robes and short fez-style hats and both proudly display their watches and hold small rings of beads entwined between their fingers. The men appear to be clutching white documents close to their bodies, which are hardly visible against the brilliant white robes that they are wearing. They appear to have entered the studio to mark a form of graduation. Apart from their difference in size they almost perfectly mirror each other in clothing and pose.

The captions for the three photographs from Bamako inform the reader that they are silver prints made in 1974 from original negatives and are on loan from a private collection. As a small group reproduced on the pages of the catalogue for the exhibition, these photographs stand out from the rest both in terms of quality and composition. The first is by far the most accomplished image technically. From the tight composition, it is not immediately evident that it is in fact a studio portrait, but the lighting and formal composition suggest that the photographer is skilled in his craft. The black skin tones of the sitters resonate with detail. The young man wears a pinstripe jacket over a white shirt, while the woman wears a fitted dress with a floral design and frilly neckline. The backdrop is a floral, William Morris-type design. The couple present themselves stylishly for the camera, and are photographed posing with their faces cheek to cheek. The man's body is mostly obscured as he is positioned behind the woman with his hand resting gently on her hip. Their intimacy is relayed further by the fact that the woman has lowered the left-hand shoulder of her dress in a gesture of self-confidence and assertive sexuality, reinforced by the inquisitive expression on her face. Her eyes convey a slight degree of hostility. The naked shoulder can be read as a seductive invitation to her intended audience, but the look in her eyes ultimately acts as a visual counter-narrative to the message delivered by the off-the-shoulder dress. Her pose can be read as a forward and transgressive act, especially if we consider the religious and cultural position of women in 1950s polygamous Bamako. She wears an array of accessories: necklaces, earrings and a headscarf. They are modern in design and may well be fashionable objects. She is identified here as a modern 'Bamakois' (Diawara 1998).

The expression on the young man's face is one of enthusiasm for the camera and his eyes are alert to the photographic encounter. He seems to project an aura of innocence, through his enthusiastic gaze and his gentle touch of the woman's hip; he may be slightly intimidated by the moment. His gesture and look contradict the woman's edgy suggestion of arrogance, and there appears to be tension in the relationship between them. Where she is a powerful, confident woman, he seems overly youthful and boyish. This tension between the different expressions on the couple's faces and the physicality of their exchange carries a visual charge. The way she presents herself to the camera transforms the woman into a modern African subject representing a powerful confidence and strong sexuality that eclipse the boyish man. As a photograph now dislocated from its place of origin and its intended original purpose, it has the capacity to be read as a metaphorical prologue for Malian independence and youthful liberation. As a visual sign, it acts as a rejection of the weighty conditions of colonisation that rendered the African subject childlike and of indigenous religious custom that hindered women's progress.

Given Magnin's specialism in African art and his extensive travels across Africa in researching *The Magicians of the Earth*, a photograph of this nature and visual quality would clearly have represented an irresistible object that was ripe for further enquiry – especially given that he had not previously visited Mali. At *Africa Explores*, the caption supplied by the curator and the private collector suggests that the original negatives may well still exist and that additional prints may be available to be bought. Crucially, then, these three 'unknown' photographs on display in New York in 1991 proved to be decisive and catalytic factors in the extraction of photography from West Africa and its re-presentation and commodification in Europe and North America. It is these three photographs from Bamako that provided the subsequent impetus for one of Europe's leading curators, André Magnin, working for one of Europe's wealthiest art collectors, Jean Pigozzi, to enquire further into the authorship of the works with the idea of owning them.

During *The Magicians of the Earth* exhibition, Jean Pigozzi met André Magnin and together they founded the C.A.A.C. (Contemporary African Art Collection), commonly known as the Pigozzi Collection, which is based in Geneva. Magnin states that this was done 'at a time when non-western contemporary art was not known and not apprehensible in the international art scene. [By 1991] André Magnin is the C.A.A.C.'s curator and artistic director' (Magnin n.d.). And while visiting the *Africa Explores: 20th Century African Art* exhibition with Pigozzi, Magnin encountered these photographs, which led him to travel to Mali to locate the photographer. Magnin flew to Bamako on 7 March 1992. While staying at the Hotel Tennessee, he employed Taihrou, a local guide, to help him. They drove to Bagadadji, Thirtieth Street, where an as yet undiscovered photographer, Malick Sidibé, recognised the photographer's work and took Magnin directly to Seydou Keita. In a voice that echoes the historical colonial joy of discoveries of potential new products and markets, Magnin recalls his meeting with Keita in classic colonial schoolboy tones: 'Such were the moments of my African photography adventure' (Magnin 1998, p.22).

The encounter between Magnin and Keita marked a decisive moment in Seydou Keita's work, one that pushed his art towards a more complex relationship with the photography world outside of

Bamako. The critical meetings – Pigozzi with Magnin, and Magnin with Keita – created the perfect conditions for the extraction and exploitation of Keita's work. This was the moment of Keita's photographic relocation – the arrival of his work in the West, which, through the agency of Magnin, brought it towards the marketplace – and it was the moment of Keita's photographic dislocation (his work's extraction and 'invention'). The encounter between Magnin and Keita also represented the resignification of Africa and its history within photography, along with its cultural appropriation, as almost 1000 negatives from Keita's studio were taken north from Bamako towards Paris with Magnin. It was during this exchange and journeying that new ideas arose concerning what African photography might be and might become, and it was through the 'discovery' of Keita that these new African works entered the lexicon of the European and North American cultural and commercial megaspaces, such as the Solomon R. Guggenheim Museum.

The frenzy in the West (Rips 2006), and the art market's excitement in the discovery and recognition of Keita's photography, was followed shortly afterwards by a similar enthusiasm for the works of Malick Sidibé and then later still the autoportraits produced by Samuel Fosso, a studio photographer from the Central African Republic. This intense interest positioned these photographers as the dominant photographic presence within the West, when it came to the collecting, promoting and displaying of photography from Africa throughout the 1990s and the early part of the 2000s, in both private and public cultural institutions across Europe and North America. At least for a while, this field of interest eclipsed the political and critical intensity of African documentary photography, which was well established in South Africa and was epitomised by the photographers working for *Drum* magazine in the 1950s and the foundation of the Market Photo Workshop in 1989. This latter project was hugely influential in providing Santu Mofokeng and other black South Africans with their first structured photography education.

A critical point we have to consider when we look at the rise of Keita, Sidibé and Fosso is that, collectively, their works offer a less harrowing view and therefore more palatable perspective on the impact of Europeans in Africa. What South African photographers like Bob Gosani, Peter Mugubane, Ernest Cole and later Santu Mofokeng offer the European viewer, through their work, is a constant reminder of the dark side of European presences on the continent. Their photography emerged primarily from the struggle against the violence of the 1948 Apartheid laws in South Africa.

What Magnin discovered in his African photography adventure was a different, pleasurable photographic space that, as far as the visual was concerned, reflected well on the time of the French colonising force in Mali. Keita was 'poor, [and] made prints, using a 5-by-7-inch view camera, by placing the negative directly against the photographic paper, used his bed sheet as a backdrop, and photographed outdoors using available light' (Rips 2006). And yet the (French Sudanese) Malian, African subjects he framed become, when presented out of context from their original commission as pocket-sized prints, translocated objects. As such they are re-readable as African subjects, mildly content in their slow mimetic journey to modernity, a journey that is managed by a colonising force, in reality and temporally ever-present, but which is rendered absent in popular readings of Keita's work. Given the original purpose of these photographs, as 'a type of private correspondence' for the French Sudanese (Rips 2006), they have worked well on the contemporary and romantic French imagination concerning memories of Africa. This is because they allow a safe and absent image to emerge of the French colonising selves. The romance of Henri Matisse is evoked, rather than an image of violent colonial occupation that Algeria, Mali's neighbour, has come to represent. Keita's subjects, through the agency of Magnin, are read as a people in transition, moving from one African temporality – the old French Sudanese subject – towards the new, modern European, Malian identity, moulded suitably and benevolently by the French. The fascination with Keita's work in France and beyond may possibly lie in the fact that his photographs unconsciously produce a unique visualisation of the degrees of 'success' that the French colonial processes of assimilation managed to achieve. Represented as objects for purchase by European galleries, the photographs are tainted by the fact that they bring forth the myth of the happy native. As images repurposed within the context of the European commercial gallery, they ultimately work against, in a Fanonian sense, the processes of decolonising the mind.

Also in 1991, the celebrated French photographer Françoise Huguier was increasingly working on extended personal photo projects in Africa and, while in Mali, she too encountered the work of Seydou Keita. Huguier's biography states that she 'discovers and contributes to popularizing the works of both the photographers Seydou Keita and Malick Sidibé' ('Françoise Huguier – Biography' n.d.). The first public popularising moment for Keita's work was achieved in 1993, when Huguier introduced it to Louis Mesplé, the Artistic Director of the Rencontres Internationales de la Photographie, Arles. Mesplé, in turn, invited Huguier to curate a large-scale audio-visual programme for the Arles photography festival in the summer of 1993. This was the first significant public display of Keita's photographs in Europe in which he was credited as the author in front of an influential, knowledgeable and international photographic audience. The projection took place in the old Antique Theatre in Arles at around 9 p.m. Dominique Anginot from Lux Modernis in Paris designed the audio-visual installation. Keita's images were projected hugely across the multi-storey high screen, and were dramatically accompanied by a live solo performance on guitar and vocals from one of Mali's rising stars in the world music scene, Mama Sissoko. Sissoko sat as a lone figure in traditional Malian robes playing his melancholic electric guitar interspersed with his high-pitched vocals, constructing a mesmerising fusion of rock guitar and traditional song, and building a wall of sound that complemented the slow slide transitions of the work on display. Sissoko was dwarfed by the giant-sized images from Keita's studio projected behind him. The audience was captivated by frame after frame of Keita's portraits. One of the songs that Sissoko sang was specially written for and dedicated to the work of Keita:

> *Oh Mother!*
> *Oh Mother, all human beings*
> *Are born from you*
> *And we owe You everything.*
> *Look, look at Seydou:*
> *How did he live and how*
> *Did he do? …*

The song goes on to praise Keita's 'probity and fortitude'. The display of Keita's work was organised along simplistic visual motifs that occurred within the works: cars, mopeds, bicycles, cigarettes and other Western consumer goods were the unifying indexical signs that drove the narration of the projection. Although the work had been 'discovered' and presented, few were really able to translate it at this juncture, and at the projection in Arles, the work was ultimately positioned within the realm of the exotic, as the names of the sitters, along with the social and political context for the photographs, were markedly absent. The 'Bamakois' were presented as a nameless body, or as nameless bodies.

This context in turn contributed to the project's success, and, that night, Keita's work was literally the 'Talk of the Town' (Diawara 1998). Throughout the remaining days of the festival, Keita's presentation eclipsed interest in the more major exhibitions being staged in Arles that year, such as the works of Richard Avedon and Larry Fink. It was evident that a new chapter in African photography had been opened up in the mainstream theatre of European photography, and within the heart of its oldest and most celebrated international festival.

As part of her Malian encounters, Huguier also developed the concept of a biennial for African photography, titled *Rencontres de Bamako*, which was successfully held in Bamako in 1994, primarily with funding from the Paris-based state-funded cultural agency 'Afrique en Créations'. The event attracted a significant amount of interest from France's photography elite, who attended *en masse*, re-creating the atmosphere of Arles in Bamako. Their collective visual presence at the festival in Bamako was representative of a caricature of postcolonial cultural exchanges: sunglasses, straw Panama hats and expensive white linen abounded among the visiting Parisian delegates. The cultural highlight of the event was formal recognition from Alpha Oumar Konaré, president of Mali, who inaugurated the festival by cutting a ribbon and making both Seydou Keita and Malick Sidibé guests of honour, in recognition of their significant work behind the camera. In a photograph taken by Abbas, the Iranian, Paris-based Magnum photographer, Huguier can be seen standing next to the president as he cuts the ribbon. On his other side is an elated-looking French diplomat. The photograph captures well the power relations at work across the event.

Bamako continues to play an important part in the display and discovery of African photography, but it remains dependent and under the ultimate control of l'Institut Français. Its impact on the local Bamako communities is, even after twenty years, problematic; few locals actively engage with the exhibitions programme.

With the international *succès fou* of two studio photographers from Bamako, Seydou Keita and Malick Sidibé, whose work found new life and, quite literally, global recirculation in galleries and museums in the 1990s, photography has played an important role in securing critical and curatorial as well as popular interest in modern and contemporary African art. Photography and photographers from Africa have not only benefited from, but have in many instances clearly driven, the current trend. (Bajorek & Haney 2010, p.264)

It is doubtful if African photographers are economically and institutionally able to currently drive trends in the appreciation of Africa's photographic history, and the benefits gained from such a project, both financial and cultural, need careful consideration. Long before 1991 and the 'discovery of Seydou Keita' and the establishment of *Rencontres de Bamako* in 1994, trends were fixed through specific cultural and curatorial displays of African photographic subjects and practices were managed by strong market-led interest in African works from Eurocentric private collectors, galleries, government-funded cultural agencies and philanthropic entrepreneurs. These trends disproportionately dictate, even today, the terms of African photographic image reception, and dangerously reproduce the historical, cultural, hierarchical and political disavowal embedded within the histories of photography and its associated and problematic colonialities. These are in need of deeper forensic enquiry concerning the colonial conditions of power that surround the history of reading African photographic production and display.

Picture Credits

Figures 1, 2, 3, 4: Photograph held as part of the Alice Seeley Harris Archives, Congo Reform Association Campaigns, in the archives of Anti-Slavery International, London.

Figure 5: Photograph reproduced by permission of Bristol Archives.

Figure 6: Reproduced by permission of the National Center for Civil and Human Rights, Atlanta, Georgia.

Figure 7: ©Imperial War Museum (Art.IWM PST 16284).

Figure 8: ©Imperial War Museum (Art.IWM PST 16285).

Figure 9: ©Imperial War Museum (Art.IWM PST 15417).

Figure 10: ©Imperial War Museum (Art.IWM PST 15795) and ©Imperial War Museum (MH 11389).

Figure 11: *Picture Post*. Reproduced by permission of Getty Images, Hulton Archive.

Figure 12: *Picture Post*. Reproduced by permission of Getty Images, Hulton Archive.

Figures 13, 14, 15, 16, 17: Reproduced by permission of Archiv Robert Lebeck.

Figures 18, 19, 20, 21: Wayne Miller, Magnum Photos.

Figure 22: Reproduced by permission of the artist, Joy Gregory.

Figure 23: Rotimi Fani-Kayode, reproduced courtesy of Autograph London.

Bibliography

'1943 – a race that there will be' (n.d.), http://www.detroits-great-rebellion.com/Detroit---1943.html (accessed 30 June 2014).

Adi, H. (1995), 'Pan-Africanism in Britain: Background to the 1945 Manchester Congress', in H. Adi & M. Sherwood (eds), *The 1945 Manchester Pan-African Congress Revisited*, London: New Beacon Books, pp.11-32.

Allen, J. (n.d.), 'Without Sanctuary', http://withoutsanctuary.org/movie_text.html (accessed 19 June 2014).

Allen, J. (2000), *Without Sanctuary: Lynching Photography in America*, Santa Fe, New Mexico: Twin Palms.

Amkpa, A. & Garb, T. (2013), *Distance and Desire: Encounters with the African Archive*, Göttingen: Steidl.

Anderson, C. (2003), *Eyes On the Prize: the United Nations and the African American Struggle for Human Rights, 1944-1955*, Cambridge and New York: Cambridge University Press.

'An Introduction to Lantern History: The Magic Lantern Society' (n.d.), http://www.magiclantern.org.uk/history/history01.php (accessed 4 September 2015).

Anon. (n.d.), 'United We Win', http://www.bucknell.edu/x36355.xml (accessed 20 August 2012).

Apenszlak, J. (1943), *The Black Book of Polish Jewry: An Account of the Martyrdom of Polish Jews Under the Nazi Occupation*, New York: American Federation for Polish Jews in Cooperation with the Association of Jewish Refugees and Immigrants from Poland.

Araeen, R., & Chambers, E. (1988), 'Black Art: A Discussion', in R. Araeen (ed.), *Third Text*, London: Kala Press, pp.51-77.

Arendt, H. (1970), *On Violence*, San Diego: Harcourt Publishers.

Atlantic Charter, 14 August 1941 (accessed at http://avalon.law.yale.edu/wwii/atlantic.asp).

Austin, R. (2005), 'An Extraordinary Generation: The Legacy of

William Henry Sheppard, the "Black Livingstone" of Africa', http://www.cairn.info/revue-afrique-et-histoire-2005-2-page-73. htm#no45 (accessed 9 August 2013).

Azoulay, A. (2015), 'Archive', in A. Downey (ed.), *Dissonant Archives: Contemporary Visual Culture and Contested Narratives in the Middle East*, London: I. B. Tauris, pp.194-214.

Bachrach, S. D. & Kuntz, D. (2004), *Deadly Medicine: Creating the Master Race*, Washington, DC: United States Holocaust Memorial Museum.

Baer, U. (2005), *Spectral Evidence: the Photography of Trauma*, Cambridge, MA: MIT Press.

Baer, U. (2014), 'Ernest Cole's House of Bondage', *Grey Gazette*, vol. 15, issue 1, New York: Grey Art Gallery, New York University.

Bailey, D. A. & Hall, S. (1992), *Ten 8 – Critical Decade*, Photo Paperback, vol. 2, no. 3, Birmingham: Ten 8.

Bajorek, J. & Haney, E. (2010), 'Eye on Bamako: Conversations on the African Photography Biennial', *Theory, Culture & Society*, vol. 27, nos 7-8, pp.263-84.

Baker, M. (1986), *Re3ections of the Black Experience*, London: GLC.

Bales, K. (1999), *Disposable People: New Slavery in the Global Economy*, Berkeley, CA: University of California Press.

Barlet, O. (2000), *African Cinemas: Decolonizing the Gaze*, London: Zed Books.

Barson, T. (2006), *Making History: Art and Documentary in Britain from 1929 to Now*, London: Tate Publishing.

Barthes, R. (1981), *Camera Lucida: Re3ections on Photography*, New York: Hill and Wang.

BBC (2011), 'Profile: Arab League', http://news.bbc.co.uk/1/hi/world/middle_east/country_profiles/1550797.stm (accessed 2 April 2014).

Berger, M. (2011), *Seeing Through Race: a Reinterpretation of Civil Rights Photography*, Berkeley, CA: University of California Press.

Bernard-Donals, M. (2004), 'Forgetful Memory and Images of the Holocaust', *College English*, vol. 66, no. 4, pp.380-402.

Bey, D. (1979), 'Dawoud Bey's Harlem, USA', http://www.studio-museum.org/exhibition/dawoud-beys-harlem-usa (accessed 20 September 2015).

Bianchini, F. (1987), 'GLC R.I.P.: Cultural Policies in London 1981-1986', *New Formations: A Journal of Culture, Theory & Politics*, no. 1, pp.103-17.

Bishton, D. (1991), *Digital Dialogues: Photography in the Age of Cyberspace*, Photo Paperback, vol. 2, no. 2, Birmingham: Ten 8.

Böttger, T. & Koetzle, M (1999), *Robert Lebeck: Vis-à-vis*. Göttingen: Steidl Verlag.

Brenson, M. (1991), 'Africans Explore Their Own Evolving Cultures', *New York Times*, 17 May, www.nytimes.com/1991/05/17/arts/review-art-africans-explore-thier-own-evolving-cultures.html (accessed 10 July 2015).

Briggs, A. & Burke, P. (2010), *Social History of the Media: From Gutenberg to the Internet*, Cambridge: Polity.

Burgin, V. (1982), *Thinking Photography*, London: Macmillan.

Cairns, H. A. C. (1965), *Prelude to Imperialism: British Reactions to Central African Society: 1840-1890*, London: Routledge & Paul.

Campany, D. (ed.) (2007), *Art and Photography*, London: Phaidon Press.

Caven, H. (2001), 'Horror in Our Time: Images of the Concentration Camps in the British Media, 1945', *Historical Journal of Film, Radio and Television*, vol. 21, no. 3, pp.205-53.

Chambers, E., Abdu'Allah, F., Forrester, D., Joseph, T., & Lancashire Probation Service (1994), *Us an' Dem: a Critical Look at Relationships Between the Police, the Judiciary and the Black Community*, Lancashire Postcard Box Set, Preston: Lancashire Probation Services.

Charny, I. (1999), *Encyclopedia of Genocide*, Santa Barbara: ABC-CLIO.

Churchill, W. (1940), 'We Shall Fight on the Beaches', 4 June 1940, https://winstonchurchill.org/resources/speeches/1940-the-finest-hour/we-shall-fight-on-the-beaches/.

Churchill, W. (1942), 'From the Archive: Mr Churchill on Our One Aim', *The Guardian*, originally published 11 November 1942, https://www.theguardian.com/theguardian/2009/nov/11/churchill-blood-sweat-tears.

Cole, E. (1967), 'Grey Art Gallery, NYU', https://greyartgallery.nyu.edu/wp-content/uploads/2016/04/ErnestCole_Grey_PressRelease_CURRENT.pdf (15 September 2015).

Connerton, P. (2009), *How Modernity Forgets*, Cambridge: Cambridge University Press.

Corbey, R., & Leerssen, J. T. (1991), *Alterity, Identity, Image: Selves and Others in Society and Scholarship*, Amsterdam & Atlanta, GA: Rodopi.

Cramerotti, A. (2009), *Aesthetic Journalism: How to Inform Without Informing*, Bristol: Intellect.

David, S. (2011), 'British History in Depth: Slavery and the "Scramble for Africa"', BBC, http://www.bbc.co.uk/history/british/abolition/scramble_for_africa_article_01.shtml (accessed 11 August 2013).

DeGroot, G. (2013), *The Sixties Unplugged: A Kaleidoscopic History of a Disorderly Decade*, Cambridge, MA: Pan Macmillan.

Deliss, C., & Mutumba, Y. (2014), *Foreign Exchange (or, the Stories you Wouldn't Tell a Stranger)*, Zurich: Diaphanes.

Deroo, E. (n.d.), 'BBC Radio 4 – Document: White Liberation Gallery', BBC, http://www.bbc.co.uk/radio4/features/document/gallery/french-colonial-soldiers/index.shtml#gallery4376 (accessed 22 November 2012).

Derrida, J., & Prenowitz, E. (1996), *Archive Fever: A Freudian Impression*, Chicago, IL: University of Chicago Press.

Diawara, M. (1998), 'Talk of the town: Seydou Keita' *Artforum International*, vol. 36, issue 6, February 1998, pp.64-71, https://www.questia.com/magazine/1G1-20544482/talk-of-the-town (accessed 10 August 2015).

Dinnersten, L. (1993), 'Antisemitism in Crisis Times in the United States: The 1920s and 1930s', in S. Gilman & S. Katz, *Anti-Semitism in Times of Crisis*, New York: New York University Press, pp.212-26.

Douzinas, C. (2000), *The End of Human Rights: Critical Legal Thought at the Turn of the Century*, Oxford: Hart Publishing.

Dower, J. W. (1986), *War Without Mercy: Race and Power in the Pacizc War*, New York: Pantheon Books.

Doy, G. (2000), *Black Visual Culture: Modernity and Post-Modernity*, London and New York: I. B. Tauris.

Drabinski, J. E. (2011), *Levinas and the Postcolonial Race, Nation, Other*, Edinburgh: Edinburgh University Press.

Drake, S. C., & Cayton, H. R. (1945), *Black Metropolis: A Study of Negro Life in a Northern City*, New York: Harcourt Brace.

Du Bois, W. E. B. (1945), *Color and Democracy: Colonies and Peace*, New York: Harcourt Brace.

Du Bois, W. E. B. & Gibson, D.B. (1996), *The Souls of Black Folk*, New York: Penguin Books.

Du Bois, W. E. B. & Aptheker, H. (1997), *The Correspondence of W. E. B. Du Bois,* Volume 3, Amherst, MA: University of Massachusetts Press.

Dubow, S. (2008), 'Smuts, the United Nations and the Rhetoric of Race and Rights', *Journal of Contemporary History*, vol. 43, no. 1, pp.45-74.

Dunelm, H. (1936), Introduction, in *The Yellow Spot: The Extermination of the Jews in Germany*, London: Victor Gollancz.

Edwards, E. (2001), *Raw Histories: Photographs, Anthropology and Museums*, Oxford: Berg.

Eede, J. (2013), 'For All Peoples of the World Are Men', Survival International, http://www.survivalinternational.org/articles/3208-bartolome (accessed 21 October 2013).

Eisenman, S.F. (2007), *The Abu Ghraib Eﬀect*, London: Reaktion Books.

Engels, D. & Van Peel, B. (dir.) (2011), *Boyamba Belgique*, http://icarusfilms.com/new2011/bb.html (accessed 23 April 2014).

Fabian, J. (1983), *Time and the Other: How Anthropology Makes its Object*, New York: Columbia University Press.

Fani-Kayode, R. (1992), 'Traces of Ecstasy', in D. A. Bailey & S. Hall (eds), *Ten 8 – Critical Decade*, Photo Paperback, vol. 2, no. 3, Birmingham: Ten 8, pp.64-71.

Fani-Kayode, R., Hirst, A., Sealy, M., & Pivin, J. L. (1996), *Rotimi Fani-Kayode & Alex Hirst*, Paris: Revue Noire.

Fanon, F. (1961), *Les Damnés de la Terre*, Paris: Maspero.

Fanon, F. (1963), *The Wretched of the Earth*, London: Penguin.

Fanon, F., & Bhabha, H. (1986), *Black Skin, White Masks*, London: Pluto Press.

Faram, Mark D. (2009), *Faces of War: The Untold Story of Edward Steichen's WWII Photographers*, New York: Caliber.

Feinstein, S. (2005), *Absence/Presence: Essays and Reﬂections on the Artistic Memory of the Holocaust*, Syracuse, NY: Syracuse University Press.

Foucault, M. (1991 [1975]), *Discipline and Punish: The Birth of the Prison*, London: Penguin.

Foucault, M. & Gordon, C. (1980), *Power/Knowledge: Selected Interviews and Other Writings 1972-1977*, New York: Harvester Wheatsheaf.

Francis, A. (1985), *The Black Triangle: the People of the African Diaspora*, London: Seed.

'Françoise Huguier – Biography' (n.d.), http%3A%2F%2Fen.francoisehuguier.com%2Fbiographie.html (accessed 10 July 2015).

Frindéthié, M. K. (2009), *Francophone African Cinema: History, Culture, Politics and Theory*, Jefferson, NC: McFarland.

Gaonkar, D. (2001), *Alternative Modernities*, 2nd revised edition, Durham, NC: Duke University Press.

Gates, Jr, H. L. (n.d.), 'What Was Black America's Double War?', PBS, www.pbs.org/wnet/african-americans-many-rivers-to-cross/history/ what-was-black-americas-double-war/ (accessed 22 September 2014).

Giefer, T. (dir.) (2010), *Death Colonial Style: The Execution of Patrice Lumumba*, Wheeling, IL: Film Ideas.

Gilman, S. L., & Katz, S. T. (1993), *Anti-Semitism in Times of Crisis*, New York: New York University Press.

Gilroy, P. (2004), *Between Camps: Nations, Cultures and the Allure of Race*, London: Routledge.

Gilroy, P. (2007), *Port City: on Exchange and Mobility*, Bristol: Arnolfini.

Grant, K. (2001), 'Christian Critics of Empire: Missionaries, Lantern Lectures, and the Congo Reform Campaign in Britain', *Journal of Imperial and Commonwealth History*, vol. 29, issue 2, pp.27-58.

Gray, J. (2013), *The Silence of Animals: On Progress and Other Modern Myths*, London: Allen Lane.

Green, M. (1946), 'Defining Moment: The *New Yorker*'s "Hiroshima" Issue', 31 August, http://www.ft.com/cms/s/0/6cb83724-b464-11dd-b780-0000779fd18c.html (accessed 16 May 2015).

Gupta, S. (2007), 'The Foundation of Autograph ABP – Diary Notes', in *Autograph ABP October 2007*, London: Autograph ABP, p.2.

Gupta, S., interview, unpublished, conducted by Mark Sealy in 2015.

Hacking, J. & Campany, D. (2012), *Photography: The Whole Story*, Munich: Prestel.

Hall, C. (1992), *White, Male and Middle-Class Explorations in Feminism and History*, Cambridge and Malden, MA: Polity Press.

Hall, S. [1973] (1980), 'Encoding/Decoding', in Centre for Contemporary Cultural Studies (ed.), *Culture, Media, Language: Working Papers in Cultural Studies, 1972-79*, London: Hutchinson, pp.128-38.

Hall, S. (1978), *Policing the Crisis: Mugging, the State, and Law and Order*, London: Macmillan.

Hall, S. (1984), 'Reconstruction Work: Images of Post War Black Settlement', *Ten 8*, vol. 2, no. 3, Birmingham: Ten 8, pp.2-9.

Hall, S. (1988), 'New Ethnicities', in K. Mercer (ed.), *Black Film British Cinema*, London: ICA, pp.27-31.

Hall, S. (1990), 'Black Narcissus', essay commissioned by Autograph ABP for the exhibition *Autoportraits*, held at Camerawork London in 1990.

Hall, S. (1991), 'June 1991 Autograph ABP Newsletter | Autograph ABP', Autograph ABP, http://www.autograph-abp-shop.co.uk/ newspapers/june-1991 (accessed 20 September 2015).

Hall, S. (1992), 'New Ethnicities', in J. Donald & A. Rattansi (eds), "Race", Culture, and Diꭵerence, London: Sage, pp.252-59.

Hall, S. (1993), 'Vanley Burke and the Desire for Blackness', in M. Sealy (ed.), Vanley Burke: A Retrospective, London: Lawrence & Wishart, pp.12-15.

Hall, S. (1995), 'Negotiating Caribbean Identities', New Left Review, vol. 1, no. 209, pp.3-14.

Hall, S. (2008), 'The Missing Chapter – Cultural Identity and the Photographic Archive', an unpublished lecture recorded by Autograph ABP on 21 May 2008.

Hall, S. (2012), in J. Akomfrah (dir.), The Un2nished Conversation, London: Autograph ABP.

Hall, S., Maharaj, S., Campbell, S., & Tawadros, G. (2001), Modernity and Diꭵerence, London: Institute of International Visual Arts.

Hall, S. (2001), 'The Social Eye of Picture Post, 1972', in G. Jordan (ed.), 'Down the Bay': Picture Post, Humanist Photography and Images of 1950s Cardiꭵ, Cardiff: Bute Town History and Arts Centre.

Hall, S., & Sealy, M. (2001), Diꭵerent, London: Phaidon Press.

Headrick, D. R. (1981), The Tools of Empire: Technology and European Imperialism in the Nineteenth Century, Oxford: Oxford University Press.

'Hennessy History – Double Victory Campaign-1', (n.d.), http://hennessyhistory.wikispaces.com/Double+Victory+Campaign-1 (accessed 16 August 2012).

Hersey, J. (1946a), 'Hiroshima', The New Yorker, http://www.newyorker.com/magazine/1946/08/31/hiroshima (accessed 16 May 2015).

Hersey, J. (1946b), Hiroshima, New York: Knopf.

Hitler, A (1925), Mein Kampf, Munich: Eher Verlag.

Hixson, W. L. (2002), The American Experience in World War II. Volume 10: The American People at War: Minorities and the Second World War, New York: Routledge.

Hochschild, A. (2000), King Leopold's Ghost: A Story of Greed, Terror, and Heroism in Colonial Africa, London: Papermac.

hooks, b. (1992), Black Looks: Race and Representation, London: Turnaround.

Imperial War Museum (n.d.a), 'A tank worker from Nigeria,' object description, http://iwm.org.uk/collections/item/object/33288 (accessed 20 June 2014).

Imperial War Museum (n.d.b), 'From India to Play her Part in Britain's

Medical Service', object description, https://www.iwm.org.uk/ collections/item/object/33289 (accessed 22 February 2019).

Imperial War Museum (n.d.*c*), 'Our Allies the Colonies: Royal West African Frontier Force', object description, https://www.iwm.org. uk/collections/item/object/32642 (accessed 22 February 2019).

International Center of Photography (2012), 'Rise and Fall of Apartheid: Photography and the Bureaucracy of Everyday Life' https://www.icp.org/files/exhibition/credits/sites/default/files/ exhibition_pdfs/icp_apartheid_press_0.pdf (accessed 23 October 2015).

International Center of Photography (2008), 'Archive Fever: Uses of the Document in Contemporary Art', media release, https://www. icp.org/sites/default/files/exhibition/credits/sites/default/files/exhibition_pdfs/Archive_PRESS.PDF (accessed 22 February 2019).

Jacobsen, Ó. (2014), *Daniel J. Danielsen and the Congo: Missionary Campaigns and Atrocity Photographs*, Ayrshire: Brethren Archivists and Historian Network (BAHN).

Jacobson, M. (2009), 'Looking Jewish, Seeing Jews', in L. Back & J. Solomos (eds), *Theories of Race and Racism: A Reader*, London: Routledge, pp.238-56.

Kennedy, L., & Patrick, C. (eds) (2014), *The Violence of the Image: Photography and International Con3ict*, London: I. B. Tauris.

Kilson, M. & Hill, A.C. (1969). *Apropos of Africa: Sentiments of Negro American Leaders on Africa from the 1800s to the 1950s*, London: Frank Cass.

Klose, F. (2013), *Human Rights in the Shadow of Colonial Violence: the Wars of Independence in Kenya and Algeria*, Philadelphia: University of Pennsylvania Press.

Kruse, K. M., & Tuck, S. G. N. (2012), *Fog of War: the Second World War and the Civil Rights Movement*, Oxford & New York: Oxford University Press.

Kühl, S. (1994), *The Nazi Connection: Eugenics, American Racism, and German National Socialism*, New York: Oxford University Press.

Laughton, C. (dir.) (1955), *The Night of the Hunter*, San Fernando Valley: United Artists.

Lauren, P. G. (1988), *Power and Prejudice: the Politics and Diplomacy of Racial Discrimination*, Boulder: Westview Press.

Lauren, P. G. (2003), *The Evolution of International Human Rights: Visions Seen*, 2nd edition, Philadelphia: University of Pennsylvania Press.

Laurent, H. (1961), 'In the Struggle for Independence', https://www.marxists.org/subject/africa/lumumba/reminiscences/laurent/independence.htm (accessed 10 November 2014).

Lebeck, R. (2008), *Tokyo, Moscow, Léopoldville*. Göttingen: Steidl.

Legum, C. (1965), *Pan-Africanism: a Short Political Guide*, New York: Praeger.

Levinas, E. (1979), *Totality and In2nity: an Essay on Exteriority*, The Hague: M. Nijhoff Publishers.

Levinas, E. (1987), *Time and the Other*, Pittsburgh: Duquesne University Press.

Levinas, E. (2006), *Humanism of the Other*, Champaign: University of Illinois Press.

Life (1945), vol.18, no.19, 7 May 1945.

Light, K., & Tremain, K. (2010), *Witness in Our Time: Working Lives of Documentary Photographers*, Washington, DC: Smithsonian Books.

Lindqvist, S., & Tate, J. (2007), *'Exterminate All the Brutes': One Man's Odyssey into the Heart of Darkness and the Origins of European Genocide*, New York: New Press.

Linfield, S. (2010), *The Cruel Radiance: Photography and Political Violence*, Chicago: University Of Chicago Press.

Lowe, P. (2012), 'Picturing the Perpetrator', in G. Batchen, M. Gidley, N. K. Miller, & J. Prosser (eds), *Picturing Atrocity: Photography in Crisis*, London: Reaktion Books, pp.189-200.

Lumumba, P. (1958), 'Speech at Accra', www.blackpast.org/1958-patrice-lumumba-speech-accra (accessed 12 December 2014).

Lumumba, P. (1960a), 'Speech at the Ceremony of the Proclamation of the Congo's Independence, 30 June 1960', https://www.marxists.org/subject/africa/lumumba/1960/06/independence.htm (accessed 31 July 2013).

Lumumba, P. (1960b), 'Statement at the Closing Session of the Belgo-Congolese Round Table Conference, 20 February 1960', https://www.marxists.org/subject/africa/lumumba/1960/02/statement.htm (accessed 17 November 2014).

McGuigan, J. (1996), *Culture and the Public Sphere*, London: Routledge.

McWhirter, C. (2011), *Red Summer: the Summer of 1919 and the Awakening of Black America*, New York: Henry Holt & Co.

Magnin, A. (n.d.), 'André Magnin: A Prospecting Life', www.caacart.com/about_am_en.php (accessed 10 July 2015).

Magnin, A. (1998), *Malick Sidibé*, Zurich: Scalo.

Major, G. (1973), 'Society World', *Jet*, vol. 44, no. 9, 24 May 1973, https://books.google.co.uk/books?id=H7EDAAAAMBAJ&prints ec=frontcover&source=gbs_ge_summary_r&cad=0#v=onepage& q&f=false (accessed 18 September 2015).

Martens, K. (2000), *Pioneering North America: Mediators of European Culture and Literature*, Würzburg: Königshausen & Neumann.

Mauro, A. (2014), *Photoshow: Landmark Exhibitions that De2ned the History of Photography*, Rome: Contrasto.

Maxwell, E.A. (2000), *Colonial Photography and Exhibitions: Representations of the Native and the Making of European Identities*, Leicester: Leicester University Press.

Memmi, A. (2003), *The Colonizer and the Colonized*, London: Earthscan.

Menefee, S. (1944), *The Gazette and Daily*, York, Pennsylvania, p.15, https://www.newspapers.com/newspage/66246340/ (accessed 17 July 2014).

Mercer, K. (1996), 'Eros and diaspora', in M. Sealy & J. L. Pivin (eds), *Rotimi Fani-Kayode & Alex Hirst*, Paris: Revue Noir, pp.108-22.

Miller, W. (1958), *The World is Young*, New York: Ridge Press.

Miller, W.F. (2000), *Chicago's South Side 1946-1948*, illustrated edition, Berkeley, CA: University of California Press.

Miller, W. F., & Daiter, S. (2008), *Wayne F. Miller: Photographs 1942-1958*, New York: powerHouse Books.

Mirzoeff, N., & McClintock, A. (1998), *The Visual Culture Reader*, London: Routledge.

Mitchell, W. J. T. (2006), *What Do Pictures Want? The Lives and Loves of Images*, Chicago: University of Chicago Press.

Mitchell, W. J. T. (2012), *Seeing Through Race*, Cambridge, MA: Harvard University Press.

Mofokeng, S. & Campbell, J.T. (2013), *The Black Photo Album: Look at Me: 1890-1950*, New York: Walther Collection.

Mudimbe, V. Y. (1988), *The Invention of Africa: Gnosis, Philosophy and the Order of Knowledge*, Bloomington: Indiana University Press.

Mudimbe, V.Y. (1992), *The Surreptitious Speech: Présence Africaine and the Politics of Otherness*, Chicago: University of Chicago Press.

Muir, R. & Deakin, J. (2014), *Under the In3uence: John Deakin, Photography and the Lure of Soho*, London: Art/Books.

Mukonoweshuro, E. G. (1991), *Colonialism, Class Formation, and Under-development in Sierra Leone*, Lanham: University Press of America.

Mulvey, L. (1975), 'Visual Pleasure and Narrative Cinema', *Screen*, vol. 16, pp 6-18.

Museum for African Art and New Museum (1991), 'Africa Explores Twentieth Century African Art', http://archive.newmuseum.org/ index.php/Detail/Occurrence/Show/occurrence_id/206 (accessed 10 July 2015).

Natanson, N. (1997), 'From Sophie's Alley to the White House: Rediscovering the Visions of Pioneering Black Government Photographers', *Prologue*, http://www.archives.gov/publications/ prologue/1997/summer/pioneering-photographers.html (accessed 6 April 2015).

Nault, D.M. (2012), '"At the Bar of Public Sentiment": The Congo Free State Controversy, Atrocity Tales, and Human Rights History', www.academia.edu/1470271/_At_the_Bar_of_Public_ Sentiment_The_Congo_Free_State_Controversy_Atrococity_ Tales_and_Human_Rights_History (accessed 2 August 2013).

Newcomb, H. (2014), *Encyclopedia of Television*, London: Routledge.

Newkirk, P. (2015), *Spectacle: the Astonishing Life of Ota Benga*, New York: Amistad.

'New Museum – Digital Archive Africa Explores: 20th Century African Art', http://archive.newmuseum.org/index.php/Detail/ Occurrence/Show/occurrence_id/206 (accessed 10 July 2015).

Nzongola-Ntalaja, G. (2002), *The Congo: From Leopold to Kabila: A People's History*, London: Zed Books.

Oberleitner, G. (2015), *Human Rights in Armed Con3ict: Law, Practice, Policy*, Cambridge: Cambridge University Press.

Oguibe, O. ((2002), 'Photography and the Substance of the Image', in N. Mirzoeff (ed.), *The Visual Culture Reader*, 2nd edition, London: Routledge, p.566.

O'Hagan, S. (2013), 'Wayne Miller Obituary', *The Guardian*, 31 May, http://www.theguardian.com/global/2013/may/31/wayne-miller (accessed 22 February 2015).

Oliver, R. A., & Atmore, A. (2005), *Africa Since 1800*, Cambridge: Cambridge University Press.

Padmore, G. (1947), 'Colonial and Coloured Unity: A Programme of Action; History of the Pan-African Congress', https://www.marx-ists.org/archive/padmore/1947/pan-african-congress/index.htm (accessed 5 August 2011).

Peres, M. R. (2007), *The Focal Encyclopedia of Photography: Digital*

Imaging, Theory and Applications, History, and Science, Amsterdam and Boston, MA: Elsevier/Focal Press.

Philips, M. (2005), 'Introduction', in A. Francis, N. Kenlock, & C. Phillips, *Roots to Reckoning: the Photography of Armet Francis, Neil Kenlock, Charlie Phillips*, London: Seed Publications, p.4.

Picture Post, 'Africa Speaks in Manchester', 10 November 1945, article text by Hilda Marchant, pp.19-20. (Photos by John Deakin/Picture Post/Hulton Archive/Getty Images)

Pieterse, J. N. (1992), *White on Black: Images of Africa and Blacks in Western Popular Culture*, New Haven: Yale University Press.

Pinney, C., & Peterson, N. (2003), *Photography's Other Histories*, Durham, NC: Duke University Press.

Polish Ministry of Information (1942), *The German New Order in Poland*, London: Hutchinson & Co.

Pollock, G. (2012), 'Photographing Atrocity: Becoming Iconic', in G. Batchen, M. Gidley, N. K. Miller, & J. Prosser (eds), *Picturing Atrocity: Photography in Crisis*, London: Reaktion Books, pp.65-78.

Procter, J. (2004), *Stuart Hall*, London and New York: Routledge.

Quinn, A. (2014), 'Under the Influence: John Deakin, Photography and the Lure of Soho by Robin Muir – Review', *The Guardian*, 22 May, https://www.theguardian.com/books/2014/may/22/under-the-influence-john-deacon-soho-review (accessed 5 October 2014).

Ribalta, J., Museu d'Art Contemporani (Barcelona, Spain) & Museu Colecção Berardo (Lisbon, Portugal) (2008), *Public Photographic Spaces*, Barcelona: Museu d'Art Contemporani de Barcelona.

Rigby, T. (dir.) (2009), *The World is Young*, Stanford: Stanford University.

Rips, M. (2006), 'Who Owns Seydou Keïta?', *New York Times*, 22 January, http://www.nytimes.com/2006/01/22/arts/who-owns-seydou-keita.html (accessed 10 August 2015).

'Robert Lebeck photography' (n.d.), http://lebeck.de/noflash/en/africa.html (accessed 18 February 2015).

Rodger, G. (1994), *Humanity and Inhumanity: Photographic Journey of George Rodger*, London: Phaidon Press.

Samuels, S. (2006), 'Strange Fruit: Lynching, Visuality and Empire', *NKA: Journal of Contemporary African Art*, Special Issue, issue 20, http://www.nkajournal.org/ (accessed 17 September 2013).

Sarikaya, D. (2011), 'The Construction of Afro-Caribbean Cultural Identity in the Poetry of Linton Kwesi Johnson', *Journal of Caribbean Literatures*, vol. 7, pp.161-75.

Satre, L. J. (2005), *Chocolate on Trial: Slavery, Politics, and the Ethics of Business*, Athens, OH: Ohio University Press.

Scarry, E. (1985), *The Body in Pain: The Making and Unmaking of the World*, Oxford & New York: Oxford University Press.

Sealy, M. (2010), 'Black Star and the Civil Rights Movement – Mark Sealy Interviews Bob Fitch and Matt Herron', https://vimeo.com/57218854 (accessed 18 September 2015).

Sebba, A. (1994), *Battling for News*, London: Sceptre.

Sekula, A. (2002), 'Reading the Archive: Photography between Labour and Capital', in L. Wells (ed.), *The Photography Reader*, London: Routledge, pp.443-52.

Shephard, B. (2006), *After Daybreak: The Liberation of Belsen, 1945*, London: Pimlico.

Sherwood, M. (2012), 'Pan-African Conferences, 1900-1953: What Did "Pan-Africanism" Mean?', *The Journal of Pan-African Studies*, vol. 4, no. 10, pp.106-26.

Sithole, N. (1959), *African Nationalism*, London: Oxford University Press.

Sliwinski, S. (2006), 'The Childhood of Human Rights: The Kodak on the Congo', *Journal of Visual Culture*, vol. 5, pp.333-63.

Slocombe, R. (2010), *British Posters of the Second World War*, London: Imperial War Museum.

Smith, S. M. (2004), *Photography on the Color Line: W.E.B. Du Bois, Race, and Visual Culture*, Durham, NC: Duke University Press.

Sontag, S. (1973), *On Photography*, New York: Farrar, Straus and Giroux.

Spurr, D. (1993), *The Rhetoric of Empire: Colonial Discourse in Journalism, Travel Writing, and Imperial Administration*, Durham, NC: Duke University Press.

Senate Revolution (S.Res.) 39 (2005), '(109th): Lynching Victims Senate Apology Resolution', https://www.govtrack.us/congress/bills/109/sres39/text (accessed 1 June 2014).

Stamatov, P. (2013), *The Origins of Global Humanitarianism: Religion, Empires, and Advocacy*, Cambridge & New York: Cambridge University Press.

Steichen, E (1955). *The Family of Man*, Museum of Modern Art New York, 24 January-8 May 1955.

Sturken, M. (2001), *Practices of Looking: an Introduction to Visual Culture*, Oxford & New York: Oxford University Press.

Sullivan, P. (2005), 'Robert McNeill Dies at Age 87; D.C. Photographer of Black Life', *Washington Post*, 29 May, http://

www.washingtonpost.com/wp-dyn/content/article/2005/05/28/ AR2005052800950.html (accessed 16 May 2015).

Tagg, J. (1989), 'Totalled Machines: Criticism, Photography and Technological Change', *New Formations*, no. 7 (Spring 1989), pp.21-34.

Taylor, C. (1994), 'The Politics of Recognition', in C. Taylor, & A. Gutmann (eds), *Multiculturalism: Examining the Politics of Recognition*, Princeton: Princeton University Press, pp.25-74.

Taylor, J. (1999), 'Shock Photos', in D. Brittain (ed.), *Creative Camera: Thirty Years of Writing*, Manchester: Manchester University Press, pp.296-300.

Thompson, T.J. (2012), *Light on Darkness: Missionary Photography of Africa in the Nineteenth and Early Twentieth Centuries*, Grand Rapids, MI: W.B. Eerdmans.

Tomlinson, R. (1993), 'Obituary: King Baudouin I of the Belgians', *Independent*, http://www.independent.co.uk/news/people/obituary-king-baudouin-i-of-the-belgians-1458724.html (accessed 5 October 2014).

Twain, M. (1970 [1905]), *King Leopold's Soliloquy: A Defense of His Congo Rule*, New York: International Publishers.

Twomey, C. (2012), 'Severed Hands: Authenticating Atrocity in the Congo, 1904-1913', in G. Batchen, M. Gidley, N. K. Miller, & J. Prosser (eds), *Picturing Atrocity: Photography in Crisis*, London: Reaktion Books, pp.39-50.

Twomey, C. (2014), 'The Incorruptible Kodak: Photography, Human Rights and the Congo Campaign', in L. Kennedy & C. Patrick (eds), *The Violence of the Image: Photography and International Conflict*, London: I. B. Tauris, pp.9-33.

UC Berkeley Office of Public Affairs (1998), 'More About...Visual Highlights of Black Chicago', 14 January, https://www.berkeley.edu/news/berkeleyan/1998/0114/more_about.html.

Vanthemsche, G. (2012), *Belgium and the Congo, 1885-1980*, Cambridge: Cambridge University Press.

Victoria and Albert Museum (2013), 'Staying Power', http://www.vam.ac.uk/page/s/staying-power/ (accessed 19 July 2015).

Vogt, R. (2014), 'Belgium: A Nation State Without a National Identity', in R. Vogt, W. Cristaudo, & A. Leutzsch (eds), *European National Identities: Elements, Transitions, Conflicts*, New Brunswick: Transaction.

Ward, J. W., & Butler, R. (2008), *The Richard Wright Encyclopedia*, Westport, CT: Greenwood Press.

Weizman, E. (2012), *The Least of All Possible Evils: Humanitarian Violence from Arendt to Gaza*, London: Verso.

Wells, H. G. (1914), *The War that Will End War*, London: F. & C. Palmer.

West, C. (1987), 'Marxist Theory and the Specificity of Afro-American Oppression', in C. Nelson & L. Grossberg (eds), *Marxism and the Interpretation of Culture*, Urbana: University of Illinois Press, pp.17-26.

WGBH PBS (n.d.), 'American Experience. Eleanor Roosevelt' http://www.pbs.org/wgbh/americanexperience/features/general-article/eleanor-riots/ (accessed 22 May 2014).

Wilkerson, I. (2014), 'Mike Brown's Shooting and Jim Crow Lynchings Have Too Much in Common: It's Time for America to Own Up', *The Guardian*, 25 August, https://www.theguardian.com/commentisfree/2014/aug/25/mike-brown-shooting-jim-crow-lynchings-in-common (accessed 15 September 2015).

Willenbrock, H. (2008), 'Africa – The Awakening', in R. Lebeck, *Tokyo, Moscow, Léopoldville: Photographs by Robert Lebeck*, Göttingen: Steidl.

Willis-Thomas, D. (2002), *Re3 ections in Black: A History of Black Photographers, 1840 to the Present*, New York and London: W.W. Norton & Co.

Willsdon, D., & Costello, D. (2008), *The Life and Death of Images: Ethics and Aesthetics: Exchanges on Art and Culture*, London: Tate Publishing.

Witte, E., Craeybeckx, J., & Meynen, A. (2009), *Political History of Belgium: From 1830 Onwards*, Brussels: Asp/Vubpress/Upa.

Wolly, B., & Burke, K. (n.d.), 'Edward Steichen's World War II Photographers' (video), *Smithsonian Magazine*, http://www.smithsonianmag.com/videos/category/arts-culture/edward-steichens-world-war-ii-photographers (accessed 7 April 2015).

Wood, M. (2000), *Blind Memory: Visual Representations of Slavery in England and America*, London: Routledge.

Wright, R. (1945), 'Introduction', in S. C. Drake & H. R. Cayton (eds), *Black Metropolis: A Study of Negro Life in a Northern City*, New York: Harcourt Brace, pp.17-34.

Young, R. J. C. (1995), *Colonial Desire: Hybridity in Theory, Culture, and Race*, Abingdon: Routledge.

Young, R. J. C. (2010), *Postcolonialism*, Oxford: Oxford University Press.

Zelizer, B. (1998), *Remembering to Forget: Holocaust Memory Through the Camera's Eye*, Chicago, IL: University of Chicago Press.

PHOTOGRAPHIC ARCHIVES CONSULTED

Anti-Slavery International, Thomas Clarkson House, The Stableyard, Broomgrove Road, London SW9 9TL – Alice Seeley Harris Archives.

Autograph ABP, Rivington Place, London EC2A 3BA – Rotimi Fani-Kayode Archives.

The Bodleian Library, Broad St, Oxford OX1 3BG – Alice Seeley Harris Archives.

Getty Images, 101 Bayham St, London NW1 0AG – *Picture Post* Magazine Archives.

Imperial War Museum, Lambeth Rd, London SE1 6HZ – War Posters Archives.

Magnum Photos Ltd, 63 Gee St, London EC1V 3RS – Wayne Miller Archives.

Ryerson Image Centre, 33 Gould St, Toronto, ON M5B 1E9, Canada – Black Star Photo Agency Archives.

Ryerson Image Centre, 33 Gould St, Toronto, ON M5B 1E9, Canada – *Life* Magazine Archives.

Acknowledgements

I would like to thank the following organisations and individuals for their generosity and support throughout the journey of this publication, without which this book would not have been possible.

The Arts & Humanities Research Council for awarding grant funding to support the research and study. My supervisors at Durham University in the School of Modern Languages and Cultures: Professor Jonathan Long, to whom I would like to express my deepest gratitude for his patience, intellectual generosity and insightful calm and structural thinking during the research and writing of this text. Thank you. Also, the late Professor Andrea Noble for her initial guidance, planning and support, and Professor Ed Welch for encouraging me to enter a programme of study at Durham University. I would also like to thank Ms Lucia Luck, Secretary in the School of Modern Languages, for being incredibly helpful at all times. My family – the book would not have been possible without the support of my family: Sheila McIntyre and the late Austin Antony Sealy. Thank you to Shona Illingworth, my wife, for her encouragement, patience and endurance. Thank you to my children, Alina and Antony (Sonny) Sealy. Thank you to all my colleagues at Autograph ABP for invaluable support throughout the project – special mention to Renee Mussai, Holly Tebbutt and Tom O'Mara. Organisations and individuals who have helped with the photography and image usage: Matthew Butson, Vice President, Getty Images, Hulton Archive; Bob Ahern, Director, Getty Images, Hulton Archive; Cordula Lebeck of Archiv Robert Lebeck; Anti-Slavery International London, Alice Seeley Harris Archive; the Imperial War Museum, London; Sophie Wright and Hamish Crooks at Magnum Photo Inc.; Jayne Bucknell at Bristol Archives; Joy Gregory; the National Center for Civil and Human Rights, Atlanta, USA; Rotimi Fani-Kayode and Alex Hirst. The editors at Lawrence and Wishart: Katharine Fletcher, Katharine Harris and Sally Davison. My editor over many years, Linda Schofield.

Index